THE SOCIAL FOUNDATIONS OF WORLD TRADE

As the former head of the WTO Pascal Lamy has highlighted, world trade traditionally involves state-to-state contracts and is based on an anachronistic "monolocation" production/trade model. It therefore struggles to handle new patterns of trade such as global value chains, which are based on a "multilocation" model. Although it continues to provide world trade on a general level with a powerful heuristic, the traditional "rationalist" approach inevitably leaves certain descriptive and normative blind spots. Descriptively, it fails to explain important ideational factors, such as culture and norms, which can effectively guide the behavior of trading nations with or without material factors such as interests and utilities. Normatively, the innate positivism of the traditional model makes it oblivious to the moral imperatives of the current world trading system, such as development. This book emphatically redresses these blind spots by reconstructing the WTO as a world trade community from a social perspective.

SUNGJOON CHO is Professor of Law at IIT Chicago-Kent College of Law, where he teaches international law, international trade law, international business transactions, and comparative law.

CAMBRIDGE INTERNATIONAL TRADE AND ECONOMIC LAW

Series Editors

As the processes of regionalization and globalization have intensified, there have been accompanying increases in the regulations of international trade and economic law at the levels of international, regional, and national laws.

The subject matter of this series is international economic law. Its core is the regulation of international trade, investment and cognate areas such as intellectual property and competition policy. The series publishes books on related regulatory areas, in particular human rights, labor, environment and culture, as well as sustainable development. These areas are vertically linked at the international, regional, and national level, and the series extends to the implementation of these rules at these different levels. The series also includes works on governance, dealing with the structure and operation of related international organizations in the field of international economic law, and the way they interact with other subjects of international and national law.

Books in the series:

The Social Foundations of World Trade: Norms, Community, and Constitution
Sungjoon Cho

Public Participation and Legitimacy in the WTO
Yves Bonzon

The Challenge of Safeguards in the WTO
Fernando Piérola

General Interests of Host States in International Investment Law
Edited by Giorgio Sacerdoti, Pia Acconci, Mara Valenti and Anna De Luca

The Law of Development Cooperation: A Comparative Analysis of the World Bank, the EU and Germany
Philipp Dann

WTO Disciplines on Subsidies and Countervailing Measures: Balancing Policy Space and Legal Constraints
Dominic Coppens

Domestic Judicial Review of Trade Remedies: Experiences of the Most Active WTO Members
Müslüm Yilmaz

International Organizations in WTO Dispute Settlement: How Much Institutional Sensitivity?
Marina Foltea

Public Services and International Trade Liberalization: Human Rights and Gender Implications
Barnali Choudhury

The Law and Politics of WTO Waivers: Stability and Flexibility in Public International Law
Isabel Feichtner

African Regional Trade Agreements as Legal Regimes
James Thuo Gathii

Processes and Production Methods (PPMs) in WTO Law: Interfacing Trade and Social Goals
Christiane R. Conrad

Non-Discrimination in International Trade in Services: 'Likeness' in WTO/GATS
Nicolas Diebold

The Law, Economics and Politics of Retaliation in WTO Dispute Settlement
Edited by Chad P. Bown and Joost Pauwelyn

The Multilateralization of International Investment Law
Stephan W. Schill

Trade Policy Flexibility and Enforcement in the WTO: A Law and Economics Analysis
Simon A. B. Schropp

THE SOCIAL FOUNDATIONS OF WORLD TRADE

Norms, Community, and Constitution

SUNGJOON CHO

CAMBRIDGE
UNIVERSITY PRESS

CAMBRIDGE
UNIVERSITY PRESS

University Printing House, Cambridge CB2 8BS, United Kingdom

Cambridge University Press is part of the University of Cambridge.

It furthers the University's mission by disseminating knowledge in the pursuit of education, learning and research at the highest international levels of excellence.

www.cambridge.org
Information on this title: www.cambridge.org/9781107036611

First published 2015

A catalogue record for this publication is available from the British Library

Library of Congress Cataloguing in Publication data
Cho, Sungjoon, author.
The social foundations of world trade : norms, community and constitution / Sungjoon Cho.
pages cm – (Cambridge international trade and economic law ; 15)
ISBN 978-1-107-03661-1 (hardback)
1. Foreign trade regulation – Social aspects. 2. International economic relations – Social aspects. I. Title.
K3943.C517 2014
382′.9–dc23
2014021020

ISBN 978-1-107-03661-1 Hardback

To my family

CONTENTS

PREFACE

This book is the culmination of what I have tried to convey, explicitly and implicitly, about the world trading system since I began my graduate study in 1996. In a nutshell, this book explores and utilizes a *social* perspective of the WTO and its operation. Here, WTO members are defined as social, rather than rational, actors. The seed of this perspective was sown in my pre-academic career as a trade official. What I witnessed in Geneva could not be explained exclusively by calculation, strategies, and interests. While these factors did loom large, an undeniably real, if not always overt, social dynamic was also present. Even when driven by strategic considerations, WTO members had to know WTO norms to square their positions within the normative framework. Trade officials were obliged to learn all the relevant WTO agreements, decisions, case law, and other practices, even before they established the strategies. Not every move made by WTO members appeared to be out of calculation: in fact, most members seemed to be doing what they were doing because they took the actions for granted in the most unspectacular fashion. They were speaking the WTO language (norms).

Indeed, we can explain the WTO and its operation in a non-rational, non-consequentialist manner.[1] Rather than dismissing rationalism, this alternative – social – framework complements it by offering constructive criticism on the former's inevitable paradigmatic blind spots. While indubitably beneficial, rationalism might degenerate into scientism if it is not hardened by such criticism. After all, values and ideas are not apologetic epithets, nor should they be equated with simple-mindedness. This book proposes a new optic that spotlights hitherto under-diagnosed problems within the WTO community, such as development failure. From a disciplinary standpoint, this book gathers insights from post-Weberian interpretive sociology, informed by phenomenology, as well as sociology's recent scholarly reincarnations in the area of International

[1] See, notably, Martha Finnemore, *National Interests in International Society* (1996).

Relations (IR), such as constructivism. Readers might identify in this book footprints of intellectual legacies pioneered by Edmund Husserl, Max Scheler and Alfred Schutz. In addition, this book is inspired by Anthony Gidden's concept of "structuration,"[2] which Alexander Wendt applied in the IR field. Thus, this book emphasizes the mutual construction of agency and structure. While the social structure represented by the WTO language shapes WTO members' actions, their *inter*actions simultaneously constitute the very structure of the WTO. As Pierre Bourdieu would have noticed, while the gravitational force from the WTO field wields symbolic power over WTO members, it is the very members that often defy such gravity and reconstruct the field.

This book's methodological approach is intentionally eclectic. I introduce diverse theoretical lenses that explain particular social aspects of the WTO operation. While this book features each theory's fortes, it also heeds each theory's inevitable ontological assumptions.[3] For example, Chapter 4, which discusses the *intra*-community dynamics, relies mainly on symbolic interactionism, developed by George Herbert Mead and Herbert Blumer, as it focuses on interaction in the form of discourse and the accompanying symbolization via norms *qua* language. In contrast, Chapter 5, addressing the *extra*-community dynamics, draws on structuralism–functionalism, along the intellectual heritage of Émile Durkheim and Niklas Luhmann, as it deals with the WTO's configuration with its environment.

At this juncture, a note of caution is in order. Some observations and arguments from the social science literature cited in this book do not necessarily dovetail with the unique context of the WTO. Indeed, social science literature often focuses on particular organizations or events. Although I am fully attentive to the risk of contextual mismatch, I still take a liberal approach in citation, as if a *bricoleur* would. After all, essential paradigmatic insights from social science that this book aims to draw tend to outweigh the risk of clutter. Nonetheless, I tender my apologies if any of such citation does violence to those original works.

As my profuse references indicate, I am not the first one who has brought a sociological inquiry to the world trade system. Nor do I intend

[2] Anthony Giddens, *The Constitution of Society: Outline of the Theory of Structuration* (1984).

[3] See Jonathan A. Turner, "Review Essay: The Theory of Structuration," 91 (1986) *American Journal of Sociology* 967.

to put the last word on this endeavor. My sincere hope is that this work will, in its own right, illuminate parts of the field worth re-examining.

In reaching this point, this book was touched by so many great minds. Joseph Weiler, my mentor and the main supervisor from my doctoral study, taught me the importance of "thinking about thinking" in an osmotic manner and constructed my academic identity. My other supervisors, Anne-Marie Slaughter and William Alford, who later became my good friends, were always sources of backing and encouragement. I also have to thank John Jackson, José Alvarez and Don Regan, my teachers from my years in Ann Arbor, whose excellent teaching and thoughtful guidance empowered me to continue my academic pursuit in Cambridge, Massachusetts. I am so grateful to Alexander Wendt for his special support in this project. As a stranger in the IR field, in particular constructivism, I benefited greatly from his gracious advice in writing this book. My close friend and colleague, David Gerber, took all the trouble to read the whole manuscript and gave me many critical suggestions, which were instrumental in finishing this book. Ever since I began my academic career in the law school, I have turned to David on a wide range of questions. He has always been considerate and supportive. I am blessed that my office is next to his. Moshe Hirsch and Jeffrey Dunoff not only endorsed my thesis in its early stage, but also offered me a number of valuable suggestions throughout the writing process.

I am also indebted to a number of outstanding scholars from whom I learned so much in various venues and occasions. In deep appreciation, I write down their names here, with sincere apologies to those whom I might impudently omit: Harold Koh, Peter Katzenstein, John Gerard Ruggie, Martha Finnemore, Petros Mavroidis, Ernst-Ulrich Petersmann, Steve Charnovitz, David Gantz, Rob Howse, William Davey, Thomas Cottier, Claire Kelly, Oona Hathaway, John Barceló III, Greg Shaffer, Joel Trachtman, Alan Sykes, Keith Hylton, Tom Ginsberg, Andrew Guzman, Debra Steger, Seung Wha Chang, Joost Pauwelyn, Paul Stephan, Frank Garcia, Larry Helfer, Karen Alter, Richard Steinberg, John McGinnis, Jide Nzelibe, Philip Nichols, Chris Brummer, David Zaring, Rachel Brewster, Anu Bradford, Terry Halliday, Bruce Carruthers, Ian Hurd, Jürgen Kurtz, Susan Frank, Amelia Porges, Mark Wu, Fiona Smith, Julia Qin, Chi Carmody, Lorand Bartels, James Gathii, Padideh Ala'i, Chantal Thomas, Thomas Lee, Andrew Lang, Tomer Broude, Simon Lester, Won-Mog Choi, Dukgeun Ahn, Jaemin Lee, Markus Wagner, Pasha Hsieh, Joe Conti, Jason Yackee, Elizabeth Trujillo, Sonia Rolland, John Ohnesorge, Sida Liu, and Alex Huneeus.

Additionally, I thank Kevin McClure, Cecilia Suh, Tiffany Eng, Rosalyn Essen, Kathleen Mallon, Jacob Radecki and Laura Caringella for their dedicated assistance in research and proofreading this book. My wholehearted thanks to Kim Hughes and the staff of Cambridge University Press for their patience and hard work. Finally, I dedicate this book to my family, whose love and sacrifices sustain my life.

Parts of this book are based on some of my past publications, such as Sungjoon Cho, "Breaking the Barrier between Regionalism and Multilateralism: A New Perspective on Trade Regionalism," 42 (2001) *Harvard International Law Journal* 419; Sungjoon Cho, "Linkage of Free Trade and Social Regulation: Moving Beyond the Entropic Dilemma," 6 (2005) *Chicago Journal of International Law* 625; Sungjoon Cho, "A Quest for WTO's Legitimacy," 4 (2005) *World Trade Review* 391; Sungjoon Cho, "From Control to Communication: Science, Philosophy and World Trade Law," 44 (2011) *Cornell International Law Journal* 249; Sungjoon Cho, "Beyond Rationality: Toward a Sociological Construction of the World Trade Organization," 52 (2012) *Virginia Journal of International Law* 321; Sungjoon Cho, "Reinventing the Development Wheel of the World Trading System," 16 (2013) *Journal of International Economic Law* 481; Sungjoon Cho and Claire R. Kelly, "Are World Trading Rules Passé?" 53 (2013) *Virginia Journal of International Law* 623; Sungjoon Cho, "How the World Trade Community Operates: Norms and Discourse," 13 (2014) *World Trade Review* 685; Sungjoon Cho, "An International Organization's Identity Crisis," 34 (2014) *Northwestern Journal of International Law and Business* 359.

1

Introduction: reconstructing the world trading system

No science can be more secure than the unconscious metaphysics which tacitly it presupposes.

– Alfred North Whitehead[1]

I. Overview: making sense of world trade in the twenty first century

A. *The contract model and its discontents*

International trade has become an integrated part of our everyday lives. Many, if not all, of the foods we eat and the clothes we wear today are consequences of trade, one way or another. Not a single day passes without contemporary media covering several reports on world trade. During the past six decades of the modern trading system, the volume of world trade increased more than twenty times.[2] During the same period, the average tariff rate on manufactured products in developed countries decreased from 40 percent to less than 4 percent.[3] It appears that those rounds of trade negotiations for the past six decades have paid off.

The typical pattern of conventional trade negotiations is reciprocal bargain. For example, Country A would cut its own tariffs on goods that Country B exports in return for the latter cutting its tariff on goods that the former exports. In other words, each country's market opening, measured by tariff concession, was (and still is) the price that the country paid to gain its own market access to its trading partner. Indeed, political

1 Alfred North Whitehead, *Adventures of Ideas* (1967), p. 197.

2 World Trade Organization (WTO), "The WTO in Brief (Part 1), The Multilateral Trading System: Past, Present and Future," www.wto.org/english/thewto_e/whatis_e/inbrief_e/inbr01_e.htm (last visited November 4, 2013).

3 WTO, "The World Trade Report 2007" (2007), pp. 207, n.53, 209.

scientists and legal scholars alike have long regarded the world trading system, represented by the General Agreement on Tariffs and Trade (GATT) and more recently the World Trade Organization (WTO), as a contract among its sovereign signatories.[4] The GATT members in fact labeled themselves as "contracting" parties. The chief goal of this world trade contract is to liberalize trade and to monitor protectionism.

The contract model makes sense at least for the following three reasons. First, reciprocal bargains on tariff reduction have historically been a main engine for market opening, as discussed above. Second, this agency-oriented model enables scholars to build sophisticated theories using various econometric methodologies (models). Third, traditional public international law also deems a treaty, such as the GATT and the WTO, a sovereign contract, as stipulated in the Vienna Convention on the Law of Treaties.[5]

However, the traditional state-to-state contract model has recently become anachronistic as it hardly captures the new pattern of trade. The prototypical GATT was based upon single-country production, a "monolocation production" model of trading patterns, while the contemporary equivalent is, by far, more complex, as it involves value-added production in multiple countries, that is, a "multilocation production" model.[6] Until relatively recently, most products were harvested or manufactured entirely in a single country and shipped to another country. For example, if Argentina produced and shipped wheat to England, this trade was understood as if Argentina exported and England imported. Under this unsophisticated trading paradigm, trade policies were prone to capture by domestic producers, as trading nations competed against each other to maximize net exports (exports minus imports).[7]

[4] See, e.g., John W. Evans, "The General Agreement on Tariffs and Trade," 22(1) (1968) *International Organization*, 72. *Cf.* Jutta Brunnée and Stephen J. Toope, "Constructivism and International Law," in Jeffrey L. Dunoff and Mark A. Pollack (eds.), *Interdisciplinary Perspectives on International Law and International Relations: The State of the Art* (2012) (observing that both realists and neo-liberal institutionalists consider international law as instrumental and thus secondary to power and interest).

[5] Vienna Convention on the Law of Treaties, May 23, 1969, 1155 UNTS 331; Draft Articles of State Responsibility on the Internationally Wrongful Acts, in Report of the International Law Commission, 53rd Sess., UN Doc. A/56/10; GAOR, 56th Sess., Supp. No. 10 (2001).

[6] See WTO, "Made in the World," tinyurl.com/8ydmkfv (last visited February 20, 2012); see also Paul Krugman, "The Move Towards Free Trade Zones," (November/December 1991) *Federal Reserve Bank of Kansas City, Economic Review*, 5, 15–18, available at tinyurl.com/kpn7e9e.

[7] See "International Trade Policy," *World Savvy Monitor*, (October 2008), tinyurl.com/blbfxyf.

Now, the old production-trade model has increasingly become unsustainable with the advent of new trade realities, such as the global factory.[8] For example, Indian textiles may be shipped to China, turned into clothes, and eventually exported to the United States. Recent technological innovations and other logistic breakthroughs have facilitated this new trend.[9] In this new production and trade pattern, global business is "nonterritorial . . ., decentered yet integrated space-of-flows, operating in real time."[10] Under these circumstances, each negotiating country might not be able to represent a single, converging national position, considering the complicatedly disparate nature of interest matrices held by numerous economic players participating in various global value chains (GVCs).

Likewise, the GVC revolution has also altered the nature of trade barriers. Within GVCs, not only direct barriers but also those barriers between third parties may clog an upstream or downstream flow of international commerce.[11] In other words, any remote, unknown trade restriction by an anonymous trading nation might affect one's own trade interest. This new possibility eloquently demonstrates the hidden yet firmly existent organic interconnection among economic actors, both state and individual, within the contemporary world trading system. It would be in any trading nation's interest not to disrupt these tightly knit value chains.[12]

This transformed trade reality goes beyond the typical assumption of the contract model. Here, it is nearly impossible to satisfy the cardinal condition for reciprocity, i.e., equivalence, which is the baseline postulate

[8] Network Global Agenda Councils, World Economic Forum, Report 2011–2012, *Global Trade System*, available at tinyurl.com/mrqrbgf.

[9] APEC Policy Support Unit, Asia Pacific Economic Cooperation, Issues Paper No. 1, Concepts and Trends in Global Supply, Global Value and Global Production Chains (2012), p. 7, available at tinyurl.com/mavm95d.

[10] Sungjoon Cho, "Linkage of Free Trade and Social Regulation: Moving Beyond the Entropic Dilemma," 5 (2005) *Chicago Journal of International Law*, 625, 668 n.187; John Gerard Ruggie, "Territoriality and Beyond: Problematizing Modernity in International Relations," 47 (1993) *International Organization* 139, 172.

[11] See OECD, WTO, and UNCTAD, "Implications of Global Value Chains for Trade, Investment, Development, and Jobs," (Prepared for the G20 Leaders' Summit) (August 6, 2013), www.oecd.org/trade/G20-Global-Value-Chains-2013.pdf.

[12] See Fredrik Erixon, Dir., "Paper Presentation at ISDP Conference in Beijing: The Twilight of Soft Mercantilism: Europe and Foreign Economic Power," European Centre for International Political Economy (Jul. 2009), p.3 available at tinyurl.com/mcsth22 (observing that serious disruptions of global commerce based on dense production networks tend to threaten economic welfare of trading nations).

of the contract model.[13] The reciprocal balance, which connects trading nations in a mechanical, not organic, manner, would be very difficult, if not impossible, to compute. In fact, conventional trade statistics cannot accurately picture the new trade landscape as it is predicated on the monolocation production model that focuses mainly on gross volume of export and import.[14] It is prone to a mercantilist state-to-state rivalry for trade surplus, yet incapable of portraying underlying sophisticated transnational business transactions.

Moreover, the contract–bargain model tends to naturalize protectionism as an inevitable status quo. The model remains largely neutral to protectionism as a normative concern. Note that the transition to free trade has never been fully completed. Although states agreed to lower levels of protection through negotiations over time, they did not relinquish primarily protectionist stances *vis-à-vis* each other.[15] While trade is more open and fewer barriers now exist than during the interwar period,[16] the current system is still a *managed* trade system[17] with a *quid pro quo* negotiation structure that pits one party against another.[18] This structural deficiency has been dramatically exposed in the aftermath of the global financial crisis, which has spread rampant protectionism across trading nations.[19] While

[13] Robert O. Keohane, "Reciprocity in International Relations," 40 (1986) *International Organization,* 1, 17.

[14] *See* Pascal Lamy, Director-General, "Keynote Address at the Launching of the WTO and IDE-JETRO Joint Publication 'Trade Patterns and Global Value Chains in East Asia'," WTO (June 6, 2011), available at tinyurl.com/kadq9dl.

[15] See Sanford Gaines, "The WTO's Reading of the GATT Article XX Chapeau: A Disguised Restriction on Environmental Measures," 22 (2001) *University of Pennsylvania Journal of International Economic Law,* 739, 833 (("The GATT is replete with qualifications and exceptions that soften the effect or limit the reach of even its central tenets."); Robert Batemarco, "Why Managed Trade is Not Free Trade," 47 (1997) *Freeman* 488, 488–9, available at tinyurl.com/knk3248 (explaining that after the Second World War, politicians began to move away from free trade and back toward protectionist ideals, while still remaining in a world of managed trade).

[16] See Craig K. Elwell, Cong. Research Serv., RL 32059, *Trade, Trade Barriers, and Trade Deficits: Implications for US Economic Welfare* (2006), p. 6.

[17] See Robert Howse, "From Politics to Technocracy – and Back Again: The Fate of the Multilateral Trading Regime," 96 (2002) *American Journal of International Law,* 94, 97.

[18] See Daniel Ikenson, "Made on Earth: How Global Economic Integration Renders Trade Policy Obsolete", in *Trade Policy Analysis* (Cato Inst., No. 42, 2009), p. 10, available at tinyurl.com/mbtfydl.

[19] See OECD, WTO, and UNCTAD, "Report on G20: Trade and Investment Measures," (Mid-October 2012 to Mid-May 2013), June 17, 2013, available at www.oecd.org/daf/inv/investment-policy/9thG20report.pdf. [hereinafter "Report on G20"]; Simon J. Evenett, "Protectionism's Quiet Return: GTA's Pre-G8 Summit Report," June 12, 2013, available at www.globaltradealert.org/12th_GTA_Report.

trade-facilitating measures have declined, trade-restrictive measures have surged. Only 20 percent of past crisis measures have been removed.[20]

Worse still, the debacle of the Doha Round negotiations, which instilled a sense of helplessness into the WTO, reveals the fatal flaw of the traditional contract–bargain framework. The contract model is inherently insensitive to normative concerns, such as "development." You are never safe when your neighbor's house is burning. "(P)overty anywhere constitutes a danger to prosperity everywhere."[21] This collective risk is yet another confirmation of the undeniable fact that our existences are all connected. In fact, such a flash of enlightenment spurred the launch of the Doha Development Round shortly after the 9/11 terrorist attacks. The Doha Round's ill fate should not be trivialized as yet another anecdote of a deal fallen apart, as would be perceived by the contract model. The Doha Ministerial Declaration emphasized that the Doha Round is a "development" round that should focus on eliminating the chronic agricultural protection practiced by developed countries.[22] This normative mandate quickly evaporated, however, as main stakeholders in developed countries increasingly considered the Doha mandate as mere charity.[23]

To most developed countries, the Doha Round is simply another "commercial" deal in which they should increase their access, or exports, to emerging markets.[24] Under this mindset, each negotiating country holds its

[20] Report on G20, *supra* note 19.

[21] Constitution of the International Labor Organization, Annex (Declaration Concerning the Aims and Purposes of the International Labor Organization), (1944), ¶ I(c), available at www.ilo.org/public/english/about/iloconst.htm#annex.

[22] "International trade can play a major role in the promotion of *economic development* and the *alleviation of poverty*. We recognize the need for all our peoples to benefit from the increased opportunities and welfare gains that the multilateral trading system generates. The *majority* of WTO members are *developing countries*. We seek to place their needs and interests at the heart of the Work Programme adopted in this Declaration." World Trade Organization, Ministerial Declaration of 14 November 2001, WT/MIN(01)/DEC/1, 41 ILM (2002), p. 746 (emphasis added).

[23] See David S. Christy, Jr., "Round and Round We Go . . .," (Summer 2008) *World Policy Journal*, 19, 24 (contending that "[a]ffixing the label 'development' to the Round may have warmed a few hearts, but it has not filled any bellies."); Simon J. Evenett, "What Can Researchers Learn from the Suspension of the Doha Round Negotiations in 2006?" (University of St. Gallen Department of Economics, Discussion Paper No. 2007–17, 2007), p. 5 (observing that the ambiguous and confusing "development" mandate of the Doha Round discouraged corporate executives from attending WTO Ministerial Conferences).

[24] International Center for Trade and Sustainable Development, "Political Positioning Dominates Opening Day of WTO Talks," *Bridges Daily Update*, July 22, 2008, available at tinyurl.com/l48oqtx.

own version of reciprocal balance. Also, negotiating countries often strategically formulate artificial concessions to be used as bargaining chips in a trade negotiation.[25] Then, add the fact that low-hanging fruits had already been picked in past negotiations and therefore the Doha trade negotiations were left with some of the hardest nuts to crack. No wonder reciprocity did not work! In sum, the normative dilemma centers on the very notion of reciprocity on which a contractarian (rationalist) model is based.[26]

B. *Embracing a new (social) framework*

These predicaments notwithstanding, the contract model has long been a virtual orthodoxy. Thus, there has hardly been any serious discussion on what the world trading system really *is*. Note that this inquiry exceeds a mere polemic. The basic image of the WTO among its observers tends to determine observers' perceptions and even their judgment of the WTO and its various operations. This basic assumption also shapes a pathway to the future of the WTO. What we believe in the first place often works as a self-fulfilling prophecy.[27]

Indeed, a number of legal and institutional changes borne of the evolution of the modern world trading system tend to justify a new (social) framework as those changes represent the emergence of organic solidarity within the WTO system. This is why it is imperative, for the purpose of this book, to fully appreciate that the conventional orthodoxy of the world trade contract is of a historical legacy. The prototype of the modern trading system, i.e., the GATT, was launched as a contract (agreement). Yet, the subsequent transformation from the GATT to the WTO has brought a number of structural changes that might not be fully fathomed by the original contract model.

[25] See John W. Evans, *The Kennedy Round in American Trade Policy: The Twilight of the GATT*, (1971), pp. 31–2.

[26] Throughout the book, rationalism connotes any theoretical framework that postulates a state as a rational (preference-maximizing) actor, including neorealism, neoliberalism, and rational choice theories. Regarding a comprehensive discussion on rationalism and its limits, *see* Peter J. Katzenstein *et al.*, "International Organization and the Study of World Politics," in Peter J. Katzenstein *et al.* (eds.), *Exploration and Contestation in the Study of World Politics* (1999), p. 30. For greater details, see Chapter 2.

[27] *Cf.* Amartya Sen, "Capitalism beyond the Crisis," *New York Review of Books* (March 26, 2009) (observing that the blind faith in the self-corrective market process contributed to the outbreak of the recent financial crisis); Donal MacKenzie, *An Engine, Not a Camera: How Financial Models Shape Markets* (2006) (arguing that financial models may actually create a new reality in the form of new markets).

Against this backdrop, this book argues that the contract model, despite its powerful heuristic, does not exhaust an account of why a WTO member behaves, and *should* behave, in a certain way. Non-material factors, such as ideas and norms, can also effectively guide state behaviors. From this standpoint, WTO members conduct most routine activities, ranging from various committee meetings to dispute settlement proceedings, not necessarily because their cost-benefit analyses instruct them to behave that way, but more because those activities are simply what they believe are the most appropriate as informed by the WTO's long-lasting customs and practices. The book aims to animate the latter social framework and offers a different narrative from the contract model, i.e., the world trade "community."

Note that I use the term "contract" throughout the book in its traditional, rationalist meaning. This definition, albeit narrow, adequately captures what most political scientists and international lawyers postulate over an international treaty or international organization, such as the WTO.[28] Of course, I do acknowledge that in the domestic law of contracts a much broader notion of contract, such as a long-term contract or relational contract, is widely accepted.[29] According to the approach taken by this book, the latter (broader) concept of contract has already entered into the realm of social framework in that it takes "relations" seriously in addition to, or despite, specific reciprocity represented by the former (narrow) concept.[30] In fact, this is where the rational and social approach may converge.

The first step toward a new framework of the world trade community is to appreciate the importance of communication among its participants, be they WTO members or individual economic players. Here, WTO norms may offer these participants an operable *lingua franca* by which to perceive, recognize, and understand one another. A discourse based on trade norms enables, and thus empowers, trading nations and private economic actors alike to reflect upon others' behaviors, decide on their own courses of action, and thus interconnect with one another. Note that this discourse model is not a mere aspirational hypothesis.

[28] See, e.g., Ian Hurd, *International Organizations: Politics, Law, Practice* (2011), p. 26 (viewing that contractualism presents the "marriage of positivism in international law and realism in IR [International Relation] theory").

[29] See infra Section VII.

[30] Mark Granovetter, "Economic Action and Social Structure: The Problem of Embeddedness," 91 (1985) *American Journal of Sociology* 481, 491 (observing that a sociological approach prioritizes "relations" over "transactions").

In fact, the evolution of the WTO dispute settlement system for the past six decades has dramatically increased the potential for trade discourse, both by expanding its scope and improving the level of clarity. Beyond merely arbitrating particular adversarial disputes between members, the WTO adjudicative discourse "communitiz[es]"[31] what would have been bilateral resolutions and eventually builds a common (trade) law that guides the future behaviors of the entire WTO membership.

In the WTO community human reason is not limited to an instrumental rationality centering on strategic self-interest. On the contrary, the WTO's "communicative rationality,"[32] through the connectedness and interdependence of our collective existence, elucidates how each member engages other members via cognitive, norm-oriented interactions, such as inquiries, responses, arguments, persuasion, deliberation, and perspective-taking. Therefore, in the WTO community, trade norms do not always represent mere accounts of exogenously given sovereign wills. Instead, trade norms may also emerge endogenously through internal communication among participants of the world trading community. These participants, or interlocutors, include not only state actors, but also individual economic players, such as importers, distributors, bankers, insurers, retailers, wholesalers, warehouse operators, shippers, and consumers. In this context, the new model corresponds with the WTO's ultimate purpose stipulated in the WTO Agreement, an "integrated, more viable, and durable multilateral trading system."[33]

Reflecting on the very nature of trade further substantiates the social approach to the WTO. Indubitably, trade is essentially a mutual enterprise. Without exporters, there would be no forwarders; without forwarders, there would be no shippers; without shippers, there would be no bankers to transact letters of credit; without bankers, there would be no importers; without importers, there would be no distributors; without distributors, there would be no warehouse owners; without warehouse owners, there would be no wholesalers; without wholesalers, there would be no retailers; without retailers, there would be no consumers of foreign products. Of course, this sequence can go in reverse, that is to say, without consumers of foreign products, there

[31] See Pascal Lamy, "The Place of the WTO and Its Law in the International Legal Order," 17 (2006) *European Journal of International Law* 969.

[32] *Cf.* Jürgen Habermas, *On the Pragmatics of Social Interaction: Preliminary Studies in the Theory of Communicative Action* (Barbara Fultner trans., 2001), p. 97.

[33] Marrakesh Agreement Establishing the World Trade Organization, April 15, 1994, 1876 UNTS, p. 154, at pmbl. [hereinafter "WTO Agreement"].

would be no retailers; without retailers, there would be no wholesalers; and so on. Importantly, this mutuality is more of an ontological nature, rather than an instrumental one. Without mutuality, the very concept of trade would be inconceivable. In a trade enterprise, each economic player "act[s] upon" each other.[34] This mutuality naturally results in shared grounds among participants of trade, comprised of a common language, common norms, and eventually a community. This book demonstrates that trade is, after all, a *social* phenomenon.

The social foundations of world trade that this book explores go beyond a mere academic endeavor. In fact, it has strong practical implications. For example, the contract model tends to naturalize protectionist trade politics. According to this conventional model, a trade policy is simply an externalized version of its domestic political status quo, that is to say, political economy equilibrium as a result of complicated bargains among interested parties. Such equilibrium, whatever it is, becomes the national interest. Yet if you are an American CEO whose production chain spans across the world, the conventional model may enervate your business. Then, you might think that this parochialism is indeed against free trade principles. Even though you are an *American* CEO, your country's trade policy hurts you. In fact, any protectionist trade policy benefits no one but a very narrowly defined set of special interest groups, such as domestic producers and their lobbyists, which James Madison aptly described as "factions."

As an American CEO, you may also be proud of your global supply chain in that it helps different people in different countries to make their ends meet. Suppose you could purchase yarn from India, have it woven and sewn in Bangladesh, have it dyed and printed in Mexico and, finally, have it shipped to New York. Here, if this shirt were to enter into the United States without any trade barriers, everyone involved in this global supply chain, including Indian yarn producers, Bangladeshi weavers and Mexican printers, wins. Each of them participates in this world trade community and profits from such participation in every niche. In this sense, you are a *global* CEO in its most genuine sense. If only domestic governments could see the world trading system through the same optic! If they did so, their titular national interests would converge with the global interest. Alas, in reality, powerful domestic industries have successfully lobbied domestic governments to prevent this ideal scenario from happening.

[34] This is what phenomenological sociologists dub "intersubjectivity." Alfred Schutz and Thomas Luckmann, *The Structures of the Life-World*, Vol. 1, (Richard M. Zaner & H. Tristram Engelhardt, Jr. trans., 1973), p. 5.

In this regard, the social framework the book proposes deeply concerns the future of the world trading system. The Doha crisis has sounded a clarion call for reflection for a good deal of scholars and commentators. Many of them have proposed various changes in how WTO members should conduct trade negotiations.[35] Critically, however, one should not expect to save the world trading system by simply altering the subject or the negotiation style. The old bargaining approach, such as "single undertaking," if left unchecked, will continue to naturalize itself: its self-fulfilling prophecy will determine the WTO's institutional pathway. What is truly necessary at this point is more than a scattered array of stop-gap proposals: there must be a structural change in the way in which we understand the nature of the WTO and its norms. In response to the urgent call for a fundamental rethinking of the WTO, this book proposes that we transform the way in which we perceive the world trading system. A different social reality will emerge from our new way of thinking about the world trading system.

Importantly, this book does *not* claim that the social framework always works. Under certain circumstances, brute material factors may simply obviate any illustrative room for ideational factors. Nor should the adoption of the social framework automatically translate into benign outcomes. While the lack of socialization might motivate a rational actor to locate loopholes in every norm to evade it, socialization among "people of the same trade" often leads to a conspiracy to monopolize the market, as Adam Smith complained a long time ago.[36] Indeed, certain business crimes, such as embezzlement, presuppose preexisting relationships of trust.[37] The Hobbesian problem, based on the state of nature, might be smaller in scale than a massive betrayal of trust, as seen in the Madoff Ponzi scheme. Likewise, conflicts, not cooperation, among WTO members might be also detected even under the social framework. Although the world trading system has matured enough to exhibit a complicated structure susceptible to sociological inquiries, concrete

[35] See, e.g., Aaditya Mattoo and Arvind Subramanian, "A Crisis Calls for a 'Crisis Round'," *Wall Street Journal Asia*, March 25, 2009, at 14 (urging WTO members to expand the current Doha Round agenda, including such issues as government procurement and climate change); David Kleimann and Joe Guinan, "The Doha Round: An Obituary," Global Governance Programme Policy Brief, European University Institute (June 2011) (proposing that the single undertaking principle be relaxed to salvage worthy agendas, such as trade facilitation).

[36] Adam Smith, *Wealth of Nations* (1776, Andrew Skinner ed., 1979), pp. 232–3.

[37] Granovetter, *supra* note 30, at 491.

empirical confirmations may vary depending on particular factual circumstances. After all, we still suffer the Doha debacle after the six decades' evolution of the modern world trading system.

Nonetheless, some of the most challenging regulatory disputes faced by the WTO today, ranging from genetically modified organisms to renewable energy subsidies, tend to require long-term, socio-cultural solutions, which tend to be unfathomable under the contract model. The new social framework appears to be better equipped to deal with these modern challenges. In this regard, the recent attempt by some WTO members to eliminate tariffs on certain environmental goods, such as solar panels and wind turbines, is noteworthy.[38] This enterprise was originally initiated by the Asia-Pacific Economic Cooperation (APEC), which is an informal, non-binding forum whose operational logic harbors no conventional reciprocal bargaining. In September 2012, the APEC Leaders decided to cut applied tariff rates on certain environmental goods to 5 percent or less by 2015.[39] Importantly, this rare voluntarism, which might not be reduced solely to reciprocity, derives from the APEC members' *shared* normative vision related to climate change and sustainable development. Now, this shared spirit has reverberated to the WTO in an expanded fashion. Once this WTO pact on liberalizing trade in environmental goods takes effect, the benefits will be shared among *all* WTO members, including those who did not participate in the negotiation.[40] In sum, trade talks can connote not only the conventional reciprocal bargain but also discursive properties of consultation, persuasion and learning.[41] This is the social dimension that this book aims to explore.

II. The historical legacy of the contract model

A. *The origin of the world trade contract*

The environment surrounding the WTO, and its predecessor the GATT, has changed over time. The environment's historical development sheds light on the GATT/WTO's own transformation, which has generated

[38] Daniel Pruzin, "U.S., Others Launch Global Talks on Free Trade in Enviro Goods; China on Board," *Bloomberg* (January 24, 2014).

[39] Asia-Pacific Economic Cooperation (APEC), "Leaders' Declaration, Annex C - APEC List of Environmental Goods" (September 8–9, 2012), available at www.apec.org/Meeting-Papers/Leaders-Declarations/2012/2012_aelm/2012_aelm_annexC.aspx.

[40] Daniel Pruzin, "Key WTO Ministers Cite Need for 'Realism, Pragmatism' in Setting Post-Bali Work Plan," *Bloomberg* (January 25, 2014).

[41] See Sungjoon Cho and Claire R. Kelly, "Promises and Perils of New Global Governance: A Case of the G20," 12 (2012) *Chicago Journal of International Law*, 491.

a distinctive institutional mission at each critical juncture. Such a defining moment, which may be dubbed a constitutional moment, is so unique and powerful that its legacy tends to characterize the nature of the GATT/WTO.[42] Ever since its inception in the 1940s, the modern world trading system has struggled to adapt itself to the altering environment so as to survive, i.e., to remain relevant. This unremitting process of challenge and response between the GATT/WTO and its environment builds up the GATT/WTO's unique identity.

Now, let us go back to the Big Bang moment of the modern international economic system. The Industrial Revolution, which originated in England in the eighteenth century and subsequently spread to other corners of the world, heralded an era of mass production, ever-expanding global trade and an exceptional level of prosperity. Yet this unparalleled economic expansion proved to be a mixed blessing. The newly-accumulated wealth of nations hurled major European powers into a Hobbesian competition. Mercantilism, often symbolized as the beggar-thy-neighbor policy, prevailed as a misguided canon to enrich nations. Mercantilism begat imperialism, which in turn led to the First World War.

Then, after the short-lived "Roaring Twenties," the Great Depression hit the United States. In what appears to be the most disastrous trade policy ever in modern history, the United States attempted to escape this quagmire by invoking the old protectionist specter. It enacted the notorious Smoot-Hawley Tariffs Act of 1930, which significantly raised tariffs for most imported goods. This protectionist zeal was highly contagious. The US trading partners, starting with the United Kingdom, swiftly followed suit. This chain reaction of protectionism eventually wreaked havoc on world trade, which subsequently shrunk by nearly two-thirds.[43] The consummate economic balkanization and the subsequent miseries sowed the seed for totalitarianism, which eventually contributed to the outbreak of the Second World War.[44]

[42] *Cf.* David Collier, *Shaping the Political Arena: Critical Junctures, the Labor Movement, and the Regime Dynamics in Latin America* (1991), p. 29; Stephen D. Krasner, "Sovereignty: An Institutional Perspective," 21 (1988) *Comparative Policy Studies*, 66, 67.

[43] Edward C. Luck, "American Exceptionalism and International Organization: Lessons from the 1990s," in Rosemary Foot *et al.* (eds.), *US Hegemony and International Organizations: The United States and Multilateral Institutions* (2003), pp. 25, 39 (quoting remarks by the former US Trade Representative Charlene Barshefsky on the US trade policy and the WTO on March 2, 2000).

[44] See Patricia Clavin, "The Triumph of Regionalism over Globalism: Patterns of Trade in the Interwar Period," in Till Geiger and Dennis Kennedy (eds.), *Regional Trade Blocs, Multilateralism, and the GATT: Complementary Paths to Free Trade* (1996), pp. 31–3.

The Second World War provided the Allies, in particular the United States, a moment of self-enlightenment. They realized that a well-operating global trading system was a necessary, if not sufficient, condition for peace and security. Such collective realization prompted the establishment of the world trading system "the Bretton Woods system" for the first time in history, as a pillar of the post-war international economic architecture. The original ambition was to create the International Trade Organization (ITO), which would have addressed even unemployment and anti-competition issues. Ironically, however, it was this very ambition that thwarted the ITO project. The US Congress feared that the ITO would wield too much power on domestic regulatory matters. Despite the demise of the ITO, the GATT was salvaged, laying the groundwork for the world trading system for the next five decades.

Against the painful historic lesson, the foremost aspiration in the minds of GATT framers was to prevent destructive protectionism. Therefore, the GATT was designed to attain the "substantial reduction of tariffs and other barriers to trade and . . . the elimination of discriminatory treatment in international commerce."[45] This might be deemed the first-generation mission of the modern trading system. The historic agenda of trade liberalization was so powerful that the GATT developed a culture of pro-trade bias that prioritized trade values over other non-trade (social) values.[46] For example, GATT Articles I, III, and XI protect free trade values as primary obligations, while domestic measures to protect social values, such as the environment or public health, may be justified subsequently only as "exceptions" under Article XX.

Classical international economic theories appear to largely support this general proposition. According to these theories, trade leads each participant to specialize in products with which it retains comparative, although not necessarily absolute, advantages over its trading partner.[47] Such specialization reduces the average cost to produce goods for trade due to the economies of scale. The collective welfare of trading nations increases when trading partners exchange specialized goods through voluntary exchange (export and import) because in so doing resources

45 General Agreement on Tariffs and Trade, October 30, 1947, 61 Stat. A-11, 55 UNTS 194, at pmbl. [hereinafter "GATT"].

46 Concerning the use of the term "pro-trade bias," see Hannes L. Schloemann and Stefan Ohlhoff, "'Constitutionalization' and Dispute Settlement in the WTO: National Security as an Issue of Competence," 93 (1999) *American Journal of International Law*, 424, 451.

47 See Charles P. Kindleberger, *International Economics* (5th edn, 1973), pp. 17–21.

are reallocated in a more efficient manner than in a pre-trade (autarky) situation. Therefore, every country taking part in this game of exchange, be it rich or poor, is expected to increase its welfare.

Against the aforementioned historical and theoretical background, the GATT framers created a global contract among trading nations that established a negotiation forum to manage world commerce.[48] The painful historical lesson from the interwar economic balkanization drove this contract to eliminate trade barriers gradually via reciprocal bargains and monitor protectionism. This was the first-generation mission of the modern world trading system embodied in the GATT. Yet, as its main logic remains a bargain, the global contract is prone to a neorealist structure based on the Hobbesian assumption that the international system represents a perpetual struggle between the *Self* and the *Other*.[49] It is prone to neo-mercantilist competition, as trading nations are obsessed with exportation and allergic to importation. Here, the titular national interest tends to be defined misguidedly as some producers' parochial interest, as it largely ignores other parts of public interest, such as consumers' and consuming industries' welfare.[50]

Special interests mobilize material power to assert themselves.[51] Moreover, the contract and negotiation characteristics of the global

[48] Robert O. Keohane and Joseph S. Nye, Jr. characterized this global trade contract as a "club." See Robert O. Keohane and Joseph S. Nye, Jr., "The Club Model of Multilateral Cooperation and the World Trade Organization: Problems of Democratic Legitimacy," in Roger B. Porter *et al.* (eds.), *Efficiency, Equity, and Legitimacy: The Multilateral Trading System at the Millennium* (2001). Ferdinand Tönnies defined this type of contractarian entity as "*Gesellschaft.*" Ferdinand Tönnies, *Community and Society (Gemeinschaft und Gesellschaft)* (Charles P. Loomis trans. and ed., 1957), reprinted in Marcello Truzzi, *Sociology: The Classic Statements* (1971), pp. 145–54 [hereinafter "*The Classic Statements*"].

[49] See Timothy J. McKeown, "Firms and Tariff Regime Change: Explaining the Demand for Protection," 36 (1984) *World Politics*, 215, 216.

[50] See Sonia E. Rolland, "Are Consumer-Oriented Rules the New Frontier of Trade Liberalization?," 55(2) (2014) *Harvard International Law Journal* (focusing on "consumers," rather than producers, in understanding the nature of trade liberalization).

[51] See Jürgen Habermas, *Between Facts and Norms: Contributions to a Discourse Theory of Law and Democracy* (William Rehg trans., 1996), p. 150. Rationalism's characteristic positivist position, which emphasizes material factors, such as power, interests, and utilities, as a main determinant for state behaviors, exhibits an ironic parallel with the Marxist mechanistic economic determinism between substructure and superstructure. Although most sociologists resisted such radical determinism, the sociological concern for the "relationship" between thought and its underlying reality persisted, as seen in Max Scheler's work. See Peter L. Berger and Thomas Luckmann, *The Social Construction of Reality: A Treatise in the Sociology of Knowledge* (1966), pp. 6–7.

contract tend to put its operation at the mercy of power dynamics among contracting parties. Simply put, a trading nation is likely to enjoy a better bargain if it is a superior, more powerful party than its counterpart in a contract. Under this structure, the powerful party might be tempted to circumvent fundamental free trade principles, such as the prohibition of trade distortion via subsidies, by neglecting or refusing to discipline those protectionist practices.

Nonetheless, the GATT was a great success in many aspects. By the 1970s, world trade grew 8 percent on average annually, which contributed dramatically to world economic growth in general. Tariffs on industrial products have fallen steeply and now average less than 5 percent in most industrial countries.[52] After its five decades of operation, world trade was twenty-two times the level it was at the time of the GATT's inception.[53]

B. *World trade transformed and the contractarian dilemma*

Rationalism underlying the contract model does make an important contribution in explaining how the WTO works. Its deductive methodology based on parsimony is useful because it can abstractify complicated trade relations and generate a number of theories. Nonetheless, it is vital to lay bare what the rationalist framework leaves behind. The old framework is useful *despite*, not because of, its omission.[54] Such omission could be descriptive or normative.

First of all, recent changes in both economic and cultural dynamics on a global scale have provided strong propellants for a *gestalt* shift in how we perceive and comprehend the world trading system.[55] In what might be considered an illustration of the "postnational constellation,"[56] cross-border investment and global sourcing – engineered by technological and financial/economic revolutions as well as the subsequent market integration – appear to have weakened the monopolistic notion of state

[52] WTO, "Understanding the WTO (Basics): The Case for Open Trade," www.wto.org/english/thewto_e/whatis_e/tif_e/fact3_e.htm (last visited November 4, 2013).

[53] WTO, "The WTO in Brief (Part 1), The Multilateral Trading System: Past, Present and Future," www.wto.org/english/thewto_e/whatis_e/inbrief_e/inbr01_e.htm (last visited November 4, 2013).

[54] *Cf.* Amartya Sen, *On Ethics and Economics* (1987), p. 8.

[55] Jürgen Habermas, *The Divided West* (Ciaran Cronin trans., 2006), p. 161.

[56] *Ibid.*; see also Rafael Domingo, "Gaius, Vattel, and the New Global Law Paradigm," 22 (2011) *European Journal of International Law* 627, 638 (arguing that state-centric international law theories contradict open and transnational trade).

sovereignty that has often obstructed the free flow of goods and services. After all, ever-expanded cross-border, transnational activities tend to make the old mercantilist model, based on territorial sovereignty, increasingly anachronistic. This new phenomenon forces us to pierce the veil of a state so as to better observe what is really happening underneath.

Likewise, the conventional *quid pro quo* bargain has become rather ineffective in dealing with new trade barriers, i.e., non-tariff barriers (NTBs). Traditional trade barriers, such as tariffs, are relatively easy to bargain over through reciprocal bargaining because they are quantifiable and calculable. However, NTBs, which are mostly domestic regulations, are basically unquantifiable. Tackling them requires a deep understanding of trading partners' regulatory cultures and backgrounds. Given the situation, dialogue, not bargain, is the key to any solution.[57] In this regard, those successes in past trade negotiations tend to render little comfort: they mostly reaped low-hanging fruits (tariffs), leaving the hardest nuts to crack (NTBs).

Moreover, the old framework is incapable of embracing non-material elements in understanding trading nations' behaviors. Yet, the institutional development of the GATT/WTO for the last six decades has revealed the burgeoning non-material (ideational) elements in constructing the GATT/WTO. Decades of institutional evolution under the GATT have begun to form a new legal dynamic, one changing from power-oriented to norm-oriented.[58] The GATT slowly evolved into something more than a mere contract: its parties would not easily walk away from the GATT to avoid the onus of obligations.[59] Here, norms can be understood as a collective representation of values and identities that are constituted in a community, not merely as a pre-programmed contractual invention measured by a legal equivalent of the *Mètre des Archives*.

[57] "Economic, social and technological advances have resulted in higher consumer demand for food safety and posed new challenges in managing globally fragmented supply chains. Food safety measures have proliferated as a tool to respond to these challenges. As a consequence, various approaches to mitigate possible negative trade impacts, such as harmonization of standards, equivalence and commitment to a set of rules, are receiving widespread attention." WTO, "World Trade Report" (2012), available at www.wto.org/english/res_e/booksp_e/anrep_e/world_trade_report12_e.pdf.

[58] John H. Jackson, *The World Trading System: Law and Policy of International Economic Relations* (1997), pp. 109–11.

[59] Debra P. Steger, "Afterword: The 'Trade and . . .' Conundrum – A Commentary," 96 (2002) *American Journal of International Law*, 135, 137.

C. *Normative neutrality of the world trade contract*

Also, the contract model is characteristically neutral to normative concerns. Basically, it is a positive framework that attempts to explain the causes of (rational) state behaviors based on self-interest, not to prescribe or proscribe them. Therefore, when the contract model functions as a *modus operandi* for state behavior, it is vulnerable to the cooperation breakdown, as the Doha crisis painfully substantiates. Egoistic states, in particular powerful ones, basically externalize their domestic interests and preferences in trade negotiations. Insofar as states' short-term national interests, which are often captured by domestic rent-seekers, guide their actions, the WTO might not achieve its original normative goals, such as "an integrated, more viable and durable multilateral trading system."[60] If left unchecked, the WTO *qua* contract risks forming a fatal path, as economic players base their future behaviors not on long-term factors, such as norm-based stability, but rather on myopic parameters, such as political contingencies.

Recall the original mission of the Doha *Development* Round. Before the Doha Round was launched, developed countries had been sluggish in implementing their Uruguay Round commitments. Most developed countries had continued to maintain high trade barriers to imports on those primary, labor-intensive products, which would cost developing countries over $100 billion per year, twice the total sum of foreign aid from North to South.[61] Developing countries increasingly believed that the Uruguay Round had failed to realize the goal of substantial and sustainable economic development. Against this background, the Doha Ministerial Declaration (2001) states that:

> International trade can play a major role in the promotion of *economic development* and the *alleviation of poverty*. We recognize the need for all our peoples to benefit from the increased opportunities and welfare gains that the multilateral trading system generates. The *majority* of WTO members are *developing countries*. We seek to place their needs and interests at the heart of the Work Programme adopted in this Declaration.[62]

Nonetheless, this initially emphatic allegiance to development in the Doha Round quickly evaporated. Some observers from developed countries even

[60] WTO Agreement, *supra* note 33.

[61] Nicholas Stern, "Foreword to Globalization, Growth, and Poverty: Building an Inclusive World Economy," A World Bank Policy Research Report, (2002), pp. 9, 53.

[62] Ministerial Declaration: The Fourth WTO Ministerial Meeting P 6, WTO, WT/MIN(01)/DEC/1 (November 20, 2001), ¶ 2 (emphasis added).

believe that the very development label distanced powerful stakeholders (businesses and industries), who tend to think that the Doha trade talks would be mere charity and thus find little incentive to participate.[63] Developed countries lobbied by these powerful business interests basically perceive the Doha Round as yet another commercial negotiation in which they could press for market opening by big developing countries, such as China, India, and Brazil.[64]

While leaders of developed countries continued to advocate the vital cause of development, this lip service never materialized at the negotiation table.[65] In the meantime, developing countries refused to make concessions before developed countries tabled substantial commitments in the area of agricultural protection.[66] It was this brinkmanship that frequently deadlocked the negotiation process.[67]

Yet developing countries are not without the mercantilist mindset. Certain major developing countries opposed the idea of a stand-alone trade facilitation agreement because they wanted reciprocal concessions from developed countries.[68] Likewise, their resistance against the reduction of industrial tariffs is also rooted in their fear of foreign imports, not only from developed but also from fellow developing countries. For example, Brazil worries about the influx of Chinese goods once the former lowers

[63] See Christy, *supra* note 23, 19, 24 (contending that "affixing the label 'development' to the Round may have warmed a few hearts, but it has not filled any bellies."); Evenett, *supra* note 23, p. 5 (observing that the ambiguous and confusing "development" mandate of the Doha Round discouraged corporate executives from attending WTO Ministerial Conference).

[64] "Political Positioning Dominates Opening Day of WTO Talks," *Bridges Daily Update* (Internationanl Center for Trade and Sustainable Development), July 22, 2008 [hereinafter "Political Positioning Dominates"].

[65] See Alan Beattie, "G8 Mood and Doha Talks 'Show Disconnect'," *Financial Times,* July 8, 2005, 4 (claiming that there was a "bizarre disconnect between the enthusiastic rhetoric from G8 leaders in Gleneagles on pushing ahead with trade talks and intransigence from negotiators that has brought the Doha round almost to a halt").

[66] See "Members Try to Convert Dalian Effort into Negotiations Breakthrough," *Bridges Weekly Trade News Digest,* 9 (International Center for Trade and Sustainable Development), July 20, 2005, 2 (noting insistence by developing nations that some of their demands be met in agriculture before moving forward on non-agricultural market access, and citing "demands that the EU reduce subsidies and open its markets to foreign farm products").

[67] See "The Doha Round Cruising Along," *Financial Times,* July 15, 2005, 12 (claiming that brinkmanship would once have led to a last-minute deal, "but the sheer breadth of the current round of trade talks, coupled with the involvement of no less than 148 countries, forecloses that option").

[68] "WTO Members Should Quickly Conclude Trade Facilitation Deal, Development Bank Chiefs Say," *Bridges Weekly Trade News Digest,* No. 26, Jul. 4, 2012, 16 available at ictsd.org/i/news/bridgesweekly/137544/.

industrial tariffs for the latter's products. In fact, the still largely un-free South–South trade is a critical obstacle for development.[69] Also, by refusing to boldly embrace opening the market, developing countries tend to situate themselves in an adverse position to pressure developed countries to drop chronic protectionism, such as tariff peaks in the Doha Round talks.

As self-interest becomes a cardinal criterion for our behaviors, we are encouraged to anticipate the worst in our trading partners, which may in turn generate the worst from us.[70] From this mindset arises the so-called "fear of relative loss," the misguided obsession based on an entropic, zero-sum assumption that others' gain is our loss. Such latent fear complicates cooperation, even in the face of common welfare generation.[71] It feeds a self-fulfilling prophecy[72] because thinking of others as potential enemies or objects of manipulation is soon reciprocated by others, thereby locking us in a Hobbesian cycle.[73] Once the reality turns Hobbesian, rationalism can perfectly explain it, hence self-justifying and self-perpetuating the zero-sum system.

Ominously, the recent financial crisis has only fueled a protectionist struggle, which some predict might precipitate a zero-sum world.[74] The crisis protectionism that has recently been rampant across trading nations betrays underlying egocentric state behaviors.[75] This fatal

[69] See Raj Bhala, "Resurrecting the Doha Round: Devilish Details, Grand Themes, and China Too," 45 (2009) *Texas International Law Journal*, 1, 121 (agreeing with the United States that South–South trade must increase and poor countries must lift themselves out of poverty in part by trading more with each other); see also Chad P. Bown, "Emerging Economies and the Emergence of South–South Protectionism," World Bank Policy Research Paper (WPS 6162) (August 10, 2012), available at econ.worldbank.org/external/default/main?pagePK=64165259&piPK=64165421&theSitePK=469382&menuPK=64166093&entityID=000158349_20120810083452 (observing that the resumption of emerging countries' exports after the repeal of other emerging countries' temporary trade barriers is slow).

[70] Robert Frank, *Passions with Reason* (1988), p. xi.

[71] Alexander Wendt, *Social Theory of International Politics* (1999), pp. 102–3.

[72] Andre Kukla, "*The Structure of Self-Fulfilling and Self-Negating Prophesies*," 4 (1994) *Theory and Psychology*, 5.

[73] Hayward Alker, *Rediscoveries and Reformulations* (1996), pp. 184–206; John Vasquez, *The War Puzzle* (1993); Alexander Wendt, "Anarchy Is What States Make of It: The Social Construction of Power Politics," 46 (1992) *International Organization* 391.

[74] See Gideon Rachman, "Welcome to a Zero-Sum World," in *The World in 2011* (2010), p. 85.

[75] See OECD, WTO, and UNCTAD, "Report on G20: Trade and Investment Measures (Mid-October 2012 to Mid-May 2013)," June 17, 2013, available at www.oecd.org/daf/inv/investment-policy/9thG20report.pdf; Simon J. Evenett, "Protectionism's Quiet Return: GTA's Pre-G8 Summit Report," June 12, 2013, available at www.globaltradealert.org/12th_GTA_Report.

feedback loop tends to delay or even hinder what is gradually to come, i.e., the ever-integration of the global trading system. Worse, the Doha Round, as *the* longest trade round ever, has unfortunately bred defeatism in the minds of WTO members. A global trade bargain appears to be elusive as long as WTO members are caught in a mercantilist spell and refuse to question, rather than reflexively accept, the traditional concept of national interests. How were these interests formed in the first place? Do, or *should*, only a handful of well-connected domestic producers determine the titular national interests?

In sum, the old, rationalist mindset dies hard. As long as trading nations believe that the WTO is a contract based on reciprocal bargaining, the world trading system will still be at the mercy of the same mercantilist evil it tried to exorcize when it was established six decades ago. Trading nations, rich and poor alike, are eager to open others' markets, while remaining reluctant to open their own.

III. A new framework: the world trade community

One might be tempted to reckon a quick fix to those blind spots by improving certain institutional aspects of the WTO operation or by changing the way in which WTO members negotiate. For example, some scholars criticize the current WTO decision-making process as antiquated and propose that the current Green Room process be modified both to better represent WTO members and to facilitate decision-making in general.[76] Other scholars argue that more topical issues, such as climate change and exchange rates, should be added to the current negotiation agendas.[77] Given that all these proposals require heavy dosages of political capital to fully materialize, expecting the completion of the Doha Round through them would be tantamount to waiting for *deus ex machina* in the form of political serendipity.[78]

In contrast, the approach proposed by this book is of a more fundamental nature. This book argues that WTO members should adopt a new

[76] Kent Jones, *Doha Blues: Institutional Crisis and Reform in the WTO* (2010).

[77] Regarding positions in favor of the expansion of the WTO's agenda, see Joost Pauwelyn, "New Trade Politics in the Twenty First Century," 11 (2008) *Journal of International Economic Law* 559, 572; see also Mattoo and Subramanian, *supra* note 35 (proposing that the WTO should mobilize its enforcement mechanism in addressing the exchange rate issues).

[78] "Waiting for Better Alignment of Political Constellations," 14 *Bridges*, September 2010, available at ictsd.org/i/news/bridges/84951/.

way of perceiving the world trading system. It calls for a novel social framework to complement, if not supplant, the old one. Contemplating an alternative framework requires us to defy the dominant, and thus unquestioned, assumptions so as to observe the unobservable.[79] After all, one can see only what his or her mind is prepared to comprehend. So often, a methodology, if left unchallenged, can turn into an unspoken ontology.[80] In sum, our failure to question the conventional image of the WTO, which is a global contract driven by self-interest, tends to simply conform to it,[81] and therefore to dismiss the rhetorical power embedded in WTO norms.[82]

This book adopts a sociological approach based on the notion of intersubjectivity. My own subjectivity, such as what I intend or believe, is communicated to, and perceived by, my counterpart. How I think of my counterpart will form his or her own subjectivity on me. This mirroring process is a hallmark of social relation.[83] With this new social framework, I intend to draw attention to our communicative capability expressed in the emerging public sphere of the world trade community: WTO members increasingly rely on meaning-based public reason in the form of ideas and norms in the everyday operation of the WTO.[84] This collective self-reflection can break the vicious circle of positivist defeatism and herald in a new organizational sense of direction.

Suppose that a WTO member notifies the WTO Secretariat of its new technical regulation under the Agreement on Technical Barriers to Trade (the TBT Agreement). Such a notification may prompt a subsequent inquiry by another member, which will be followed by reason-giving by the original regulating member. What are these actions? How can we understand them? Why are they doing this? One possible interpretation,

[79] Wendt, *supra* note 71, p. 5 ("[A]ny facts we collect will be shot through with ontological assumptions about what we are looking at that are not easily falsified."). *Ibid.* p. 37.

[80] *Ibid.*, p. 35.

[81] *Ibid.*, p. 89; see also Anne-Marie Slaughter and Steven R. Ratner, "The Method Is the Message," 93 (1999) *American Journal of International Law* 410, 410 (observing that a choice of a "method" as an "applied theory" reveals "a set of choices" about what kinds of problems to address).

[82] *Cf.* Paul Schiff Berman, *Global Legal Pluralism: A Jurisprudence of Law beyond Borders* (2012), p. 21 (emphasizing the rhetorical power of law, rather than coercion).

[83] Wendt, *supra* note 71, p. 327.

[84] Regarding general discussion on communication, public sphere, and identity, see Marc Lynch, *State Interests and Public Spheres: The International Politics of Jordan's Identity* (1999); Heinz Kohust, "Creativeness, Charisma, and Group Psychology," in Heinz Kohust (ed.), *Self-Psychology and the Humanities* (1985), pp. 209–11 (1985); Wendt, *supra* note 71, pp. 375–6.

informed by the conventional framework, might be that those actions serve the interests of the parties involved, perhaps by preventing a potential dispute and thus lowering transaction costs. One might even say that WTO members in fact envisioned all these utilitarian consequences and programmed this mechanism (notification and reason-giving) in a contract labeled the TBT Agreement.

Plausible as this explanation may be, it would not exhaust the explication, or justification, of those actions. How salient would such interest calculus be in reality? Would WTO members press a mental calculator every moment for every action like this one? What if an alternative action, such as the refusal to respond to an inquiry, would actually be more profitable than complying with the TBT procedure? In that case, would the recipient party always decide not to respond? More fundamentally, what factors would determine whether and when a choice of action is truly profitable or not? What constitutes the so-called "interest" in a given situation? Perhaps, being agnostic about what the interest might be, the recipient country responds simply because it believes that is the way it is. This habituated, taken-for-granted attitude is possible because the recipient country finds certain *meanings* from the original inquiry as well as its response. From this perspective, their dialogue in the TBT Committee broadens and reinforces their social bond.

Importantly, the main theme of this book is opportune as it sheds light on the nascent global trade reality, such as GVCs. Under GVCs, many different economic players from many different countries are involved in producing any given product. Under this new reality symbolized by cross-border mergers and acquisitions (M&As) and global sourcing, the conventional distinction between made-in-America and made-in-China has increasingly become less significant.[85] Such groundbreaking transformation naturally highlights the old framework's bracketed assumptions since the contract model, which focuses on state-to-state reciprocal bargaining, cannot fully explain this sophisticated phenomenon transpiring beyond borders. The community model is better positioned to explicate these behind-the-border trade activities because the new model includes these shadow actors (individual economic players) as critical to the community.

The recent global financial crisis has only amplified this fateful bonding within the global trading system. While the crisis has negatively affected developing countries and their businesses, the post-crisis

[85] Daniel Ikenson, "Made on Earth: How Global Economic Integration Renders Trade Policy Obsolete," *Trade Policy Analyses, Cato Institute*, December 2, 2009, p. 5.

situation, which is often dubbed the "new normal,"[86] has ironically put developing countries and their businesses in a solution-making position on account of their enormous growth potential superior to crisis-stricken developed countries.[87] Developing countries must fully realize their development potential by actively connecting with the WTO's community – by mainstreaming international trade. Considering the emerging link between GVCs and development,[88] this mainstreaming of trade becomes increasingly essential for the sake of development.[89]

From a theoretical standpoint, the community framework of the WTO warrants a "constructivist" interpretation, which has widely been adopted by IR scholars in the area of international economy.[90] Under constructivism,[91] how WTO members understand their national interests within the context of the WTO's object and purpose would depend on the WTO's norms and social structure. In other words, the norms and social structure of the WTO constitute its members' interests and preferences.[92] WTO membership does not merely confer a sum of rights and privileges, such as the national treatment and the most-favored nation principles, under the WTO agreements. It also connotes various social benefits, such as belongingness, assurance, and even prestige, derived from a certain social status within the world trading system. This explains why so many countries, in particular developing countries, such as China,

[86] See Ian Davis, "The New Normal," *McKinsey Quarterly*, March 2009, available at www.mckinseyquarterly.com/The_new_normal_2326.

[87] Robert Zoellick, "Pittsburgh Should Be a Turning Point for the Poor," *Financial Times*, September 24, 2009.

[88] "Lamy Lauds $200 Billion Mobilized in Aid for Trade Funding," *WTO News*, January 16, 2013, available at www.wto.org/english/news_e/sppl_e/sppl262_e.htm; see also Oliver Cattanen *et al.* (eds.), *Global Value Chains in a Postcrisis World: A Development Perspective* (2010).

[89] See generally Sungjoon Cho, "Reinventing the Development Wheel of the World Trading System" (reviewing Sonia E. Rolland, *Development at the World Trade Organization* (2012)), 16 (2013) *Journal of International Economic Law* 481.

[90] See Rawi Abdelal *et al.*, "Introduction," in Rawi Abdelal *et al.* (eds.), *Constructing the International Economy* (2010), p. 2 (highlighting constructivism's focus on "nonmaterial" factors behind state practice).

[91] Regarding constructivism, see generally Wendt, *supra* note 71; Jeffrey T. Checkel, "The Constructivist Turn in International Relations Theory," 50 (1998) *World Politics* 324, 325–6. For a comprehensive discussion on constructivism *vis-à-vis* rationalism, see Chapter 2.

[92] Regarding the inherent tension between the WTO on its own and the WTO as a member-driven organization, see Jan Klabbers, "New Logo: The Sutherland Report and the Rebranding of the WTO," 2 (2005) *International Organizations Law Review* 177, 181–3.

Vietnam, and Russia, were so eager to become WTO members. They desire to emulate the stature that previous members have achieved.[93]

IV. The intra-community dynamics of the world trade community

A. *Trade norms as a communicative medium*

The first step toward a social framework of the world trading system is to appreciate the importance of communication among its participants, be they trading nations or individual economic players. Here, WTO jurisprudence offers these participants a *lingua franca* by which to communicate with one another. Discourse based on trade norms enables, and empowers, trading nations and traders alike to reflect upon others' behaviors, decide on their own course of action, and thus connect with one another. The dramatic evolution of the multilateral trading system, from a contract to a system,[94] contributed to the enrichment of trade discourse, thereby improving its general level of clarity while expanding its operative scope. Consequently, trade discourse builds social ties among those participants. Sociologists observe that this kind of discourse, as a common *modus operandi* within a community, provides participants with a strong sense of identification, safety, and comfort.[95]

The robust performance of the WTO dispute settlement mechanism, which is quite unique as an international adjudicative mechanism, eloquently demonstrates the power and potential of trade discourse. Disputants engage in deliberations and arguments based on the self-referential grammar and syntax that trade norms furnish. Disputants use trade norms as if they were a language to communicate with each other in both litigation and settlement. Third parties, even if they have no direct legal interest in a pending case, also participate in the proceeding and add their own narratives to it. In this sense, both disputants and third-party non-disputants are interlocutors in this trade discourse, which references, and at the same time generates, the discursive record

[93] *Cf.* Ann Florini, "The Evolution of International Norms," 40 (1996) *International Studies Quarterly*, 363, 375.

[94] See Sungjoon Cho, "The Nature of Remedies in International Trade Law," 65 (2004) *University of Pittsburgh Law Review*, 763.

[95] Steven Brint, "Gemeinschaft Revisited: A Critique and Reconstruction of the Community Concept," 19 (2001) *Social Theory* 1, 4.

of trade jurisprudence. In sum, trade discourse is both *juris*-dependent and *juris*-generative.

The WTO discourse operates not only through typical judicial interlocution but also through extra-judicial avenues, including various inter-governmental dialogues prescribed by WTO Agreements (e.g., TBT and the Agreement on the Application of Sanitary and Phytosanitary Measures (SPS)), such as notifications, inquiries, and reason-giving; peer review procedures under various committees and the Trade Policy Review Mechanism (TPRM); and the Secretariat's overt, and often covert, normative enterprises. For example, under the SPS Committee, WTO members may learn from and adapt to each other through exchange of information and deliberation in a way that cannot be fully captured by rationalist narratives.[96] This intersubjectivity in the form of regulatory dialogue and cooperation tends to sensitize regulating states to the external trade impact of their regulations on affected WTO members and thus persuade regulating states to modify or repeal those regulations.[97] Notably, clarification on the meaning of some SPS provisions often results from informal discussions among working-level government officials.

Perhaps the biggest contribution of the WTO jurisprudence may be that it promotes fidelity to *law*, rather than fidelity to power, and thus unites participants of the world trading system around this ideal.[98] In the absence of fidelity to law, myopic parameters, such as political contingencies, would fill in any legal vacuum.[99] Therefore, an essential element

[96] Joanne Scott, *The WTO Agreement on Sanitary and Phytosanitary Agreement: A Commentary* (2006), p. 4.

[97] *Ibid.*, p. 57.

[98] "[T]he law of international trade requires that all of their matters be dealt with in terms of principles, rather than naked animosity and power. Thus international trade law encourages the continued communication essential for cooperation among trading nation governments." Kenneth W. Abbott, "The Trading Nation's Dilemma: The Functions of the Law of International Trade," 26 (1985) *Harvard International Law Journal*, 501, 532; see also Panel Report, *United States – Sections 301–310 of the Trade Act of 1974*, ¶ 7.76, WT/DS152/R (December 22, 1999) ("The security and predictability in question are of 'the multilateral trading system.' The multilateral trading system is, per force, composed not only of States but also, indeed mostly, of *individual economic operators*. The lack of *security and predictability* affects mostly these individual operators ...") (emphasis added); cf. Jeremy Waldron, "Why Law – Efficiency, Freedom, or Fidelity?," 13 (1994) *Law and Philosophy* 259, 275–81.

[99] Sungjoon Cho, "A New Agenda for Peace: International Trade Law as a Practical Discourse," in Padideh Ala'i *et al.* (eds.), *Trade as the Guarantor of Peace, Liberty and Security?" Critical, Historical and Empirical Perspectives* (2006), pp. 63, 67–8.

of a community of law is the participants' self-consciousness of the normative context of the community's operation.[100] The ethos of communicative rationality emerging against the shared cultural background within the GATT/WTO system tends to transform the tone of trade discourse from being power-oriented to being rule-oriented, and thus constitutes the normative ground for the WTO's community.[101]

From this standpoint, trade norms are not necessarily given exogenously as a mere invention of a sovereign contract. Instead, trade norms may be self-generating, in an endogenous fashion, through a cultural discourse among participants of the world trading community. These participants, or interlocutors, include not only state actors, but also individual economic players, such as importers, distributors, bankers, insurers, retailers, wholesalers, warehouse operators, shippers, and consumers. The internalized reliance on, and also the occasional feedback to, trade norms by these shadow actors reinforces and self-legitimizes trade discourse. This social framework for the WTO community can offer an effective bulwark against the power-based realpolitik, such as unilateralism, by providing both less powerful trading nations and traders with normative – often judicial – protection. This is how the new framework contributes to the attainment of the WTO's ultimate *telos*, which is an "integrated, more viable, and durable multilateral trading system."

B. The basic law of international trade

As witnessed in the current debacle of the Doha Round talks, the empirical manifestation of the WTO discourse has not been robust enough to warrant its normative ideal. Unfortunately, WTO norms as a language still remain esoteric to most of us. They are technical, complicated, and often unintelligible, particularly to non-experts. Unarticulated and subaudible, the WTO language self-limits its value. Therefore, if the WTO language is to be shared broadly, and the legal gravitational force of WTO

[100] Laurence R. Helfer and Anne-Marie Slaughter, "Toward a Theory of Effective Supranational Adjudication," 107 (1997) *Yale Law Journal* 273, 369; see also Detlev F. Vagts, "Hegemonic International Law," 95 (2001) *American Journal of International Law* 843, 845 (observing that even a hegemon "has to operate in the highly legalized universe of the World Trade Organization").

[101] See John H. Jackson, *The Jurisprudence of GATT and the WTO: Insights on Treaty Law and Economic Relations* (2000), pp. 278–9; John Gerard Ruggie, "International Regimes, Transactions, and Change: Embedded Liberalism in the Post-War Economic Order," 36 (1982) *International Organization* 379, 404–5.

norms is to be expanded, it should become more articulated, audible, and therefore exoteric to the world. For this purpose, one might recapitulate the normative quintessence of international trade law and formulate the "Basic Law of International Trade" so that both states and private actors can more easily identify the WTO language and thus become more willing to *speak* it. The goal of the Basic Law here is not to advance any universal, dogmatic tenets of international trade law; rather, it aims to offer a salient heuristic on WTO norms. It will visualize what has already been normatively shared among WTO members and further expand the horizon of the common law of international trade.[102]

The Basic Law can be distilled from the rich WTO jurisprudence that represents the three-prong *telos* of free trade, market integration, and development. Importantly, the Basic Law is not a mere mechanical restatement of the existing WTO jurisprudence, but rather a teleological reconstruction of it. Thus, it governs how one WTO member should treat another one in trade relations. In this regard, the Basic Law may be understood as the ultimate moral authority of the WTO community. Given that this book views WTO norms as a language to be used for WTO discourse, the Basic Law may be deemed an essential syntax and grammar of the WTO language.

The Basic Law may manifest itself in two different – negative and positive – forms. A WTO member *shall not* discriminate against another member; yet, a WTO member *shall* take into consideration another member's situation. First, note that even after rounds of trade talks for the past several decades, the trying realities of political economy on the ground still undermine supreme norms of international trade, such as anti-discrimination. Therefore, the first tenet of the Basic Law is to reaffirm this backbone of free trade. The Basic Law should proscribe any kind of protectionism so that any WTO member can secure better access to others' markets for both agricultural and manufactured products. Importantly, the first tenet also paves a firm ground for international economic justice by empowering the poor to obtain effective access to the global market. In this regard, it is a superior developmental apparatus to any special trade preferences or aid: aid without free trade seldom surpasses free trade without aid.[103]

[102] See notably Joseph H. H. Weiler, *The EU, the WTO, and the NAFTA: Towards a Common Law of International Trade?* (2000).

[103] "Mixed Reaction on Trade in Financing for Development Outcome," *Bridges Weekly Trade News Digest,* March 26, 2002, p. 6, available at www.ictsd.org/weekly/02-03-26/story3.htm; Ela Soyemi, "Africa Needs Trade, Not Aid," *The Guardian*, April 17, 2010, available at guardian.co.uk.

However, even when a WTO member pursues legitimate non-discriminatory social policies, these measures may still affect another member's effective market access. For example, higher health or environmental standards in developed countries may preclude African countries' agricultural exports from accessing those markets, since African producers are often unable to comply with sophisticated regulatory standards.[104] These countries may lack both the technical and financial capacities necessary to adopt and implement such high standards. This is why the Basic Law should also manifest itself through a positive mode. This positive manifestation of the Basic Law requires a regulating importing country to take into full consideration any potential regulatory burdens that an exporting country may incur.

The ultimate goal of the Basic Law is not to establish an axiomatic norm. Rather, it attempts to schematize a basic normative structure under which the WTO system evolves. While its concrete content is subject to change, the notion is still useful in the sense that it offers coherent normative guidance on particular cases. Note that the WTO discourse, even with reference to the Basic Law, might not always produce consensus. A deeper nature of the Basic Law is to nurture WTO members' level of discursive tolerance by concretizing unshared grounds and making them ready for future accommodation.[105]

V. The extra-community dynamics of the world trade community

A. *From the world trade community to the world trade constitution*

The WTO community is not a self-contained system. It does not exist isolated from its environment comprised of other legal systems. Its external relationship with the environment is as significant as its internal operation. While the WTO community is shaped by its own intradiscourse, this external dynamic is a reflection of interdiscourse between the WTO community and other *nomoi*, be they other areas of international law or domestic legal systems.[106] Thus, fully comprehending the WTO

104 See generally John S. Wilson and Victor O. Abiola (eds.), *Standards and Global Trade: A Voice for Africa* (2003).

105 Berman, *supra* note 82, pp. 327–8.

106 Regarding "intradiscourse" and "interdiscourse," see Peter Goodrich, *Legal Discourse: Studies in Linguistics, Rhetoric and Legal Analysis* (1987), pp. 146–51.

community calls for *inter*-systemic or *inter*-institutional investigations between the WTO and other legal systems concerning such questions as how the WTO responds to non-trade systems, coined as resonance; how its norms penetrate into members' domestic legal systems, coined as internalization; and how it configures itself with regional trade agreements (RTAs), coined as defragmentation.

This book embraces the notion of the world trade "constitution" in an effort to conceptualize the WTO community's external relationship.[107] Its main analytical focus is how the world trade community defines, governs, manifests, and eventually constitutes itself in an external legal relationship with other legal systems, such as multilateral environmental treaties, domestic legal systems, and RTAs. The WTO community is constitutive in the sense that it creates a social connection with its environment that might not otherwise exist.[108] If the WTO has any meaning, it is because it constructs, and reconstructs, its own identity as well as that of another entity through a continuous interdiscourse with the latter.[109]

Modalities of these legal relationships between the WTO and other legal systems may vary. For example, a horizontal relationship between the WTO and a multilateral environmental agreement may be pluralistic in that the relationship would neither completely assimilate nor exclude the other.[110] Rather, they communicate with, and thus resonate to, each other. In contrast, a vertical relationship between the WTO and a domestic legal system may be more orderly, if not entirely hierarchical, than the horizontal relationship in the sense that a WTO member should somehow transform the WTO norms into its own law within its discretion. Also, a federalistic, not federal, relationship can emerge between the WTO and RTAs in that RTAs may complement the

[107] Regarding a similar categorization (horizontal and vertical) in explaining the mechanisms of constitutionalism, see Jeffrey L. Dunoff and Joel P. Trachtman, "A Functional Approach to International Constitutionalization," in Jeffrey L. Dunoff and Joel P. Trachtman (eds.), *Ruling the World?: Constitutionalism, International Law, and Global Governance* (2009); T. Cottier, "Limits to International Trade: The Constitutional Challenge," (2000) *American Society of International Law Proceedings* 220, 221 (viewing that a horizontal perspective on constitutionalism concerns coherence between different values, while a vertical one involves the balancing of power between different levels of government).

[108] *Cf.* Abbott, *supra* note 98, 974.

[109] *Cf.* W. Richard Scott, "Reflections on a Half-Century of Organizational Sociology," 30 (2004) *Annual Review of Sociology*, 1, 13.

[110] See notably Berman, *supra* note 82, p. 12.

WTO's operation while not losing their organizational autonomy.[111] From a social perspective, this book explores the interplay between the WTO and non-WTO legal systems, rather than attempting to measure any legal hierarchy between them.[112] The main purpose of the book is to envision possibilities for bringing WTO and non-WTO actors together into a common discursive sphere.[113]

B. *The horizontal trade constitution: resonance*

The WTO's community exists and operates as it continuously communicates with its environment, including other international legal systems that aim to achieve different non-trade goals from free trade. This *inter*discourse is critical in the WTO's evolution *qua* institution because it shapes the contour of the WTO's own identity. More often than not, certain tensions emerge between the WTO's pursuit of free trade values and other areas of social regulation that may inhibit such pursuit.

For example, the goal of protecting human health from certain risks may effectively ban foreign imports. Here, a trade value and a social value (human health) appear to cancel each other out. In this situation, which is broadly labeled "linkage" in the sense that trade is linked to human health issues, how should the WTO act? Should the WTO defer this issue to relevant regulatory organizations, such as the World Health Organization (WHO)? Or should the WTO adhere to its own value (free trade) while it simply ignores other (social) values? This trying question of linkage characterizes the WTO's horizontal constitution because the way this matter is handled eventually constitutes the WTO itself *vis-à-vis* other areas of law and institutions.

Essentially, interdiscourse as the *modus operandi* of the WTO's horizontal constitution is an extension of intradiscourse. The institutionalized forms of WTO intradiscourse, such as adjudication, extrajudicial dialogue, and consultation, also serve as valuable avenues for

[111] Sungjoon Cho, "Breaking the Barrier between Regionalism and Multilateralism: A New Perspective on Trade Regionalism," 42 (2001) *Harvard International Law Journal* 419, 453.

[112] Berman, *supra* note 82, p. 15; see also Gregory Shaffer, "A Structural Theory of WTO Dispute Settlement: Why Institutional Choice Lies at the Center of the GMO Case," 41 (2008) *New York University Journal of International Law and Politics* 1, 13 (recognizing that the term constitution may accord the WTO a false image of "global hierarchy").

[113] Berman, *supra* note 82, p. 16.

interdiscourse, such as inter-institutional communication between the WTO and other international regulatory regimes. Among these different modes of WTO discourse, adjudication tends to exhibit the most salient case for the WTO's horizontal constitution. While the WTO tribunal should not per se *apply* non-WTO norms, it can still reference or take into account those non-WTO norms in a way that narrows rhetorical distances between WTO norms and non-WTO norms.[114]

For example, although the Appellate Body in *Shrimp-Turtle* did not apply the United Nations Convention on the Law of the Sea (UNCLOS) in a technical sense, the Appellate Body did reference the UNCLOS and the Convention on International Trade in Endangered Species of Wild Fauna and Flora (CITES) to support its evolutionary interpretation of "exhaustible natural resources."[115] The point is that the WTO should be open to and should communicate with non-trade norms so long as it retains its identity as a *trade* organization. In other words, in various linkage situations, the WTO should hold its primacy over trade issues that fall within its jurisdiction.[116] In this regard, the WTO tribunal (panels and the Appellate Body) might treat those non-WTO laws as relevant fact, but not law itself.

In sum, while the world trade community should maintain its operational autonomy through its self-referential communication (intradiscourse), it should also engage in operational interaction with other areas of international law in its environment (interdiscourse). The

[114] "While WTO Panels and the Appellate Body cannot definitively determine rights and obligations under non-WTO agreements, absent some provision so providing, they can refer to and analyze such agreements to the extent it is necessary to determine rights and obligations under the WTO agreements." William J. Davey and André Sapir, "The *Soft Drinks* Case: The WTO and Regional Agreements," 8 (2009) *World Trade Review*, 1, 18.

[115] Report of the Appellate Body, *United States – Import Prohibition of Certain Shrimp and Shrimp Products*, ¶¶ 168–9, WT/DS58/AB/R (October 12, 1998) (referencing various multilateral environmental treaties in interpreting GATT Article XX (g)).

[116] Laurence Boisson de Chazournes and Makane Moïse Mbengue, "Trade, Environment and Biotechnology: On Coexistence and Coherence," in Daniel Wüger and Thomas Cottier (eds.), *Genetic Engineering and the World Trade System* (2008). The 2004 WTO Consultative Body Report (the "Sutherland Report") also highlighted that the WTO should maintain its "*sui generis*" status *vis-à-vis* other international organizations. Peter D. Sutherland *et al.*, "The Future of the WTO: Addressing Institutional Challenges in the New Millennium" (WTO Consultative Report) (2005), at ¶¶ 159–60 ("The guiding line for granting observer status to international organizations, as for cooperative agreements, is the contribution 'horizontal coordination' can offer to the activities of the WTO.").

gist of interdiscourse is for the world trade community to develop regulatory sensitivity *vis-à-vis* other communities, such as the "climate community."[117] The true challenge of the WTO's horizontal constitution is to build trust with other international law communities,[118] while at the same time effectively screening out any disguised form of protectionism.

C. *The vertical trade constitution: internalization*

The concept of constitution offers a useful heuristic apparatus with which to probe and comprehend a subtle system of governance between the WTO and its members.[119] The vertical trade constitution concerns how the WTO norms may permeate into WTO members' domestic legal systems. Mainstream public international law and International Relations (IR) theories characterize this issue as "compliance." Under this dominant framework, compliance is a particular pattern of state behavior determined by certain exogenous factors, such as power, interest, and utility. For example, according to neorealists, a state complies with international law when – *only* when – either such compliance is in its interest or non-compliance would bring to it certain disutilities, such as sanctions. This exogenous approach leads naturally to a remedial accent on compliance, which overemphasizes a binary, and judgmental, aspect of underlying obligations, namely, violation versus compliance, in the shadow of sanctions (enforcement).

[117] See Patrick A Messerlin, "Keeping the WTO Busy While the Doha Round Is Stuck," *Vox* (July 29, 2012), www.voxeu.org/article/keeping-wto-busy-while-doha-round-stuck.

[118] Franz Xaver Perrez, "Risk Regulation, Precaution and Trade," in Daniel Wüger and Thomas Cottier (eds.), *Genetic Engineering and the World Trade System* (2008), pp. 246, 274.

[119] Regarding the general use of the constitution concept, see David Schneiderman, *Constitutionalizing Economic Globalization: Investment Rules and Democracy's Promise* (2008), p. 3; Anthony Giddens, *New Rules for Sociological Method* (2nd edn, 1993). Regarding the "trade constitution," see John H. Jackson, *The World Trading System: Law and Policy of International Economic Relations* (2nd edn, 1997), p. 339; John H. Jackson, *The World Trade Organization: Constitution and Jurisprudence* (1998), pp. 101–4; John H. Jackson, "Reflections on International Economic Law," 17 (1996) *University of Pennsylvania Journal of International Economic Law*, 17, 25–8; John H. Jackson, "Perspectives on Regionalism in Trade Relations," 27 (1996) *Law and Policy in International Business* 873, 873; see also Antonio F. Perez, "WTO and U.N. Law: Institutional Comity in National Security," 23 (1998) *Yale Journal of International Law*, 301, 316–24 (1998) (discussing Professor Jackson's constitutional premise of international trade law).

However, mainstream IR theories may not capture the whole picture of states' norm conformity, in particular the discourse between the WTO norms and domestic law. They rarely address the jurisgenerative process under which the WTO discourse cascades into domestic legal systems.[120] Likewise, scholars and policymakers alike seldom probe the process in which WTO norms as the objective, social reality are "retrojected" into a stream of a subjective reality within a domestic legal system in the course of socialization.[121] Here, a social framework can help overcome such deficiency by highlighting the transmission process in which WTO members internalize the WTO discourse in an endogenous fashion. In this regard, constructivist scholars such as Harold Koh, Martha Finnemore, and Kathryn Sikkink focus on the vertical dynamics in which domestic actors learn, familiarize themselves with, and eventually assimilate international law within the domestic legal system.[122] This is a different research project from mainstream IR theories, which are basically interested in causal relationships between state behaviors and certain material exogenous factors, such as power and interest.[123]

Importantly, a hidden yet crucial connection between national welfare and global trade/development warrants a sociological investigation of the jurisgenerative discourse between the WTO community and a domestic legal system.[124] To capture this connection, it is vital to understand the teleological coherence between international trade law and

120 See Benedict Kingsbury, "The Concept of Compliance as a Function of Competing Conceptions of International Law," 19 (1998) *Michigan Journal of International Law* 345, 368 (trenchantly observing that different "theories" of international law tend to beget different views on compliance since these diverging theories have different accounts on the relationship of international law to state behaviors).

121 *Cf.* Berger and Luckmann, *supra* note 51, p. 61. Regarding a notable exception, see Robert Wolfe, "See you in Geneva! Legal (Mis-)Representations of the Trading System," 11 (2005) *European Journal of International Relations* 339 (observing that dense interactions within the SPS Committee tend to function better in enhancing WTO members' understanding of, and thus compliance with, the SPS Agreement than adjudicated decisions which are often confusing and incomprehensible).

122 Martha Finnemore and Kathryn Sikkink, "International Norm Dynamics and Political Change," 52 (1998) *International Organizations*, 887, 891; Harold Hongju Koh, "Why Do Nations Obey International Law?," 106 (1997) *Yale Law Journal* 2599.

123 Kingsbury, *supra* note 120, 368. Of course, constructivist theories on compliance may also be prone to the "rationalist criticism" in that these theories fail to explain certain conditions under which international law really becomes "effective." *Ibid.*, 359.

124 See Pauwelyn, *supra* note 77, 573 (highlighting such "consumer/citizen driven" trade politics over congressional, mercantilist producer-driven one).

domestic legal systems. Both a national economy and the global economy share the same tenet of market integration in pursuing augmented prosperity. Uninterrupted interstate commerce and the consequent creation of a single federal market have brought national prosperity to the United States. Likewise, free movement of goods and services and the resultant establishment of a common European market have also brought regional prosperity to the European Union. It is based on the same principle that global free trade among trading nations brings global prosperity. In the highly integrated and interdependent global marketplace, such free market operations in both domestic and international arenas connect and reinforce each other.

In order to preserve this essential connection between national welfare and global trade/development, domestic courts may serve as agencies for the nationalization of WTO norms. For example, a domestic litigant may sue her own government or other individuals in a domestic court for the violation of WTO norms. Granted, the WTO Agreement itself does not necessitate any self-execution or direct effect: it leaves implementation to each domestic legal system. Both the United States and the EU deny such an effect,[125] while other WTO members, such as Korea, recognize the possibility of direct applicability in the national court.[126] Yet domestic courts can still communicate with the WTO's community in the absence of a direct channel of transforming the WTO norms into domestic ones. Domestic courts, through various means and patterns, can cite, quote, or incorporate WTO norms in their own interpretation. In doing so,

[125] See Meinhard Hilf, "The Role of National Courts in International Trade Relations," 18 (1997) *Michigan Journal of International Law* 321, 338–9 (summarizing the European Court of Justice (ECJ)'s jurisprudence which denied direct applicability of GATT law); but see Carlos Manuel Vazquez, "Treaties as Law of the Land: The Supremacy Clause and the Judicial Enforcement of Treaties," 122 (2008) *Harvard Law Review* 599 (arguing that the Supremacy Clause sets a "default rule" of self-execution of all treaties, which may be reversed only by an explicit declaration of non-self-execution).

[126] See Constitution of the Republic of Korea, July 17, 1948, art. 6:1 (Korea) ("Treaties duly concluded and promulgated under the Constitution and the generally recognized rules of international law shall have the same effect as the domestic laws of the Republic of Korea"); Supreme Court [S. Ct.], 2004Chu10, September 9, 2005 (S. Kor.) ("Since General Agreement on Tariffs and Trade 1994 is an integral part of WTO Agreement which the National Assembly had given ratification and now in operation . . . according to Article VI:1 of the Korean Constitution, the effect of the treaty is equivalent to national law. Therefore, if an act by a local assembly violates GATT, it is invalid.") (translated and quoted in Ji Hyun Sohn, "The Relationship between WTO Law and National Law: Critical Analysis on Jurisprudence of Korean National Courts," 2 (2007) *Korean University Law Review* 138, 138–9).

domestic courts can synchronize their hermeneutical circle with WTO norms and thus engender domestic discourse (jurisprudence) that coheres with WTO norms.

D. *The federalistic trade constitution: defragmentation*

A social framework may justify the longstanding apprehension over ever-propagating RTAs. In particular, structural functionalism posits that parts contribute to the solidarity of a whole system.[127] From this theoretical stance, RTAs (parts) must contribute to the integrationist *telos* – "to develop an integrated, more viable and durable multilateral trading system"[128] – of the world trade community (whole). If RTAs generate negative externalities to the global trading system, they remain stumbling blocks to global trade equivalent to public *bad* of the world trade community.[129] Against this backdrop, the federalistic trade constitution pursues the institutional stability of the world trade community by defragmenting RTAs-driven compartmentalized sub-trading systems.

If the federalistic trade constitution is a newly defined social structure of the world trade community, it is its symbolic interaction among individuals and groups, such as judges and tribunals, that actually shapes such social structure.[130] Discourse, to be more precise interdiscourse, between social actors from the WTO and RTAs may defragment, or multilateralize,[131] the WTO community. Various means of interdiscourse between the WTO and RTAs are capable of broadening their shared grounds. Each mode of discourse tends to retain its own pros and cons. Negotiation has produced little progress in this area due mainly to the highly political nature of RTAs. Negotiating parties have largely avoided any binding, legislative actions in the area, although "clarifying and improving" disciplines over RTAs remains as one of the Doha Round agendas.[132] While a formal mode of discourse, such

[127] Moshe Hirsch, "The Sociology of International Economic Law: Sociological Analysis of the Regulation of Regional Agreements in the World Trading System," 19 (2008) *European Journal of International Law* 277, 290–1.

[128] WTO Agreement, *supra* note 33.

[129] Sungjoon Cho, "Linkage of Free Trade and Social Regulation: Moving Beyond the Entropic Dilemma," 5 (2005) *Chicago Journal of International Law* 625.

[130] Hirsch, *supra* note 127, 291–2.

[131] See generally Richard Baldwin and Philip Thornton, *Multilateralizing Regionalism: Ideas for a WTO Action Plan on Regionalism* (2008).

[132] World Trade Organization, Ministerial Declaration of 14 November 2001, ¶ 2, WT/MIN(01)/DEC/1, 41 ILM 746 (2002).

as adjudication, may deliver a concrete result, it tends to lack flexibility and practicality, which an informal mode of discourse, such as peer review, might be in a better position to provide. The eventual effectiveness of the federalistic trade constitution depends on the frequency, intensity, and depth of symbolic interactions engineered by these means of interdiscourse between the WTO and RTAs.

VI. Evaluation: the legitimacy of the world trade community

The final stage in reconfiguring the world trading system is to evaluate whether the new social framework proposed in this book is legitimate. Admittedly, the concept of legitimacy may be elusive. Simply, so many theories and narratives revolve around the concept. There is no single, unified definition. At least three different versions of legitimacy may exist in accordance with three different perspectives. From a legal perspective, legitimacy may denote a legal validity; from a moral-philosophical perspective, it may mean moral justifiability; from a sociological perspective, it may simply refer to Weberian social acceptability.[133] At broad brush, this book focuses on the third type of legitimacy.

For the purpose of this book, the legitimacy of the world trade community can be defined as a generalized perception among members of the community that its operation is desirable or appropriate within the social context formed by culture and norms.[134] Therefore, the WTO's legitimacy is inextricably linked to social aspects of its existence and operation, such as its intra- and extra-community dynamics. Internal legitimacy concerns the intra-community dynamics, while external legitimacy is linked to the extra-community dynamics. Each dimension of legitimacy denotes certain properties that define the evaluative concept. First, trust characterizes internal legitimacy. Internal legitimacy concerns whether or how much the intra-community dynamics of the WTO community, shaped by its norms and discourse, are acceptable to the internal actors of the community, such as WTO member states and individual economic players within them. Second, sustainability demonstrates external legitimacy. External legitimacy represents whether and how much the extra-community dynamics,

[133] David Beetham, *The Legitimation of Power* (1991), p. 11.

[134] M. Suchman, "Managing Legitimacy: Strategic and Institutional Approaches," (1995) *Academy of Management Review* 20, 571; W. R. Scott, *Institutions and Organizations* (2nd edn, 2001).

which concerns the WTO's social relationship with surrounding non-trade systems, is sustainable in the long-run.

VII. Coda: the double-helix structure of two frameworks

This book is based on a dual observation: on the one hand, the old contract framework has recently failed to capture the new trade reality; on the other hand, the old framework, if sustained, is likely to precipitate serious normative problems in the world trading system. In response, this book offers a new (social) framework.

Note that a framework is not a matter of being right or wrong. It simply presents a different way of observing the world. In this regard, each framework can be said to be right on its *own* terms. Both the old and new framework are based on different "scope conditions."[135] Based on the assumption that WTO members' preferences are fixed (in favor of trade surplus), rationalists are likely to explain the status quo in a causal fashion, such as why a particular member or a group of members behave in a particular direction. In contrast, constructivists attribute WTO members' behaviors to their social traits, such as norms and collective identities.[136]

Admittedly, paradigmatic heterogeneities between rationalism and constructivism often appear irreconcilable because they originate from differing disciplines or methodologies employing differing realms of inquiries. Thus, any paradigm tends to resist falsification by post hoc rationalization and therefore might be vulnerable to tautology.[137] For example, although rationalists might view that institutionalization would be reduced eventually to an "economy of effort,"[138] this titular economy belongs to a cognitive dimension and could not be deemed an economic action as a typical unit of analysis under rationalism.

Likewise, a social framework might be equally accused of falling into the same paradigmatic trap that this book argues a rationalist approach would tumble into: that a single fundamental drive exists behind a social action. While this book faults rationalism's preoccupation with an under-socialized, utilitarian motive behind a state action, by the same token one

[135] Ronald Jepperson *et al.*, "Norms, Identity and Culture in National Security," in Peter Katzenstein (ed.), *The Culture of National Security* (1996), p. 71.

[136] Wendt, *supra* note 71, pp. 366–7.

[137] J. I. Prattis, "Synthesis, Or, a New Problematic in Economic Anthropology," 11 (1982) *Theory and Society*, 205, 205.

[138] *Cf.* Berger and Luckmann, *supra* note 51, p. 53.

might challenge an "over-socialized" conception of a social action.[139] Mark Granovetter eloquently warned against this mechanical adherence to a singular model attributable to both under-socialization and over-socialization.[140] Obviously, this book does not view that WTO members simply follow social scripts of WTO norms in a mechanical fashion.

Notably, paradigmatic heterogeneities do not necessarily negate a possible co-existence, or even symbiosis, between rationalism and constructivism. Indeed, an intellectual dichotomy between scientific and humanistic approaches is a false one.[141] Given that each framework holds its own disciplinary merit, the WTO might be viewed as a "double-helix" structure inextricably combined by individuality and collectivity as well as material and ideational sub-structures. Mindful of this double-helix structure, this book, while advancing the community model based on social constructivism, does recognize complementary theoretical space for the contract model and rationalism. In fact, some IR scholars called for this kind of cross-framework discourse, and synthesis, so as to both broaden and deepen IR narratives.[142] Illuminating each framework's blind spots, this nuanced attitude will offer a more complete picture of an international organization than any disciplinary monopoly.[143]

The unfolding of the double-helix structure of the WTO community comes in two forms. First, one can observe that one framework complements the other framework's relative paucity. Despite its characteristic parsimony, which can deliver a powerful heuristic on state behaviors,[144]

[139] See Dennis Wrong, "The Oversocialized Conception of Man in Modern Society," 26 (1961) *American Sociological Review*, 183, 188–9.

[140] Here, I draw on Granovetter, *supra* note 30, 481, 487–9, 491, 493, 502–3, 507 ("Actors do not behave or decide as atoms outside a social context, nor do they adhere slavishly to a script written for them by the particular intersection of social categories that they happen to occupy."). *Ibid.*, 487. See also Mark A. Granovetter, "The Impact of Social Structure on Economic Outcomes," 19 (2005) *Journal of Economic Perspectives* 33.

[141] Prattis, *supra* note 137, 212.

[142] See e.g., Robert O. Keohane, "International Institutions: Two Approaches," 32 (1988) *International Studies Quarterly*, 379, 393 (advocating a synthesis between the rationalistic and reflective approaches); Checkel, *supra* note 91, 347–48 (urging constructivists to embrace a more coherent research design following the rationalistic critiques).

[143] See Ian Hurd, "Book Review," 62 (2013) *International & Comparative Law Quarterly* 771, 771 (reviewing Jeffrey Dunoff and Mark Pollack (eds.), *Interdisciplinary Perspectives on International Law and International Relations: The State of the Art* (2013)) (underscoring the need for an inter-disciplinary conversation, rather than justifying one's favored approach, as if "scoring points for the home team").

[144] Keohane, *supra* note 142, 392.

rationalism cannot exhaust such explanation and prediction.[145] For example, the same behavior, such as a WTO member's implementation of a decision by the Appellate Body, is explainable in multiple ways. A WTO member's compliance may be attributed to its calculation of the costs of non-compliance, including reputational costs (rationalism). Yet, the same compliance may be attributable simply to the state's habit, namely, to its internalized norm-abiding culture as a member of the WTO (constructivism). Under the first scenario, the decision-making process toward the compliant behavior might be a complicated one, involving many different matrices of calculation. In contrast, the decision-making under the second scenario might be rather intrinsic since it is largely cultural.

In parallel, the WTO, even as a community, may not connote an absolute collective identity. In fact, members are able to maintain their individuality, and one might observe that any collective authority extrapolated from the world trade community might not diminish each member's own rights under the WTO system.[146] Nonetheless, the context of the world trade community does modify the *terms* of such individuality.[147] After all, even a self-centered notion of individuality logically presumes the concept of community and its norms within which such individuality may have any meaning.[148]

Importantly, even a material order, be it a contract or market, is not self-generating. A material order does require a certain minimum social foundation. As Kenneth Arrow famously noted, even a simple commercial transaction necessitates an underlying trust to function.[149] One

[145] See notably Martha Finnemore, *National Interests in International Society* (1996).

[146] *Cf.* Harold Lasswell, "Future Systems of Identity in the World Community," in C. Black and R. Falk (eds.), *The Future of International Legal Order* (1972), pp. 3–31; Andrew Linklater, "The Problem of Community in International Relations," 15 (1990) *Alternatives*, 135–53.

[147] Wendt, *supra* note 71, pp. 246, 364.

[148] Charles Taylor, "Language and Society," in Axel Honneth and Hans Joas (eds.), *Communicative Action: Essays on Jürgen Habermas's The Theory of Communicative Action* (1991), p. 24 ("Subjects acting communicatively always come to an understanding in the horizon of a lifeworld ... formed from more or less diffuse, always unproblematic, background convictions ... [it] serves as a source of situation definitions that are presupposed by participants as unproblematic ... The lifeworld also stores the interpretive work of preceding generations."). See also Jürgen Habermas, "Reason and the Rationalization of Society," in 1 *The Theory of Communicative Action* 70 (Thomas McCarthy trans., 1984).

[149] Kenneth J. Arrow, "Gifts and Exchanges," 1 (1972) *Philosophy and Public Affairs*, 343, 357.

should also learn to understand the market to be able to operate within it.[150] In the same vein, the titular national interests are not simply thrust upon us: they are not just waiting to be picked. Rather, they are constructed via social processes.[151] Rationalism, such as a game theory, simply brackets social dimensions of key parameters, such as players, rules, and payoffs.[152] A game theory does not explain the identity of players (how they view themselves), the rules of game (how they form those rules), and the nature of payoffs (how they define interests). After all, answers to these socio-structural questions are vital to determine whether game theory models make any sense.

The second way of decoding the double helix structure of the WTO community is through the lens of convergence. One may compare an explanation of a phenomenon under one framework with another explanation of the same phenomenon rendered by the other framework. While the two explanations are different, one may nonetheless locate some conceptual zone of convergence where an alternative interpretation of the same phenomenon might not be entirely improbable under a different framework.[153]

For example, in the very long run, both frameworks may provide quite converging narratives on states' behaviors. The so-called "repeated game" under the rationalist framework speaks to fully habituated behavioral patterns that characterize the social framework. Here, even under the contract model, the duration and frequency of transactions could transform the nature of parties' interests. Now, the newly defined interest connotes a broader and longer-term interest that would defy any narrow, short-term calculation. One can also witness a similar phenomenon in domestic contract law, as seen in a "relational contract."[154] This is the very juncture where a commercial interest is blended with a social structure.

The juridification process in the history of the GATT/WTO reveals the second dimension of the double-helix structure. Even in its origin, the

[150] See Granovetter, *supra* note 30, 481. [151] Finnemore, *supra* note 145, p. 2.

[152] Audie Klotz, *Norms in International Relations: The Struggle against Apartheid* (1995), pp. 19–20.

[153] See, e.g., Antoine Bouet Sr. and David Laborde, "The Potential Cost of a Failed Doha Round," April 2, 2009, available at ssrn.com/abstract=1396335 (quantifying negative economic consequences of "non-cooperative" trade policies).

[154] See, e.g., Ian R. Macneil, "The Many Futures of Contract," 47 (1974) *Southern California Law Review*, 691 (defining a contract as a set of human relations from a social perspective).

GATT project was a mixture of the Kantian (community) and the Lockean (contract) perspectives.[155] It was Kantian in the sense that the interwar economic balkanization sparked a moment of enlightenment among trading nations and thus led them to agree on a grand collective project called the GATT. At the same time, however, it was also Lockean in the sense that the GATT contract was built upon rivalry. Contracting parties were constantly suspicious of each other's potential opportunistic behavior, such as cheating, which would have nullified any initial contractual terms established by painful tariff reduction negotiations. Given the dearth of trust, they wanted to program a control mechanism in the form of legal obligations to monitor and deter such cheating.[156]

Under the contract model, this pre-programmed control mechanism lowers transaction costs by reducing the negative entropy within the system, and thus enhancing the level of stability. In addition to this original design, the GATT/WTO's subsequent practice took an evolutionary path toward a less contingent rule-oriented system than what a power-oriented system would have created. Such deepening of legalization boosts trust in the system itself,[157] thereby further reducing transaction costs.

Then, what about trust in *others*? Although trust in the system should not immediately translate into trust in others (fellow trading nations), the former still tends to beget the latter. On rationalist terms, trust in others means that the risk of others' betrayals, such as cheating, is low enough to assume it is negligible.[158] Thus, one might reasonably speculate that trust in the system results in trust in others by means of reciprocity. Note that trust-inducing reciprocity is not narrow and strategic; rather, it is a broad, diffuse mode of reciprocity. Then, this newly defined notion of reciprocity features properties of social dynamics. At this very point, the original concept of game or transaction could

155 See Wendt, *supra* note 71.

156 Control is "a regulatory process by which the elements of a system are made more predictable through the establishment of standards in the pursuit of some desired objective or state." R. Leifer and P. K. Mills, "An Information Processing Approach for Deciding upon Control Strategies and Reducing Control Loss in Emerging Organizations," 22 (1996) *Journal of Management*, 113, 117.

157 S. B. Sitkin, "On the Positive Effect of Legalization on Trust," in R. J. Bies *et al.*, (eds.), *Research on Negotiations in Organizations* (1995), pp. 185, 189.

158 S. C. Currall and T. A. Judge, "Measuring Trust Between Organizational Boundary Role Persons," in *Organizational Behavior and Human Decision Processes* (1995), pp. 64, 151–70.

be converted into discourse under the community framework. Repeated discourse builds trust and provides a fertile ground for the emergence of norms.[159]

In sum, two different default patterns of sociality exist. While rationalism presupposes an asocial – atomistic, anonymous, and solipsistic – actor, social theories presume a social actor. Rationalism brackets a social process leading up to the formation of certain material conditions. Yet, WTO members are not robots. While pursuing self-interest and efficiency, they are also sentient actors who constantly struggle to find the meaning of the WTO and its operation. The WTO is not, and should not be, a mere machine run by software to ensure only the maximum systemic efficiency.

Nonetheless, two frameworks may still interlock and embrace parallel narratives on the same phenomenon or operation within the WTO system if their scopes coincide. A wide spectrum exists in each discipline depending on clinical circumstances. Low sociality under constructivism borders on a rationalist situation; high sociality under rationalism approaches a constructivist situation, as seen in the repeated games. The more these two frameworks provide converging explanations on the same social phenomenon, the closer they may approach each other. Distrust and exploitation may equally precipitate the legitimacy crisis under both frameworks: communication breakdown (constructivism) or prohibitively high transaction cost (rationalism). Likewise, the Doha debacle would end up with being both inappropriate (constructivism) and inefficient (rationalism): it would raise the community risk. Some neoliberal institutionalists even consider "ideas" as an important causal factor that determines state behaviors.[160]

Finally, it would be naïve to expect that trade norms alone would be sufficient in changing hard-core politics or commercial interest.[161] True, the WTO's community will not turn all of us into communitarians overnight. Nonetheless, it will transform, over the long haul, the way in which WTO members view domestic trade politics and trade interest, even though it may take time to fully materialize. This book argues that the world trade community, if fully developed and sustained, will impact

[159] T. K. Das and B. Teng, "Between Trust and Control: Developing Confidence in Partner Cooperation in Alliances," 23(3) (1998) *Academy of Management Review*, 491, 497.

[160] See notably Judith Goldstein and Robert O. Keohane, "Ideas and Foreign Policy: An Analytical Framework," in Judith Goldstein and Robert O. Keohane (eds.), *Ideas and Foreign Policy: Briefs, Institutions, and Political Change* (1993).

[161] I owe this insight to an anonymous reviewer.

WTO members' identities and culture as they concern trade. In this way, the world trade community is capable of bettering the welfare of many *domestic* communities, such as the United States and the EU, which still suffer from parochial protectionism.[162] In fact, this is the very constitutional effect of the world trade community that the book advocates.

[162] I owe this insight to an anonymous reviewer.

2

Two frameworks on an international organization

The purely economic man is indeed close to being a social moron.

– Amartya K. Sen[1]

This chapter sets a theoretical tone for the book. It juxtaposes two different frameworks – rationalism and constructivism – under which one can understand an international organization (IO), such as the WTO, and its operation. The chapter probes what the conventional IR theories bracket, that is to say, ideational factors, such as culture and norms, which guide state behaviors, together with material factors, such as power and interests. Based on these ideational factors, the chapter explains social dynamics among member states and how such dynamics construct collective identities of an IO. The chapter does not propose to supplant rationalism with constructivism. Rather, its main purpose is to provide a complementary narrative on an IO so as to grapple with a complete picture of an IO.

I. Prologue: how to understand an international organization

Two months after the 9/11 terrorist attacks in 2001, WTO members gathered in the Qatari capital, Doha. Prompted by the exigency of the time, they launched an audacious trade negotiation round for the main purpose of reducing or eliminating chronic agricultural protection in developed countries.[2] WTO members were desperate to send the post-9/11 world

[1] Amartya K. Sen, "Rational Fools: A Critique of the Behavioral Foundations of Economic Theory," 6 (1977) *Philosophy and Public Affairs* 336, 336.

[2] In the Doha Ministerial Declaration of 2001, WTO members highlighted that "the majority of WTO members are developing countries" and agreed to "place [developing countries'] needs and interests at the heart of the Work Programme adopted in this Declaration." World Trade Organization, Ministerial Declaration of 14 November 2001, ¶ 2, WT/MIN(01)/DEC/1, 41 ILM 746 (2002).

a clear message that would reverberate even to the marginalized lands: "development." The Doha Round still remains unfinished even after over a decade of tedious and torturous talks,[3] despite a mini-package delivered in Bali at the end of 2013.[4]

While the Doha crisis must be one of the darkest hours of the WTO's history, it offers a rare opportunity to testify about the *gestalt* of world politics. Its conventional post-mortems invariably attribute the debacle to the lack of convergence in trade interests of key negotiating members, such as the United States, the EU, China, and India.[5] This standpoint betrays a latent yet firm premise that the WTO is a functional tool that coordinates and channels its (major) members' policy positions. That is, WTO members' national interests determine what the WTO does, and perhaps more importantly, what the WTO *is*. Methodologically, this perspective reflects individualism-cum-materialism. Presupposing self-regarding, profit-maximizing state actors, it attempts to explain why states behave in a particular pattern in a particular situation. This thread of thought, loosely coined rationalism,[6] is a dominant framework among contemporary IR scholars.[7] Under a rationalist lens, the Doha Round is no more than a deal fallen apart.

[3] See generally, Sungjoon Cho, "The Demise of Development in the Doha Round Negotiations," 45 (2010) *Texas International Law Journal* 573 (analyzing the history of the Doha Round's decade-long negotiation stalemate).

[4] WTO, Bali Ministerial Declaration and Decisions, available at wto.org/English/thewto_e/minist_e/mc9_e/balipackage_e.htm.

[5] See e.g., Alan Beattie, "Hopes Fade for Accord at Doha Talks," *Financial Times*, June 22, 2011 (highlighting fissures among the US, the EU, Brazil, and China on various issues, such as cotton subsidies); International Center for Trade and Sustainable Development, "Contemplating Doha Failure, WTO Members Look to Paris Meeting for Way Forward," 15 *Bridges Weekly Trade News Digest*, May 25, 2011, p. 1, available at ictsd.org/downloads/bridgesweekly/bridgesweekly15-19.pdf (observing gaps in negotiating parties' positions as "unbridgeable"); International Center for Trade and Sustainable Development, "Deeply Divided, WTO Members to Search for Common Ground on Doha," 14 *Bridges Weekly Trade News Digest*, May 26, 2010, p. 1, available at ictsd.org/downloads/bridgesweekly/bridgesweekly14-19.pdf (pointing out that WTO members failed to agree on "common terms of engagement").

[6] Two strands of IR theories stand out under the banner of rationalism depending on main parameters: realism (neorealism) characterizes an IO as a mechanism reflecting interest of powerful states, while liberalism (neoliberalism and neoliberal institutionalism) focuses on the utilities that an IO offers to its members, such as the reduction of transaction costs. See Robert O. Keohane, "International Institutions: Two Approaches," 32 (1988) *International Studies Quarterly* 379, 381.

[7] See Jeffrey T. Checkel, "The Constructivist Turn in International Relations Theory," 50 (1998) *World Policy* 324, 324 (observing that the neorealist-neoliberal debate has been central within IR for the past decade).

Granted, it would be disingenuous to say that states do not pursue material (economic) interests. Still, however, rationalism does not, and cannot, elucidate how an IO's members form their interests in the first place. After all, an IO membership cannot be reduced simply to a bargaining privilege. It also represents a common set of beliefs shared collectively by its members, with or without cost-benefit calculations.[8] From this perspective, one might render a different interpretation of the Doha failure. The true failure might be for WTO members not to establish a shared normative ground among themselves over the Doha Development Agenda. Under this framework, the Doha Round is a failed community-building project. This book aims to animate this *social* framework that remains hitherto under-explored in international studies.[9]

Most IR scholars are trained to perceive world politics *through* state actors. The conventional framework of an IO may be best depicted as a global contract,[10] namely, a contractarian relationship established by

[8] See José E. Alvarez, "International Organizations: Then and Now," 100 (2006) *American Journal of International Law*, 324, 338 (observing that "the ideas, shared understandings, and norms (soft and hard) that emerge from participation in IOs [International Organizations] 'constrain and enable choices' for states").

[9] One of the earlier ventures to apply sociology to international law can be found in Max Huber's work. While emphasizing collective interests among states, Huber still recognized a special status of powerful states ("Machtrecht"), especially in his early work. See Jost Delbrück, "Max Huber's Sociological Approach to International Law Revisited," 18 (2007) *European Journal of International Law*, 97, 97–8, 109–11. Subsequently, Harold Lasswell and Myres McDougal also pursued "the global common interest in approximating a world public order of human dignity." Richard H. Steinberg and Jonathan M. Zasloff, "Power and International Law," 100 (2006) *American Journal of International Law*, 64, 76–7. Yet this sociological approach has often been criticized as lacking interest in the "effectiveness" of international law. *Ibid.* More recently, international scholars, in particular those who take international organizations seriously, have begun to pay more attention to a sociological framework in understanding state behaviors. For example, José Alvarez viewed compliance pull as a sociological phenomenon. Alvarez, *supra* note 8. In a similar vein, Jutta Brunnée submitted that IOs "socialize" states and lead them to internalize norms generated within IOs even without material (cost-benefit) considerations. *Ibid.* (referring to the reliance on the concept of socialization based on IO membership by Jutta Brunnée and other scholars). Robert Keohane called a sociological approach a "reflexive" approach in contrast with a rationalist approach, yet he criticized that a sociological approach generally lacks a coherent "theory." Keohane, *supra* note 6, 393.

[10] The concept of "contract" this book adopts is analogous to the notion of "*Gesellschaft*" that German sociologist Ferdinand Tönnies used. See Ferdinand Tönnies, *Community and Society (Gemeinshaft und Gesellschaft)* (Charles P. Loomis trans. & ed., 1957), pp. 223–31, reprinted in Marcello Truzzi, *Sociology: the Classic Statements* (1971), pp. 145–54 (1971). Tönnies wrote about the dichotomy between *Gesellschaft* ("society") and *Gemeinschaft*

sovereign states to achieve a certain functional goal, be it the promotion of free trade or the prevention of climate change.[11] Here, particular political outcomes may be attributed eventually to calculative individual actions, rather than internal norms provided by the IO itself.[12] To this extent, an IO may be viewed as a hollow instrument that states manipulate to attain their desired goals.[13]

True, rationalism provides a simple yet powerful heuristic on world politics.[14] One need not become a diplomat to appreciate this point. At the same time, however, it presents a rather curtailed picture of contemporary IOs and their relationships with states.[15] Most of all, rationalism's very assumption simply omits the underlying ideational properties of state action. Even states' strategic choices, which are informed by rationally structured national interests, cannot be made in a vacuum. While states do calculate,[16] they also interpret.[17] Their alleged rational choices are not to be deducted invariably from pre-defined sets of preferences.[18] There must be an explanation as to how these interests are constructed in

("community") found in human interactions and group dynamics. Tönnies defined *Gesellschaft* as an artificial human connection built by people who possessed an intent to work together, whereas *Gemeinschaft* was a natural human connection arising out of birth or family. *Ibid.*

11 *Cf.* Francis Ysidro Edgeworth, *Mathematical Physics: An Essay on the Application of Mathematics to the Moral Sciences* (1881), p. 52 (viewing that "economical calculus" in opposition to ethical deliberation was particularly relevant to "war and contract").

12 See James G. March and Johan P. Olsen, "The New Institutionalism: Organizational Factors in Political Life," 78 (1984) *The American Political Science Review* 734, 736–9 (observing that utilitarianism as an ideology interprets actions as based on calculated decisions).

13 See Kenneth A. Shepsle, "Studying Institutions: Some Lessons From the Rational Choice Approach," 1 (1989) *Journal of Theoretical Politics*, 131, 133.

14 Regarding legal scholarships applying rationalism to international law, see e.g., Jack L. Goldsmith and Eric A. Posner, *The Limits of International Law* (2005), p. 3 (arguing that international law "emerges from states acting rationally to maximize their interests").

15 Regarding general critiques on rationalist model, see Emilie M. Hafner-Burton *et al.*, "Political Science Research on International Law: The State of the Field," 106 (2012) *American Journal of International Law* 47, 81–2; Alexander Wendt, "Driving with the Rearview Mirror: On the Rational Science of Institutional Design," 55 (2001) *International Organization*, 1019; John S. Duffield, "The Limits of 'Rational Design'," 57 (2003) *International Organization* 411.

16 See Colin Hay and Daniel Wincott, "Structure, Agency and Historical Institutionalism," 46 (1998) *Political Studies* 951, 952.

17 See Stephen Bell, "Institutionalism: Old and New," in Dennis Woodward, Andrew Parkin and John Summers (eds.), *Government, Politics and Power in Australia* (2002), pp. 1, 8.

18 *Ibid.*

the first place,[19] such as through normative reference and cultural templates.[20] By the same token, states must decide where and how to use power and wealth obtained in the name of national interests.[21]

In this regard, this book defines states as social actors, more than atomistic individuals.[22] In particular, this book employs an IR version of a social framework, i.e., constructivism.[23] While admitting that power and interest still matter in terms of their causal effect on state behaviors, constructivism nonetheless emphasizes the constitutive role of ideas and norms on such material factors as power and interest.[24] In other words, it is ideas that eventually define power and interest.[25] Constructivism enables us to conceptualize a community of law comprised of norms and legal discourses.[26] Under this constructivist *Weltanschauung*, an

[19] See Kathleen Thelen and Sven Steinmo, "Historical Institutionalism in Comparative Politics," in Kathleen Thelen and Sven Steinmo (eds.), *Structuring Politics: Historical Institutionalism in Comparative Analysis* (1992), pp. 1, 8.

[20] See Bell, *supra* note 17; see also Walter W. Powell and Paul J. DiMaggio (eds.), *The New Institutionalism in Organizational Analysis* (1991).

[21] See Martha Finnemore, *National Interests in International Society* (1996), p. 2.

[22] See Alexander E. Wendt, "The Agent-Structure Problem in International Relations," 41 (1987) *International Organization* 335, 366 (arguing for a theory that posits the state as a particular kind of social actor that is "an inherently social entity, rather than as a Hobbesian primitive individual").

[23] The pedigree of constructivism dates back to the 1950s when Karl Deutsch "highlighted the importance of identity formation measured by social transactions and communications." Jutta Brunnée and Stephen J. Toope, "International Law and Constructivism: Elements of an Interactional Theory of International Law," 39 (2000) *Columbia Journal of Transnational Law* 19, 26 (quoting Peter J. Katzenstein *et al.*, "International Organization and the Study of World Politics," 52 (1998) *International Organization*, 645, 654). See generally Karl W. Deutsch *et al.*, *Political Community in the North Atlantic Area: International Organization in the Light of Historical Experience* (1957). Yet the term ("constructivism") was coined by Nicholas Onuf in 1989. See Brunnée and Toope, *supra* (citing Nicholas Greenwood Onuf, *World of Our Making: Rules and Rule in Social Theory and International Relations* (1989), Chapter 1). There are many different forms of constructivism. In this book, I draw mainly on a modest (thin) form of constructivism that Alexander Wendt developed along the line of "structurationist and symbolic interactionist sociology." Alexander Wendt, *Social Theory of International Politics* (1999), p. 1; see also Stefano Guzzini, "A Reconstruction of Constructivism in International Relations," 6 (2000) *European Journal of International Relations* 147, 148 (observing that constructivism is inherently eclectic). See also Andreas Hasenclever *et al.*, *Theories of International Regimes*, (1997), p. 136 (defining constructivism as a "knowledge-based" theory or "cognitivism").

[24] See Wendt, *supra* note 23, p. 135 (arguing that power and interest are still important but constituted more by ideas and emphasizing the constitutive, not causal, nature of ideas).

[25] *Ibid.*

[26] See Emanuel Adler, "Seizing the Middle Ground: Constructivism in World Politics," 3 (1997) *European Journal of International Relations*, 319, 327; see also Benedict Anderson, *Imagined Communities: Reflections on the Origin and Spread of Nationalism* (2nd edn, 1991).

IO's norms function as a language members use to communicate with one another, thereby understanding and predicting each other's behaviors, instead of simply attempting to outmaneuver fellow members.

II. The rationalist framework: an international organization as an instrument

A. Neorealism

The end of the Second World War heralded in an era of IOs. The unprecedented tragedy brought to nations a rare Kantian moment of collective enlightenment.[27] Most of about two hundred international organizations now operating were established *post bellum*.[28] Most conspicuously, the United Nations (UN) was created "to save succeeding generations from the scourge of war" and "to unite our strength to maintain international peace and security."[29] Many other IOs derived from the UN, such as the World Health Organization (WHO), whose goal is the "attainment by all peoples of the highest possible level of health."[30] On the economic side, the so-called Bretton Woods institutions – the International Monetary Fund (IMF), the International Bank for Reconstruction and Development (IBRD), and the General Agreement on Tariffs and Trade (GATT) – were launched to rehabilitate the war-torn international financial, economic, and trade systems.[31]

Those lofty founding principles notwithstanding, from a technical standpoint, those IOs are a product of treaties, such as the UN Charter, the WHO Constitution, and the IMF Articles of Agreement. These treaties are multi-party contracts in which sovereign states (*contracting* parties) stipulate their rights and obligations in an attempt to achieve various regulatory goals. Those sovereign states negotiate terms of such contracts, and then draft, sign, and execute them. Contracting parties engage in various types of bargains among themselves over eventual terms of those treaties during the negotiation process. Naturally, they vie to secure better terms than their fellow states.

[27] See Wendt, *supra* note 23, pp. 297–308 (describing the Kantian culture based on collective identity and "friendship").

[28] For a comprehensive history of international organizations, see Bob Reinalda, *Routledge History of International Organizations: From 1815 to the Present Day* (2009).

[29] UN Charter, pmbl.

[30] Constitution of the World Health Organization, art. 1, July 22, 1946, 14 UNTS, 185.

[31] See Reinalda, *supra* note 28.

This contractarian characterization of treaties and IOs, which is conventional under public international law,[32] is susceptible to neorealism[33] in IR theories. Although it has copious variations, neorealism basically regards an IO as an instrument that serves sovereign states' functional needs.[34] Neorealism is rationalistic to the extent that it presupposes an optimal state behavior through objective calculations.[35] Under the neorealist logic, an IO is nothing but a global contract, an artificial association that states establish for the purpose of facilitating certain pre-programmed regulatory goals.[36] An IO as a global contract basically

[32] Vienna Convention on the Law of Treaties, May 23, 1969, 1155 UNTS 331; Draft Articles of State Responsibility on the Internationally Wrongful Acts, in Report of the International Law Commission, 53rd Sess., UN Doc. A/56/10; GAOR, 56th Sess., Supp. No. 10 (2001).

[33] See Ian Hurd, *International Organizations: Politics, Law, Practice* (2011), p. 26 (viewing that contractualism presents the "marriage of positivism in international law and realism in IR theory"). Regarding variations of realism, see Richard H. Steinberg and Jonathan M. Zasloff, "Power and International Law," 100 (2006) *American Journal of International Law* 64, 73–6. The prefix "neo" denotes a contemporary version of realism and liberalism distinguished from their classical prototypes. Neorealism and neoliberalism employ the "analytical tools of microeconomics to lend greater precision." Martha Finnemore and Kathryn Sikkink, "International Norm Dynamics and Political Change," 52 (1998) *International Organization*, 887, 890 (1998). In a similar manner, rational choice (game theory) theorists also emphasize the scientific superiority of a rationalist methodology in studying international law. See Andrew T. Guzman, *How International Law Works: A Rational Choice Theory* (2008), pp. 17, 21 (praising a rational choice model as the most promising model due to its parsimony and falsifiability). However, their subtle differences are not material for the purpose of this book. Therefore, these two terminologies are used interchangeably in this book.

[34] See Gayl D. Ness and Steven R. Brechin, "Bridging the Gap: International Organizations as Organizations," 42 (1988) *International Organization*, 245, 246; Harold K. Jacobson *et al.*, "National Entanglements in International Government Organizations," 80 (1986) *The American Political Science Review*, 134, 141–59. The most radical version of realism leads to a wholly dismissive claim that "international law does not pull states toward compliance contrary to their interests." Goldsmith and Posner, *supra* note 14, p. 13. According to this position, states comply with international law only when such compliance is in sync with their interests. Harlan Grant Cohen, "Can International Law Work?: A Constructivist Expansion," 27 (2009) *Berkeley Journal of International Law*, 636, 637 (observing that rational choice scholars view states as rational actors who condition their compliance with international law on their interests).

[35] See Keohane, *supra* note 6 (citing Herbert A. Simon, "Human Nature in Politics: The Dialogue of Psychology with Political Science," 79 (1985) *The American Political Science Review*, 293, 294). Yet as Robert Keohane aptly observed, this substantive rationality is situation-specific, depending on an initial analytical setting. Thus, the realist mantra of "national interests," which found its heyday in the Cold War era, tends to presuppose an ever-present Hobbesian zero-sum conflict.

[36] See Truzzi, *supra* note 10, pp. 223–31 (viewing that where contracts become the basis of a system, it is then formed by interests).

represents an economistic model where states attempt to maximize their interests by using a rational instrument to attain certain goals.[37]

Yet the IO's innate contractarian origin, and in particular, reciprocal bargain, inevitably subject the global contract to power disparity among its members. Indeed, the analytical centrality of neorealism lies in power.[38] Powerful states tend to design IO norms in a way that best serve their own preferences and interests. Therefore, contractarian norms are exogenously imposed constraints under which states' alleged rational behaviors are strategized.[39] The neorealist framework dates back to the Cold War period when security issues dominated both public policymaking and academic debates.[40] The neorealist methodology nearly became an unspoken ontology as it was long left unchallenged.[41]

This rather inorganic view of IOs is a logical corollary to the root thesis of neorealism, which is a theory about states.[42] Under this framework, an IO could not claim its own independent ontology separate from states.[43] Even if an IO may condition or structure state behaviors by controlling the information-decision flow among states, that alone might not grant the IO autonomy.[44] According to the old framework, IOs exert no independent impact on state behavior[45] since every single output generated by an IO is made, after all, *through* and *by* states. Therefore, neorealism reveals reductionism in that its focus on individual actors

[37] See Michael N. Barnett and Martha Finnemore, "The Politics, Power, and Pathologies of International Organizations," 53 (1999) *International Organization*, 699, 702; Powell and DiMaggio, *supra* note 20; Anna Grandori, "Notes on the Use of Power and Efficiency Constructs in the Economics and Sociology of International Organizations," in Siegwart Lindenberg and Hein Schreuder (eds.), *Interdisciplinary Perspectives on Organizational Studies* (1993), pp. 61–78.

[38] Richard H. Steinberg, "Wanted – Dead or Alive: Realism in International Law," in Jeffrey Dunoff and Mark Pollack (eds.), *Interdisciplinary Perspectives on International Law and International Relations: The State of the Art* (2013), p. 150.

[39] See Lauren B. Edelman *et al.*, "The Endogeneity of Legal Regulation: Grievance Procedures as Rational Myth," 105 (1999) *American Journal of Sociology*, 406, 410–11 (observing that ideologies of rationality determine strategic responses to law).

[40] See Katzenstein *et al.*, *supra* note 23, 652; *cf.* John H. Jackson, *Sovereignty, the WTO and Changing Fundamentals of International Law* (2006), p. 59 (characterizing the sovereignty-based old assumptions of public international law as "mantras").

[41] See John Gerard Ruggie and Friedrich V. Kratochwil, "Epistemology, Ontology, and the Study of International Regimes," in *Constructing the Polity: Essays on International Institutionalization* (1998); see also Wendt, *supra* note 23, p. 35.

[42] See Barnett and Finnemore, *supra* note 37, 706. [43] *Ibid.*, 704. [44] *Ibid.*

[45] See John J. Mearsheimer, "The False Promise of International Institutions," 19 (1995) *International Security* 5, 7.

and their interactions tends to make any organizational autonomy at the collective level unessential.[46]

B. *Regime theory*

Many a scholar has attempted to overcome the aforementioned limits in the neorealist framework by exploring an alternative one. Some neorealists departed from their traditional assumptions and took an institutionalist turn. In the 1970s, an intellectual thirst for a systematic explanation of global governance amid some uncharacteristic developments, such as the relative encroachment of the US hegemony and the rise of the Organization of Petroleum Exporting Countries (OPEC), drew many scholars toward the regime theory.[47] Regime theorists define regimes as state-constructed arrangements to coordinate international behaviors in certain issue areas.[48] Therefore, a regime may constrain and condition states' behavior. In this regard, one can identify a trade regime represented by the GATT/WTO and a monetary regime represented by the IMF.

However, the lingering deficiency in the regime theory is its failure to close the discrepancy between its epistemology and ontology.[49] By definition, regimes are based on certain epistemological traits, such as the convergence of expectations among their participants. Yet the neorealist-positivist pedigree[50] in the regime theory tends to focus only on objective forces influencing state behaviors; and therefore, it trivializes the subjective, and intersubjective, elements that produce *meanings* of state behaviors and eventually constitute state identities (ontology).[51]

Therefore, the role of norms was rather passive in the regime theory since the theory regards norms as mere external variables with which to

[46] See March and Olsen, *supra* note 12, 735–6.

[47] See Friedrich Kratochwil and John Gerard Ruggie, "International Organization: A State of the Art on an Art of the State," 40 (1986) *International Organization*, 753, 759.

[48] *Ibid.* [49] *Ibid.*, 764–6.

[50] See Steven Smith, "The Discipline of International Relations: Still an American Social Science?," 2 (2000). *British Journal of Politics and International Relations*, 374, 375 (contending that positivism is so dominant as a methodology, in particular in the United States, that it tends to marginalize other epistemological approaches).

[51] Sociologists criticize the titular objective tenets of rationality, such as market efficiency or causality, as a "myth" in that they are not axiomatically correct but rather widely "shared" and "accepted" in a community. See Edelman *et al.*, *supra* note 39, 410–11; Richard W. Scott, *Organizations: Rational, Natural, and Open Systems* (2nd edn, 1987).

postulate a certain incidence, such as a state behavior.[52] Under this basically causal setting, one of the classical logics, *modus tollens*, tends to prevail. In other words, even a single counterfactual incidence may lead to the refutation of the efficacy of norms.[53] For example, the IMF helps prevent its members from manipulating their foreign exchange rates for the purpose of obtaining undue trade advantages. Here, a regime theorist may be tempted to equate an anecdote of currency manipulation with the normative bankruptcy of the IMF.

Importantly, however, rather than directly causing a certain state behavior, norms may guide or justify the behavior.[54] While regime theorists are interested in whether an IO can effectively control its members' behavior, they seldom pay attention to the importance of the "communicative dynamic" under which states justify their own behaviors as well as interpret and respond to others' behaviors *through* norms.[55] In the IMF example, it might be difficult for regime theorists to explain how other exporting countries potentially affected by such an alleged currency manipulation would demand reasons behind the measure from the devaluing country as well as how the devaluing country would respond to such a reason-giving request. The regime theory might not fully embrace the possibility of the devaluing country being persuaded and modifying its original measure as a result of this communication in a manner consistent with IMF norms.

C. *Rational choice institutionalism*

Rational choice institutionalism views an institution as a script that *ex ante* stipulates actors' strategies (choices), the sequence of these choices, and their consequences.[56] Here, an institution is nothing but a set of constraints shaping and binding actors' behaviors.[57] At the same time, rational choice institutionalism presupposes that all institutions are invariably accompanied by transaction costs and therefore can be

[52] See Kratochwil and Ruggie, *supra* note 47, 766–8. One solution to this deficiency, proposed by Kratochwil and Ruggie, might be to shift this positive epistemology embedded in the regime theory to more "interpretive strains" accentuating discourses and communication among state actors, as seen in Ernst Haas' "evolutionary epistemology" and Jürgen Habermas' "universal pragmatics." *Ibid.*

[53] *Ibid.*, 767. [54] *Ibid.* [55] See *ibid.*

[56] See Kenneth A. Shepsle, "Rational Choice Institutionalism," in S. Binder *et al.* (eds.), *Oxford Handbook of Political Institutions* (2006).

[57] See James Alt and Douglas C. North (eds.), *Institutions, Institutional Change and Economic Performance* (1990), p. 3.

replaced by alternatives through a rational (cost–benefit) analysis.[58] Under this law and economics approach, an IO may be defined as a welfare-maximizing contract in which various institutional choices are reduced to and defined by participating states' preferences and concerns of economic welfare. Thus, all institutional choices revolve around the ultimate rationalist goals of welfare maximization and transaction cost minimization.[59]

Many scholars adopt variations of rational choice institutionalism in explaining states' behaviors under IOs. For example, Joel Trachtman and Gregory Shaffer attempt to understand the drafting and interpretation of the WTO by analyzing various institutional choices made by WTO members and the WTO tribunal.[60] They focus on two dimensions of institutional choices: temporal and spatial.[61] The temporal dimension involves institutional choice-making at two different stages: a treaty drafting (*ex ante*) stage and a treaty interpretation (*ex post*) stage. Different patterns, and concerns, of institutional choices arise within each stage. The spatial dimension, meanwhile, refers to a range of decision-making processes transpiring in different institutional loci, such as domestic, regional, international, political, administrative, judicial, and market fields.

In the temporal dimension, Trachtman and Shaffer rely on efficiency concerns, such as the specification cost, central to the rationalist framework to suggest that there is an institutional choice between rules and standards in the treaty-drafting stage.[62] They assume that broader standards may be more efficient than specific rules given the specification cost inherent in drawing narrow rules.[63] In the spatial dimension, they argue that the idea of member participation involves the allocation of authority through various mechanisms ranging from the use of international standards to judicial interpretation.[64]

Here, WTO member participation is instrumental to understanding how members seek to maximize the WTO's welfare[65] because individual preferences can be inferred from behaviors like participation.[66] Under

[58] See Oliver Williamson, *The Economic Institutions of Capitalism* (1985) (using the "transaction cost" approach in analyzing institutions).

[59] See generally Sungjoon Cho, "Beyond Rationality: Toward a Sociological Construction of the World Trade Organization," 52 (2012) *Virginia Journal of International Law*, 32.

[60] See Gregory Shaffer and Joel Trachtman, "Interpretation and Institutional Choice at the WTO," 52 (2011) *Virginia Journal of International Law* 103, 105.

[61] *Ibid.*, 105–6. [62] See *ibid.*, 112. [63] See *ibid.* [64] See *ibid.*, 152.

[65] See *ibid.*, 106. [66] See *ibid.*, 108.

this position, participation offers a methodological proxy by which to measure welfare through revealed preferences. Participation concerns such cardinal economic concepts as efficiency and externalities.[67] As a result, participation-based criteria may translate eventually into welfarist terms, rather than into any social phenomenon in its genuine sense.[68]

Another scholar employing rational choice institutionalism explains why states comply with their international legal obligations. Andrew Guzman views a treaty as a contract in which self-interested states give and take concessions in order to maximize their utilities.[69] According to him, three factors – reputation, reciprocity, and retaliation – influence states' compliance with their international obligations, although reputation is the most important.[70] First, he argues that a state will be bound to a legal obligation under a treaty *only* if its payoffs (utility) from cooperation (compliance) are greater than the costs to the state.[71] Note that the cost to the state is not the cost of complying with the legal obligation itself; instead it is the cost of breach under his theory.[72] Therefore, according to this scholar, every time a state complies with a treaty obligation, it conducts a complicated calculus based on any negative impact to its reputation (credibility) resulting from its breach, any possible reciprocal breach from other states, and any potential penalties (sanctions).[73] It is this sophisticated calculation informed by reciprocity which eventually increases a state's payoffs from compliance.

Although this theory diverges from most neoclassical economists in that the former takes institutions seriously, it still considers reputation as an economic problem that requires an efficient solution and therefore omits socio-cultural investigations in its analysis of institutions.[74] For

[67] See *id.*, 107 n.5 (quoting Neil Komesar, "The Essence of Economics: Law, Participation and Institutional Choice (Two Ways)," in Sandra Batie and Nicholas Mercuro (eds.), *Alternative Institutional Structures: Evolution and Impact* (2008), pp. 165, 170).

[68] See *ibid.*, pp. 106–8. Regarding a similar approach focusing on alternative institutional settings informed by transaction costs, see Beth V. Yarbrough and Robert M. Yarbrough, *Cooperation and Governance in International Trade: The Strategic Organizational Approach* (1992), p. 22 (observing that "institutional variety in trade liberalization reflects the efficacy of alternate governance structure for different types of trade transactions in different political and economic environments.").

[69] See Guzman, *supra* note 33, pp. 25, 121 ("[o]ur basic rational choice assumptions imply that states will only enter into agreements when doing so makes them (or at least, their policy-makers) better off").

[70] See *ibid.*, 33–48, 71. [71] See *ibid.*, 55–60. [72] See *ibid.*, 86–8.

[73] See *ibid.*, 36–40, 45, 47–8.

[74] Mark Granovetter, "Economic Action and Social Structure: The Problem of Embeddedness," 91 (1985) *American Journal of Sociology*, 481, 505; see also Gregory Shaffer and

example, under the theory the reputation factor largely remains a utilitarian one: a state's reputation (credibility) is a utility itself in that it induces or facilitates future cooperation from other states.[75] Here, reputation may be analogous to a "business asset."[76] Thus, this conception of reputation denotes an instrumental, not cognitive, factor in international relations, as parallel to power or interest. It cannot explain how the surrounding social structure comprised of ideas and norms,[77] which IOs often provide, constitutes states' interest, preference, and identity over time. Instrumental rationality alone does not exhaust an understanding of states' law-abiding behavior. After all, states do comply with international law because they believe that compliance is an appropriate behavior, with or without cost-benefit calculation.

In general, rational choice institutionalism delivers a powerful heuristic on IOs and their operations. Most of all, its characteristic parsimony, namely the limitation of employed variables, not only delivers convincing narratives on an IO's present operation, but also retains a predictive force on the IO's future development. This explains why the rationalist framework is capable of generating such a good deal of significant research, such as those discussed above.

Nonetheless, the common problem with the rational choice model is that it replaces *real* actors whose rationality is, in fact, bounded[78] with flawlessly rational (hypothetical) actors.[79] As a result, although the underlying logic of rationalist theses may appear rational, it also represents a certain myth in

Tom Ginsberg, "The Empirical Turn in International Legal Scholarship," 106 (2012) *American Journal of International Law* 1, 6 (observing that rational institutionalism focuses on the facilitation of international cooperation by reducing transaction cost); see also José E. Alvarez, *The Public International Law Regime Governing International Investment* (2011), p. 138 (criticizing Andrew Guzman's "single (inadequate)" rationale behind the least-developed countries' signing of bilateral investment treaties and introducing a number of alternative motivations).

[75] See *ibid.*, 73–5. [76] Oliver Williamson, *Markets and Hierarchies* (1975), pp. 106–8.

[77] The "social structure" in this book does not connote the global material force, such as capitalism, under the "world-system" theory. See generally Immanuel Wallerstein, *The Modern World System* 1 (1974).

[78] See Edward L. Rubin, "Public Choice, Phenomenology, and the Meaning of the Modern State: Keep the Bathwater, But Throw out That Baby," 87 (2002) *Cornell Law Review* 309, 315. The idea of "bounded rationality" has alternatively been described as "cognitive loafing" or "cognitive illusions." *Ibid.*, 315–16. According to the bounded rationality argument, public officials may be motivated by objectives aside from mere reelection ("hacks"). *Ibid.*, 311, 322, 336.

[79] See Shaffer and Trachtman, *supra* note 60, 132; see generally Bo Rothstein, *Social Traps and the Problem of Trust* (2005); Fritz W. Scharpf, *Games Real Actors Play* (1997); Vivien A. Schmidt, "Taking Ideas and Discourses Seriously: Explaining Change through Discursive Institutionalism as the Fourth 'New Institutionalism'," 2 (2009) *European Political Science Review* 1.

that such logic is constructed within a narrow set of assumptions and is not axiomatic in and of itself.[80] For example, given the reality of trade negotiations, titular institutional choices are hardly deliberate or even calculated. Theories relying on the power of rational choice and efficiency do not properly characterize most political bargains because those bargains are often negotiated on a highly contingent basis across issue areas,[81] whereas the notion of efficiency is often theorized only around a specific issue. Thus, in a normal political bargaining situation, *ex ante* rational choices may be ambiguous or even nonexistent.

D. *Neoliberal institutionalism*

Neoliberalism considers private individuals or their groups as primary actors in international relations. It views states as mere proxies for individual or group preferences.[82] These domestic constituencies express their values and interests through various domestic channels, such as legislation, political actions, court decisions, or self-organizations.[83] As rational actors, neoliberalism argues, those individuals pursue competing interests as they are constrained by both material (such as resources) and non-material (such as values) circumstances.[84] Therefore, neoliberalism takes an integrated view of the relationship between the international and domestic spheres.[85] For example, neoliberal scholars believe that an understanding of the workings of international tribunals requires knowledge of the internal operations of the state actors that establish such tribunals and decide which disputes to submit or not to submit.[86]

[80] See Scott, *supra* note 51; Edelman *et al.*, supra note 39, 406, 410–11. Additionally, the rational choice model (law and economics) is often criticized for holding unrealistic assumptions as to "perfect foresight and complete information about the future." Andrew Keay and Hao Zhang, "Incomplete Contracts, Contingent Fiduciaries and a Director's Duty to Creditors," 32 (2008) *Melbourne University Law Review*, 141, 156.

[81] See Robert Howse, "Do the World Trade Organization Disciplines on Domestic Subsidies Make Sense?: The Case for Legalizing Some Subsidies," in Kyle W. Bagwell *et al.* (eds.), *Law and Economics of Contingent Protection in International Trade* (2009), p. 85.

[82] See Claire R. Kelly, "The Value Vacuum: Self-Enforcing Regimes and the Dilution of the Normative Feedback Loop," 22 (2001) *Michigan Journal of International Law* 673, 681–3.

[83] See *ibid.*

[84] See Andrew Moravcsik, "Taking Preferences Seriously: A Liberal Theory of International Politics," 51 (1997) *International Organization* 513, 516.

[85] See Anne-Marie Slaughter, "A Liberal Theory of International Law," 94 (2000) *American Society of International Law Proceedings*, 240, 241.

[86] See Laurence Helfer and Karen Alter, "The Andean Tribunal of Justice and its Interlocutors: Understanding Preliminary Reference Patterns in the Andean

The challenge that neoliberal theorists face in international relations is how to coordinate these differentiated domestic preferences among states with minimal transaction costs.[87] Neoliberal theorists view that an IO provides such a coordination mechanism among states by creating norms, reducing transaction costs, and supplying information. Accordingly, the stability of a given IO indicates that conflicting domestic preferences have been somehow coordinated.[88] For example, drawing largely on economics, such as game theory, Robert Keohane demonstrates that institutions matter since they can facilitate interstate cooperation by providing information, reducing transaction costs, and monitoring compliance.[89] In a similar vein, Robert Axelrod observes that the prisoner's dilemma could be avoided if games were repeated indefinitely, the monitoring costs were sufficiently low, and the actors' discount rates for the future were not too high.[90]

Importantly, neoliberals distinguish themselves from neorealists in that the former acknowledge certain cognitive factors, such as ideas, which may influence state behaviors, while the latter regard state behaviors simply as responses to external material forces.[91] Neoliberals acknowledge that ideas may intervene between material factors, such as power and interest, and state behaviors.[92] Thus, neoliberals are interested in the *evolving* nature of cooperation against the backdrop of increasing interdependence among states. Under the neoliberal framework, the evolution of states' interactions can develop international

Community," 41 (2009) *New York University Journal of International Law and Politics* 871 (arguing that European courts are more willing to engage with the European Court of Justice because they are empowered by the relationship, whereas Andean judges were passive).

87 Although neoliberalism offers richer narratives than neorealism, the variety, and the complexity, of actors and their preferences tend to undermine its explanatory power of causal relationship between those actors' interests and state behavior. See Katzenstein *et al.*, *supra* note 23, 658–9.

88 See Moravcsik, *supra* note 84, 537 (arguing that an international regime is stable when groups adjust so as to make domestic policy socially embedded and its reversal costly).

89 Robert O. Keohane, *After Hegemony: Cooperation and Discord in the World Political Economy* (1984) (viewing that international institutions facilitate decentralized cooperation among state actors).

90 Robert Axelrod, *The Evolution of Cooperation* (1984), p. 182 (noting the importance of monitoring actual behavior so that players are able to observe and respond to each other's choices).

91 See Adler, *supra* note 26, 321.

92 See Wendt, *supra* note 23, p. 19 (citing Judith Goldstein, *Ideas, Interests, and American Trade Policy* (1993)).

institutions to sustain their expectations and thus minimize transaction costs.[93]

Nonetheless, some believe that neoliberalism does not take these ideational parameters (ideas and norms) seriously enough to regard them as primary, namely constitutive, factors shaping the contours of material parameters such as power and interest.[94] According to these critics, under neoliberalism ideas and norms still remain only residual factors that may explain states' behaviors where power and interest cannot. In other words, neoliberals' main focus lies in the consequential (behavioral) aspects of cooperation, rather than states' culture and identities.[95] From this position, even occasional cooperation results from an instrumental motivation, not from an intrinsic collegial value.[96] After all, methodological individualism basing neoliberal institutionalism is without the "cement" that is characteristic of a social theory.[97]

III. What rationalism leaves out

A. *Descriptive omission*

The conventional IR theories on IOs share a common thesis: IOs are instruments that states create to achieve certain material goals, such as power, interest, utilities, and efficiency. It is in this context that Robert Keohane grouped these theories together and labeled them rationalism.[98] Naturally, rationalism connotes a strong microeconomic

[93] See *ibid.* [94] See *ibid.*, p. 35.

[95] See Axelrod, *supra* note 90 (regarding an "iterated" Prisoners' Dilemma game). Regarding another type of criticism on neoliberalism, in particular one related to its distinction between "liberal" and "non-liberal" states, see generally José E. Alvarez, "Behave Better: A Critique of Slaughter's Liberal Theory," 12 (2001) *European Journal of International Law* 183.

[96] See Christopher Jencks, "Varieties of Altruism," in J. Mansbridge (ed.), *Beyond Self-interest* (1990), p. 53.

[97] See Jon Elster, *The Cement of Society: A Study of Social Order* (1989).

[98] See Keohane, *supra* note 6, 381. Likewise, even neoliberalism considers norms as a "superstructure built on a material base." Checkel, *supra* note 7, 327. According to David Baldwin, the theoretical distinction between neorealists and neoliberals is far from being salient: any differences between them are of a matter of degree, not of substance. See David Baldwin, "Neoliberalism, Neorealism, and World Politics," in David Baldwin (ed.), *Neorealism and Neoliberalism: The Contemporary Debate* (1993), pp. 5–8. For example, both neorealists and neoliberals recognize that anarchy constrains state behavior, while institutions (regimes) can mitigate such constraints. (No wonder

bias[99] as it presupposes that international institutions are mediums that self-interested actors establish to maximize efficiency in attaining the actors' preferences.[100] Thus, mainstream IR theories reveal their measurement proclivity: both neorealism and neoliberal institutionalism widely adopt microeconomic methodologies that are highly susceptible to modeling and mathematical equations.[101] Therefore, conventional IR theorists pay little attention to the vast differences among IOs, such as varying degrees of effectiveness in performance across different IOs.[102]

In a similar vein, John Ruggie highlights the utilitarian framework adopted by rationalism. Ruggie critically observes that even rationalists consider ideational factors, but they consider them in terms of utilities in achieving agents' material interests.[103] As discussed above, some scholars admit that rational actors may comply with international law out of a fear of reputation costs.[104] At first glance, one might assume that a reputation seeker might easily internalize international norms for fear of loss to its reputation from non-compliance. Yet, it is a derivative form of rationalism in that reputation itself is also an exogenous factor shaping an actor's rational pay-off matrices. If the fear of such loss is somehow attenuated, as is often the case with powerful nations, it is only

that the regime theory derives from neorealism, while neoliberal institutionalism derives from neoliberalism.) What distinguishes neorealists from neoliberals is that the former are more cognizant of anarchy's constraining power than the latter, while the latter are more optimistic on institutions' cooperation-inducing power than the former. Markedly, both theories view that states desire to maximize their material interests, while paying little attention to moral considerations. See also Andreas Hasenclever *et al.*, *supra* note 23, pp. 1–2 (defining realism as a "power-based" approach and neoliberalism as an "interest-based" approach).

99 See Brunnée and Toope, *supra* note 23, 32 (observing that proponents of neorealism and neoliberalism "adopted the analytic tools of microeconomics to lend greater precision").

100 See Philip M. Nichols, "Forgotten Linkages – Historical Institutionalism and Sociological Institutionalism and Analysis of the World Trade Organization," 19 (1998) *University of Pennsylvania Journal of International Economic Law*, 461, 474; see also Jon Elster, *Nuts and Bolts for the Social Sciences* (1989), p. 22 ("Actions are valued and chosen not for themselves, but as more or less efficient means to a further end.").

101 See Finnemore and Sikkink, *supra* note 33, 889–90; *cf.* Robert W. Staiger, "Non-Tariff Measures and the WTO," WTO Staff Working Paper ERSD-2012-01, January 2012, available at www.wto.org/english/res_e/reser_e/ersd201201_e.pdf (adopting a quantitative (mathematical) methodology in understanding non-tariff barriers under the WTO system).

102 See Ness and Brechin, *supra* note 34, 247.

103 See John Gerard Ruggie, "What Makes the World Hang Together?: Neo-Utilitarianism and the Social Constructivist Challenge," 52 (1998) *International Organization* 855, 865–6 (observing that neorealists have often imported unacknowledged ideational factors and that neoliberal institutionalism "assigns a limited causal role to ideational factors").

104 See Guzman, *supra* note 33, p. 33 (arguing that reputation, along with reciprocity and retaliation, are the three costs of non-compliance with international obligations).

rational to expect relatively little compliance from the actor, if not total non-compliance.[105]

Under rationalism defined as above, material factors exogenously determine state behaviors and provide us with useful knowledge in understanding how international institutions work.[106] From a methodological standpoint, this is possible because rationalism can limit the number of variables in a theory and thus increase its explanatory power.[107] Ironically, however, this theoretical superiority is a double-edged sword. Rationalism's characteristic propensity for parsimony[108] cannot fully capture ideational contents, such as culture and values.[109] While rationalism's technical scrutiny[110] may produce many useful research projects, its epistemological hurdles tend to marginalize the significance of a social structure that is not always reducible to atomistic agencies (states).[111]

For example, rational choice theorists treat states as external objects of observation.[112] Their behaviors in a given condition constitute a set of sterilized data to be tested against a certain hypothesis in a pure, scientific manner. Here, WTO members would react to interest as mice react to food in a Skinner box. Notably, however, such data-collecting itself is not a random process. Logically, it presupposes a certain screening process concerning what kinds of actions are meaningful enough to

[105] In this context, the reputation model is vulnerable from its own rationalist camp. See Goldsmith and Posner, *supra* note 14, p. 102 (observing that the reputation discourse tends to exaggerate the theoretical determinacy of reputation over state behaviors).

[106] See Keohane, *supra* note 6 (comparing the two approaches and their respective strengths in analyzing how international institutions work and change).

[107] See Amartya Sen, *On Ethics and Economics* (1987), p. 24.

[108] See *ibid.* ("the propensity to account for all appearances from as few principles as possible").

[109] See Keohane, *supra* note 6, 392. [110] See Sen, *supra* note 107, p. 8.

[111] See notably Émile Durkheim, *Les Regles del la Methode Sociologique* (8th edn, 1927), p. 127 ("Society is not a simple sum of individuals, but the system formed by their association which represents a specific reality with its own characteristics.") (translated and quoted in Hans-Georg Moeller, *Luhmann Explained: From Souls to Systems* (2006), p. 229; Mark Gould, "Law and Sociology: Some Consequences for the Law of Employment Discrimination Deriving from the Sociological Reconstruction of Economic Theory," 13 (1992) *Cardozo Law Review* 1517, 1519; *cf.* Mark Granovetter, "Economic Action and Social Structure: The Problem of Embeddedness," 91(1985) *American Journal of Sociology* 481, 504 (observing that economists' professional commitments to atomized actions theories lead to under-socialized views of human action).

[112] This is called "methodological monism," which equates social science with natural science. See Stefano Guzzini, "A Reconstruction of Constructivism in International Relations," 6 (2000) *European Journal of International Relations*, 147, 157.

be collected and investigated. Indeed, this presupposed screening mechanism, or schema, is tacitly embedded in assumptions underlying the titular scientific investigations. Then where does this *meaning* come from in the first place? It emerges from a social, that is shared, context of WTO members. In sum, a WTO member's speech or act may not always be reduced to self-standing raw data; it is also an interpretable social action, the meaning of which is related to other members.[113]

Another descriptive omission of rationalism is its incapability of identifying an institutional *change* within an IO – how it develops and evolves internally over an extensive period of time. Although rationalism may be useful in understanding and predicting IO members' behaviors within a given matrix of preferences, it nonetheless offers very few collective possibilities to change the existing system of fixed preferences.[114] Under rationalism, change is either simply "assumed away"[115] or imposed externally upon an IO by states as a logical outcome of their altered interests and preferences.[116] Here, change is no more than an exogenous re-creation by a state, not an endogenous institutional development. For this reason, the rationalist interpretation of an IO often lacks historical and cultural insights with which one may identify the transformation of the IO system on its own terms. Thus, rationalism often offers a historically neutral solution, which reveals its functionalist attribute.[117]

Notably, however, states, as well as their actions, are in fact deeply embedded in their socio-cultural setting such that a purely utilitarian

[113] See Alfred Schutz and Thomas Luckmann, *The Structure of the Life-World 2* (Richard M. Zaner & David J. Parent trans., 1989), p. 20.

[114] See Wendt, *supra* note 23, p. 377; *cf.* Thelen and Steinmo, *supra* note 19, p. 16 (arguing that "a critical inadequacy of institutionalist analysis has been a tendency towards mechanical, static accounts that largely bracket the issue of change and sometimes lapse inadvertently into institutional determinism").

[115] See Ira Katznelson and Barry R. Weingast, "Intersections between Historical and Rational Choice Institutionalism," in Ira Katznelson and Barry R. Weingast (eds.), *Preferences and Situations: Points of Intersection between Historical and Rational Choice Institutionalism* (2005), pp. 1, 7.

[116] See Laurence R. Helfer, "Understanding Change in International Organizations: Globalization and Innovation in the ILO," 59 (2006) *Vanderbilt Law Review* 649, 661. Here, realists show strong resistance to change, at least until the tipping point of what Krasner called "punctuated equilibrium." Stephen D. Krasner, "Structural Causes and Regime Consequences: Regimes as Intervening Variables," in Stephen D. Krasner (ed.), *International Regimes* (1983), p. 1; see also Bell, *supra* note 17, p. 12.

[117] See March and Olsen, *supra* note 12, 737–8.

(profit-maximizing) framework becomes nonsensical.[118] Historical developments reflected in an IO's institutional design shape states' behaviors, which are "culturally and structurally thick, not just strategically lean."[119] Interestingly, this historicity has deprived the old framework of its *Zeitgeist* status. Recent changes in both economic and cultural dynamics on a global scale have provided strong propellants for a paradigm shift in how we perceive and comprehend IOs.[120] This shift might have been a "quiet cataclysm"[121] to those sovereigntists who were cocooned in a uniquely fertile ground to thrive in the Cold War context. In the post-Cold War world, the global market integration in tandem with the demise of political ideologies has facilitated communitarian *inter*-dependence over sovereign *in*-dependence.[122]

B. *Normative dilemma*

Certain normative dilemmas of the old framework accompany the aforementioned descriptive ones. First of all, in the contractarian structure, as is often the case in a domestic contract situation, power determines the eventual terms of the contract.[123] Naturally, the innate power disparity

118 This theoretical position is called "historical institutionalism." See Thomas A. Koelble, "The New Institutionalism in Political Science and Sociology," 27 (1995) *Comparative Politics*, 231, 237 (book review).

119 See Ira Katznelson, "The Doleful Dance of Politics and Policy: Can Historical Institutionalism Make a Difference?," 92 (1998) *The American Political Science Review*, 191.

120 See Jürgen Habermas, *Divided West* (2006), p. 161 (expressing the view that a *gestalt* shift depends on the world society's cultural and economic dynamics).

121 See John Mueller, *Quiet Cataclysm: Reflections on the Recent Transformation of World Politics* (1995).

122 For example, the "complex interdependence" model, which was touted by Joseph Nye and Robert Keohane more than three decades ago, has now earned the status of paradigm after rich empirical confirmations. See Robert O. Keohane and Joseph S. Nye, Jr., *Power and Interdependence* (2011); Peter Gourevitch, "The Second Image Reversed: The International Sources of Domestic Politics," 32 (1978) *International Organization*, 881, 893. Another clairvoyant, Edward Morse, similarly observed as early as in the seventies that modernity via interdependence changed the nature of anarchy among atomistic sovereign states and instead instilled a strong converging pattern of welfare state and legitimacy among states. See Edward Morse, *Modernization and the Transformation of International Relations* (1976); see also Wilfried Bolewski, *Diplomacy and International Law in Globalized Relations* (2007), pp. 47–8 (observing the rise of "communitarian" spirit in the twenty-first century as it replaces the old balance of power struggle).

123 See Ji Li, "From 'See You in Court!' to 'See You in Geneva!': An Empirical Study of the Role of Social Norms in International Trade Dispute Resolution," 32 (2007) *Yale Journal of International Law* 485, 488 (observing that "realists predict that the WTO is nothing more than a forum for power politics").

in the international anarchy may entail unjust outcomes. For example, even if a small WTO member prevails over a big, powerful country in a WTO dispute, the former's victory may be in vain. If the powerful country refuses to comply with the WTO tribunal's decision, the ultimate retaliation by the small country, i.e., the suspension of a tariff concession, might not work simply due to the insurmountable gap in the economic size between the two countries.[124] In a dispute involving Ecuador and the EU, a WTO panel aptly observed that:

> Given the difficulties and the specific circumstances of this case which involves a developing country Member, it could be that Ecuador may find itself in a situation where it is *not realistic or possible* for it to implement the suspension authorized by the DSB [Dispute Settlement Body] for the full amount of the level of nullification and impairment estimated by us in all of the sectors and/or under all agreements mentioned above combined. The present text of the DSU does not offer a solution for such an eventuality.

This frustrating prospect tends to deter small countries from filing complaints against powerful countries in the first place.[125]

This power disparity among IO parties is also prone to an externalization of domestic politics, in particular those of powerful nations, onto the global contract.[126] In this process, the desperate voices of powerless developing countries tend to be silenced.[127] This marginalization of developing countries within IOs raises various developmental concerns. Two interrelated, and disheartening, contemporary global trends – the widening global income gap[128] and persistent

[124] Decision by the Arbitrators under Article 22.6 of the DSU, European Communities – Regime for the Importation, Sale and Distribution of Bananas, ¶ 177, WT/DS27/ARB/ECU (Mar. 24, 2000).

[125] See Chad Bown, "Participation in WTO Dispute Settlement: Complainants, Interested Parties and Free Riders," 19 (2005) *World Bank Economic Review* 287–310; see also Andrew Guzman and Beth Simmons, "Power Plays and Capacity Constraints: The Selection of Defendants in WTO Disputes," 34 (2005) *Journal of Legal Studies* 557 (highlighting the importance of capacity constraints in preventing poor countries from suing rich countries in the WTO).

[126] See Wendt, *supra* note 23, p. 361; David H. Lumsdaine, *Moral Vision in International Politics* (1993); Justin Rosenberg, *The Empire of Civil Society: A Critique of the Realist Theory of International Relations* (1994).

[127] See Sungjoon Cho, "The WTO's Gemeinschaft," 56 (2004) *Alabama Law Review* 483, 492.

[128] See World Bank, *World Development Report: Equity and Development* (2005), p. 7; "INCOME: Global Gap Rising, World Bank Study Shows," *UN Wire* (January 18, 2002);

poverty in the least-developed countries (LDCs)[129] – tend to eclipse a triumphant halo of globalization. As the World Economic Forum (WEF) glorifies the mainstream consensus on market opening and deregulation,[130] the World Social Forum (WSF) accuses the North of enacting hypocritical economic policies and explores the possibility of an alternative world.[131]

As discussed above, the contract model is largely incapable of accommodating a genuine pro-development discourse within an IO, as its theoretical concerns remain preoccupied with an egocentric state pursuing myopic national interests. This development deficit, which is destined to materialize under the global contract, even invites criticism along the lines of neo-imperialism. Some development scholars condemn the global contract as an "emerging Global State"[132] or a new version of "Empire"[133] operated by a global market system without due consideration of the interests of marginalized states.

Conceivably, some might point to the eventuality of "hegemonic unilateralism"[134] or even certain merits of a "well-meaning hegemon,"[135] a role allegedly shouldered by the United States during the Cold War era. For example, an empirical analysis illustrates the importance of egalitarian considerations in the outcome of the GATT Tokyo Round trade negotiation.[136] This analysis demonstrates that during the Tokyo Round negotiation, which took place during the 1970s, the Swiss proposal highlighting equity and fairness in tariff reductions prevailed over the

Louis Charbonneau, "UN Sounds Alarm on Worsening Global Income Disparities," *Reuters* (January 29, 2014).

129 See UN Millennium Project, *Investing in Development: A Practical Plan to Achieve the Millennium Development Goals* (2005), Chapter 2; Charlotte Denny, "US Blocks Brown-led Drive for Increase in Aid," *Guardian Unlimited* (January 23, 2002), available at www.guardian.co.uk/business/story/0,3604,637808,00.html (reporting that 2.8 billion people on earth live on less than $2 a day).

130 See *World Economic Forum*, available at www.weforum.org (last visited February 20, 2012).

131 See *World Social Forum*, available at www.nadir.org/nadir/initiativ/agp/free/wsf (last visited February 20, 2012). The WSF is "opposed to neo-liberalism and to domination of the world by capital and any form of imperialism." "Charter of Principles," *World Social Forum India*, available at www.wsfindia.org/?q=node/3 (last visited February 20, 2012).

132 B. S. Chimni, "A Just World under Law: A View from the South," 22 (2007) *American University International Law Review*, 199, 201.

133 Michael Hardt and Antonio Negri, *Empire* (2000), p. xi.

134 Habermas, *supra* note 120, p. 183. 135 *Ibid.*, p. 116.

136 See Kenneth S. Chan, "The International Negotiation Game: Some Evidence from the Tokyo Round," 67 (1985) *Review of Economics and Statistics*, 456.

US's efficiency approach.[137] Some scholars translate such prevalence of egalitarianism in the Tokyo Round as a small price the United States paid for having an open global economy.[138] Considering the US's hegemonic status in the middle of the Cold War, this observation sounds quite plausible. However, even this hegemonic view no longer stands valid. After the Cold War ended and the post-hegemonic era began, such strategic (hegemonic) egalitarianism declined in what Jagdish Bhagwati termed the "diminished giant syndrome."[139]

In sum, the contractarian logic of the old framework is prone to normative problems linked inevitably to the inherent power disparity among parties in an IO's operation.

IV. A new framework: an international organization as a "community"

A. *A social framework*

The new framework aims to overcome the over-determinacy of rationalism, a system driven by an individuated agency (state) structure defined by material factors, such as power, interests, and utilities. As discussed above, while these conventional IR theories hold analytical prowess due mainly to parsimony, they nonetheless pay scant attention to certain social factors, such as normative structures, that various social dynamics among states create.[140]

Critically, the new framework does not merely represent an aggregate interrelationship of states; rather, it denotes a certain collectivity, namely, a community that endogenously constructs those states'

[137] See *ibid.*

[138] See Ethan B. Kapstein, "Power, Fairness, and the Global Economy," in Michael Barnett and Raymond Duvall (eds.), *Power in Global Governance* (2005), pp. 80, 95. Regarding a similar observation that powerful nations bargain some constraints for the long-term stability of the international society, see Joseph A. Conti, "Learning to Dispute: Repeat Participation, Expertise, and Reputation at the World Trade Organization," 35 (2010) *Law and Social Inquiry*, 625, 633; Joel P. Trachtman, "Embedding Mutual Recognition at the WTO," 14 (2007) *Journal of European Public Policy*, 780; Kenneth W. Abbott and Duncan Snidal, "Why States Act through Formal International Organizations," 42 (1998) *Journal of Conflict Resolution* 3.

[139] Jagdish Bhagwati, "The Diminished Giant Syndrome: How Declinism Drives Trade Policy," 72 (1993) *Foreign Affairs*, 22.

[140] Martha Finnemore, "Norms, Culture, and World Politics: Insights from Sociology's Institutionalism," 50 (1996) *International Organization* 325, 462.

perception of values, norms, and even their collective identities.[141] The internal dynamics among social actors in a community both condition and constitute their own perception of challenges and responses, which conventional IR theorists tend to discount.[142] For example, although a regime is pre-programmed by states, it nonetheless cannot dispense with a certain institutional structure based on which states interact. This interaction naturally requires intersubjectivity among actors, which is basically social and thus remains irreconcilable with the regime theory's reductionist (individualist) ontology.[143]

The social framework is capable of probing those issues that rationalism removes from the research agenda on account of the latter's own assumptions.[144] As IR scholars face ever-mounting theoretical needs to reflect social constructions in their own research programs, sociology offers a uniquely powerful set of narratives on the role of culture and norms in international life that cannot be found in conventional IR theories.[145] While conventional IR theories begin with isotropic actors (states) sharing similar pre-determined interests, a social framework views that social structure constructs those actors.[146] Indeed, IR scholars have only recently begun to pay belated attention to various social aspects of political life. For example, some refined versions of neoliberalism appear to converge with main tenets of constructivism.[147] "Sociological liberalism" highlights the constructive effects of transnational coalitions on the domestic definition of interests.[148] In contrast with traditional liberalism, sociological liberalism takes seriously ideational incentives defined by communication.[149]

Moreover, political scientists have recently incorporated the social framework in earnest into various strands of institutionalism. Often dubbed "new institutionalism," these recent strands of institutionalism feature certain logics different from rationalism. While rationalism, or

[141] See Guy E. Swanson, "An Organizational Analysis of Collectivities," 36 (1971) *American Sociological Review*, 607 (arguing that collectivities can be classified according to their organization's fundamentals for making decisions and taking action).

[142] See *ibid.* [143] See Kratochwil and Ruggie, *supra* note 47.

[144] See Finnemore, *supra* note 140, 337 (observing that realism and neoliberalism treat certain questions as assumptions and remove them from the research agenda whereas institutionalism's framework allows questions about issues such as the origin and nature of states).

[145] See *ibid.* [146] See *ibid.*, 333.

[147] See Joseph S. Nye, Jr., "Neorealism and Neoliberalism," 40 (1988) *World Politics* 235, 238.

[148] See *ibid.*, 246. [149] See *ibid.*, 250.

rationalist institutionalism, represents the logic of calculation,[150] "historical institutionalism" and "sociological institutionalism" connote the logic of path-dependence and the logic of appropriateness, respectively.[151] First of all, historical institutionalism focuses on a historical path-dependency of an organization in its creation and evolution into an integrated system.[152] While still recognizing a strategic dimension of individual actors' dynamics in an organization, historical institutionalism also highlights the cultural properties that an organization provides, such as cognitive frameworks for interpretation.[153] It provides background material as to how social actors as sentient agents instill past practices (and norms) with contextualized meanings, generate knowledge, and respond to external challenges.[154]

Likewise, sociological institutionalism highlights how broadly defined institutions, such as norms, shape states' behaviors by providing them with the "cognitive scripts, categories and models" that are vital for those behaviors.[155] According to sociological institutionalism, an organization's

[150] Vivien Schmidt observes that in exceptional cases some rationalist scholars, such as Judith Goldstein, do turn to the notion of ideas when they fail to explain institutional change through interests only. For example, those scholars seem to view that ideas can determine interests by clarifying goals in advance. Yet, they still fail to demonstrate why some ideas are chosen over others. See Schmidt, *supra* note 79, at 4; see also Judith Goldstein, *Ideas, Interests, and American Trade Policy* (1993).

[151] Schmidt, *supra* note 79, 1 (arguing that that historical institutionalism concentrates on political institutions and their development through "regularized patterns and routinized practices" subject to a "logic of path-dependence" and that sociological institutionalism focuses on social agents who act based on a "logic of appropriateness"). Rationalists often explain path-dependence by "sunk costs." If new programs are not profitable enough to justify forsaking all the irretrievable past investments (sunk costs) in the old path, the old path survives. See Arthur L. Stinchcombe, *Constructing Social Theories* (1968), pp. 120–1; Ira Katznelson, "The Doleful Dance of Politics and Policy: Can Historical Institutionalism Make a Difference?," 92 (1998) *The American Political Science Review*, 191.

[152] See Nichols, *supra* note 100, 475–82 (submitting that historical institutionalism's definitive characteristic is its attenuated path dependency, which places an emphasis on the historical path taken by an institution in its creation and development).

[153] See Peter A. Hall and Rosemary C. R. Taylor, "Political Science and the Three New Institutionalisms," 44 (1996) *Political Studies*, 936, 939.

[154] See Schmidt, *supra* note 79, 9 (viewing that the background information offered by a historical institutionalist examination can illustrate how sentient actors instill rules with contextualized meanings, construct understandings, or create ideas that "lead to the 'layering' of one institution over another, the 'reinterpretation' of an institution, or the 'conversion' of agents to another institution").

[155] See Hall and Taylor, *supra* note 153, 948 ("Sociological institutionalism (SI) focuses on the forms and procedures of organizational life stemming from culturally specific practices, with institutions cast as the norms, cognitive frames, scripts, and meaning

creation and evolution depends on social legitimacy, which it generates in a certain cultural setting, rather than on a narrow utilitarian premise.[156] Some scholars who pursue non-rationalist logics focus particularly on the discursive dimension, such as ideas and discourse, and are often collectively dubbed the "discursive institutionalists."[157] These scholars often spotlight the ideas side, as seen in "ideational institutionalism"[158] and "constructivist institutionalism;"[159] others emphasize the discourse side, as seen in "discourse analysis"[160] or "*réferentiel*" (frame of reference).[161]

B. *Constructivism*

Sharing a similar theoretical background with the aforementioned institutionalist strands, constructivism offers a representative social theory in the IR circle. Constructivism emerged in the late 1980s as an "ideational turn,"[162] which aimed to counter materialistic theories such as neorealism and neoliberalism.[163] Many scholars observe that the rationalists' failure to predict the end of the Cold War triggered the reflective rise of constructivism.[164] This new pattern of

systems that guide human action according to a 'logic of appropriateness.'"); Schmidt, *supra* note 79, 10; see also W. Richard Scott, *Institutions and Organizations* (1995); Powell and DiMaggio, *supra* note 20; James G. March and Johan P. Olsen, *Rediscovering Institutions: The Organization Basis of Politics* (1989).

156 *See* Nichols, *supra* note 100, 485; Hall and Taylor, *supra* note 153, 949.

157 Schmidt, *supra* note 79, 1–2; see also John L. Campbell and Ove Pedersen, "Introduction," in John L. Campbell and Ove Pedersen (eds.), *The Rise of Neo-Liberalism and Institutional Analysis* (2001), pp. 1, 9–13 (discussing discursive institutionalism).

158 See Colin Hay, "The 'Crisis' of Keynesianism and the Rise of Neo-Liberalism in Britain: An Ideational Institutionalist Approach," in John L. Campbell and Ove Pederson (eds.), *The Rise of Neo-Liberalism and Institutional Analysis* (2001), pp. 193, 193–218.

159 See generally Colin Hay, "Constructivist Institutionalism," in R. A. W. Rhodes *et al.* (eds.), *Oxford Handbook of Political Institutions* (2006), pp. 56, 64–5 (discussing constructive institutionalism).

160 See Maarten Hajer, "A Frame in the Fields: Policymaking and the Reinvention of Politics," in Maarten A. Hajer and Hendrik Wagenaar (eds.), *Deliberative Policy Analysis: Understanding Governance in the Network Society*, (2003), pp. 88–112.

161 Bruno Jobert, "The Normative Frameworks of Public Policy," 37 (1989) *Political Studies* 376, 376–86.

162 Finnemore and Sikkink, *supra* note 33, 888.

163 See John Gerard Ruggie, "International Regimes, Transactions, and Change: Embedded Liberalism in the Postwar Economic Order," 36 (1982) *International Organization* 379 (observing that the prevailing interpretation of international authority, which focuses on power and a market rationality in international economic regimes, ignores phenomenological dimensions such as social purpose).

164 See Rawi Abdelal *et al.*, "Introduction," in Rawi Abdelal *et al.* (eds.), *Constructing the International Economy* (2010).

reasoning[165] begins with a "move from the model of reality to the reality of the model."[166] The new Zeitgeist that emerged after the end of the Cold War commanded attention toward an IO's ontology[167] – that is, how the reality around an IO is constituted.[168] A mere equilibrium of competing political vectors cannot fully explain the existential foundation of an IO as well as its norms.[169] An IO provides its members with social constructs, such as norms, that symbolize constitutive ideas.[170]

Constructivism captures the nascent construction of an IO as a *community*.[171] Constructivism differentiates itself from the traditional IR theories in that it focuses on certain socio-cultural (intersubjective) dynamics among states in understanding states' behaviors. This is a cognitive moment in the social process that the rationalist model has largely bracketed as it naturalized its calculative methodology as ontology.[172] Endogenous factors, such as ideas, values, and norms,[173] are central parameters to constructivism *vis-à-vis* exogenous factors such as power, interest, or domestic politics. Thus, endogenous normative self-understanding among social actors explains why states stick

165 Ian Hacking, *Historical Ontology* (2004), p. 160.

166 Vincent Pouliot, "'Sobjectivism': Toward a Constructivist Methodology," 51 (2007) *International Studies Quarterly*, 359, 363 (quoting Pierre Bourdieu, *Choses Dites (Things Said)* (1987), p. 62).

167 See e.g, Chios Carmody, Frank J. Garcia and John Linarelli (eds.), *Global Justice and International Economic Law: Opportunities and Prospects* (2011).

168 See Wendt, *supra* note 23, 22, 370–1; see also Michael Barnett and Martha Finnemore, *Rules for the World: International Organization in Global Politics* (2004), pp. 6–7 (observing that an international organization can create its own "social reality" based on norms).

169 See Kenneth W. Abbott, "The Trading Nation's Dilemma: The Functions of the Law of International Trade," 26 (1985) *Harvard International Law Journal*, 501, 520.

170 See Kenneth W. Abbott, "'Economic' Issues and Political Participation: The Evolving Boundaries of International Federalism," 18 (1996) *Cardozo Law Review* 971, 974.

171 This chapter focuses on a "legal" or "normative" community. An international community, however, is not necessarily constituted by law alone. See Bruno Simma and Andreas L. Paulus, "The 'International Community': Facing the Challenge of Globalization," 9 (1998) *European Journal of International Law* 266, 267 (warning against any wholesale adoption of "international legal community," which views a community of states exclusively as a community of international law).

172 See Wendt, *supra* note 23, pp. 367–8 (observing that rationalism "isolates an important moment in the social process, a moment of perfect subjectivity when actors choose actions on the basis of identities and interests which are for an instant given").

173 See Nichols, *supra* note 100, 504; Gardner Patterson and Eliza Patterson, "The Road from GATT to WTO," 3 (1994) *Minnesota Journal of Global Trade* 35, 41–2 (documenting how Professor John Jackson's study led to the creation of the WTO).

together beyond material incentives. The norm-based intersubjectivity awakens social actors' critical faculty of self-reflection and full appreciation of social environment.[174] This collective reflection offers an ideational foundation for a community within an IO as a public sphere in which states can discursively engage with each other and collaborate together toward collective goals.[175]

Constructivist understanding of an IO features the following basic characteristics: the emergence of a legal community, the formation of social identities, and the redefinition of national interests.

First, the emergence of a shared cultural background for IOs[176] has naturally transformed the tone of organizational discourse from power-oriented to norm-oriented, and thus it has paved the normative ground for an emerging community of law within them.[177] As seen in the history of de-colonialization and the repeal of Apartheid, norms often prevail over purely material interests, and can thus empower weak states.[178] In this sense, the biggest contribution of some IOs' dispute resolution systems and their derivative jurisprudence may be that they promote commitment to law, rather than power, and unite state members around this ideal.[179] It is under such fidelity to law that states may learn to lose

[174] See Wendt, *supra* note 23, p. 375. [175] See *ibid.* at 375–6.

[176] See Laurence R. Helfer and Anne-Marie Slaughter, "Toward a Theory of Effective Supranational Adjudication," 107 (1997) *Yale Law Journal* 273, 369.

[177] See Jackson, *supra* note 40. In his celebrated "communicative action" theory, Jürgen Habermas argued that a communicative action necessitates a shared ground of both norms and facts among social actors. See generally Jürgen Habermas, *Justification and Application: Remarks on Discourse Ethics* (Ciaran P. Cronin trans., 1993); Jürgen Habermas, *Between Facts and Norms: Contributions to a Discourse Theory of Law and Democracy* (William Rehg trans., 1992), p. 150; see also Emanuela Ceva and Andrea Fracasso, "Seeking Mutual Understanding: A Discourse-Theoretical Analysis of the WTO Dispute Settlement System," 9 (2010) *World Trade Review* 457, 468 (arguing for a Habermasian discourse-theoretical interpretation of the WTO Dispute Settlement System).

[178] See Audie Klotz, *Norms in International Relations: The Struggle against Apartheid* (1995), p. 24.

[179] *Cf.* Jeremy Waldron, "Why Law – Efficiency, Freedom, or Fidelity?," 13 (1994) *Law and Philosophy* 259, 275–81. "[T]he law of international trade requires that all of their matters be dealt with in terms of principles, rather than naked animosity and power. Thus international trade law encourages the continued communication essential for cooperation among trading nation governments." Abbott, *supra* note 169, 532; see also Panel Report, *United States – Sections 301–310 of the Trade Act of 1974*, ¶ 7.76, WT/DS152/R (January 27, 2000) ("The security and predictability in question are of 'the multilateral trading system.' The multilateral trading system is, per force, composed not only of States but also, indeed mostly, of individual economic operators. The lack of security and predictability affects mostly these individual operators...").

under the dispute resolution mechanism based on their trust in the international community of law.[180] They cultivate institutional confidence that they can prevail in the future, even though they lose today, as long as the community of law sustains. In the absence of the fidelity to law, myopic parameters, such as political contingencies, would fill in any legal vacuum.[181] Therefore, an essential element of the international community of law is the self-consciousness of participants of the apolitical properties of their operation.[182]

Second, in this new normatively conscious terrain, a collective identity of states may be formulated against a social backdrop, rather than exclusively in an atomistic player image. In a 1996 decision, the International Court of Justice (ICJ) ruled that:

> The resolutely positivist ... approach of international law ... has been replaced by an objective conception of international law, a law more readily seeking to reflect a *collective juridical conscience* and respond to the social necessities of States organized as a community.[183]

This "collective juridical conscience" is a critical foundation for a social identity intermediated by ideas and norms, which are not reduced to an individual, psychological level,[184] but instead symbolize collective

[180] See Andrew Hurrell, "International Society and the Study of Regimes: A Reflective Approach," in Volker Rittberger (ed.), *Regime Theory and International Relations* (1995), p. 59.

[181] See generally Sungjoon Cho, "A New Agenda for Peace: International Trade Law as a Practical Discourse," in Padideh Ala'i *et al.* (eds.), *Trade as Guarantor of Peace, Liberty and Security?: Critical, Historical and Empirical Perspectives* (2006), pp. 63, 67–8 (warning that a lack of discourse based on legal principles creates a "fatal legal vacuum," which tends to give rise to naked politics and peace-breaking economic balkanization).

[182] See Helfer and Slaughter, *supra* note 176, 369; see also Detlev F. Vagts, "Hegemonic International Law," 95 (2001) *American Journal of International Law*, 843, 845 (observing that even a hegemon "has to operate in the highly legalized universe of the World Trade Organization"). Regarding views that a legalized dispute settlement system tends to reduce the role of bargains based on power, see Robert Keohane, Andrew Moravcsik and Anne-Marie Slaughter, "Legalized Dispute Resolution: Interstate and Transnational," 54 (2002) *International Organization* 457; but see Maia Zehfuss, *Constructivism in International Relations: The Politics of Reality*, p. 150 (emphasizing a political nature of intersubjectivity that reflects underlying power dynamics among states).

[183] *Legality of the Threat or Use of Nuclear Weapons*, Advisory Opinion, 1996 ICJ 226, 270–1 (July 8) (Declaration of President Bedjaoui, at ¶ 13) (emphasis added).

[184] See Judith Goldstein and Robert O. Keohane, "Ideas and Foreign Policy: An Analytical Framework," in Judith Goldstein and Robert Keohane (eds.), *Ideas and Foreign Policy: Beliefs, Institutions, and Political Change* (1993), p. 3 (observing that ideas, as well as material interests, shape behavior and noting the impact of beliefs shared by large numbers of people, such as world views).

intentionality based on social interactions.[185] Based on social actors' "ontological security,"[186] this social identity shapes states' behaviors in given situations and thus defines their collective interests.[187] Therefore, under constructivism, an entity's social identity, which is key to the social reality around each actor, is shaped by the interpretive schemata uniquely structured in a given cultural context.[188] In other words, this social identity is an essential element of members' "lifeworld," which might be defined as the repository of habituated patterns of collective interpretation.[189]

Importantly, a logical corollary of these social, collective identities is a strong empathy among states, a socially mature perspective viewing the other as a "cognitive extension of the self."[190] Under constructivist conditions, states may build up diffuse, not particularized, reciprocity, which tends to discourage uncooperative behaviors and assumes costs even without immediate incentives.[191] Although this proposition may sound idealistic, it is indeed empirically proven.[192] At the same time, it should be noted that the intersubjective qualities of social identities are not necessarily cooperative; they can be conflictual, as was seen in the Cold War.[193] After all, social norms as an operational structure that guide state actions must be distinguished from any moral evaluation about such norms: slavery is also a type of social norm.[194] At the same time, however, moral effects of social norm, such as enhancing interstate cooperation and realizing common values, should not be underestimated either.

185 See Ruggie, *supra* note 103, at 869.

186 See Jennifer Mitzen, "Ontological Security in World Politics: State Identity and the Security Dilemma," 12 (2006) *European Journal of International Relations* 341.

187 See Alexander Wendt, "Collective Identity Formation and the International State," 88 (1994) *The American Political Science Review* 384, 385.

188 See Adler, *supra* note 26, at 322.

189 Christian Reus-Smit, "The Constitutional Structure of International Society and the Nature of Fundamental Institutions," 51 (1997) *International Organization* 555, 564 (quoting Jürgen Habermas, *Moral Consciousness and Communicative Action* (1991), p. 136).

190 Wendt, *supra* note 187. 191 *Ibid.* at 386.

192 See Linnda R. Caporael *et al.*, "Selfishness Examined: Cooperation in the Absence of Egoistic Incentives," 12 (1989) *Behavioral and Brain Sciences*, 683; Robyn M. Dawes *et al.*, "Clinical Versus Actuarial Judgment," 243 (1989) *Science*, 1669.

193 Wendt, *supra* note 187, 386. In this sense, constructivist thinking has been around ever since Karl Deutsch envisioned "security communities" in which social interactions among members led to unique identity formation. See Brunnée and Toope, *supra* note 23, 26; Deutsch *et al.*, *supra* note 23.

194 Finnemore, *supra* note 21, p. 128.

Collective identities built upon social norms govern behavioral patterns among actors, as seen in a language.[195] IO norms, including institutional practices and jurisprudence,[196] share similar operational patterns with a language in the sense that the structure of norms is basically self-referential. Through norms *qua* medium (language), participants' communicative competence transforms into administrative power that can effectively coordinate their behaviors.[197] In the community conceptualized within an IO, one can envision the public mentalities under which a member can shed impartial light on his or her own behavior through a critical process of perspective taking.[198]

Suppose that a state member claims that its measure is consistent with certain IO norms. Once those IO members establish a certain level of social identity, the eventual reception of this particular member's validity claim by other members depends on the discursive power of that member's communication. Its claim originates from its own perspective, which may be accepted and sustained unless refuted by another member. Another member may attempt to invalidate the measure at issue by exposing it to better arguments or different contexts.[199] Thus, norms channel social actors' behaviors via this process of reasoning, which is operated by discursive merits and generalizable rules.[200] As it happens in

[195] According to Jutta Brunnée and Stephen J. Toope, a strong sociological tradition, in particular Anthony Giddens' "structuration theory," shaped the development of constructivism. Structurationists view that agents' self-understandings of their behaviors are inseparably linked to social structures and that agents and social structures constitute each other via interaction. Brunnée and Toope, *supra* note 23, 27; see also Anthony Giddens, *The Constitution of Society: Outline of the Theory of Structuration*, (1984), pp. 281–4. Yet constructivists express a nuanced position in the causal relationship between these ideational factors and state behaviors. They do not argue that shared understandings (norms) nurtured by social structures are a direct cause of state actions: rather, they observe that these social structures "constrain and enable" state actors in their behavioral choices. Ruggie, *supra* note 103, 869. "[S]tates follow specific rules, *even when inconvenient*, because they have a longer-term interest in the maintenance of law-impregnated international community." Hurrell, *supra* note 180 (emphasis added). This position parallels with Anthony Giddens' thesis of the "duality of structure." Giddens, *supra*, pp. 25–9.

[196] See generally José E. Alvarez, *International Organizations as Law-Makers* (2005) (arguing that the age of IOs has given rise to international norms, which alter the mechanisms behind the making, implementation, and enforcement of international law).

[197] See Habermas, *Between Facts and Norms*, *supra* note 177.

[198] *Ibid.*, p. 148 (quoting Immanuel Kant, *Critique of Judgment* (John Henry Bernard trans., 1951), § 40).

[199] See *ibid.*

[200] See Friedrich V. Kratochwil, *Rules, Norms, and Decisions: On the Conditions of Practices and Legal Reasoning in International Relations and Domestic Affairs* (1991),

a language, members take these norms for granted as they share the same grammar and syntax of their communication. In this sense, the social role of norms does not necessarily translate into a Humean utility or a Hobbesian command. Rather, norms prescribe a claim that can be discursively validated.[201]

Finally, the aforementioned cognitive traits in constructivism spotlight how the titular national interest is molded into a broader community of social actors. The conventional IR theories simply treat national interest as something cast from outside and pre-specified.[202] Yet the social framework redefines the traditional national interest in much longer and broader terms than the old framework through a diffuse notion of reciprocity. As a social construct, an IO's community is not only a constraining environment to its members: it is also an enabling structure that generates and even facilitates their purposeful behaviors.[203] In this regard, national interest might even connote a systematic interest, such as the maintenance of a stabilized, norm-based system.[204] According to this new framework, the main barometer for an IO's success should be not only efficiency but also appropriateness reflecting socio-cultural norms.[205] After all, organizations exist not solely because they are efficient but because they are perceived to be legitimate social goods.[206]

p. 43 (arguing that rules and norm guide choices via deliberation and discourse on the merits and "cast in terms of universalizable rules").

201 See *ibid.*, p. 97.

202 See Ruggie, *supra* note 163, 384. In fact, this socio-idealist approach is not new; it dates backs to postwar thinkers, such as Karl Deutch, Ernst Haas, and Hedley Bull, as well as to much earlier ones, such as Hugo Grotius and Immanuel Kant. See Wendt, *supra* note 23, p. 3.

203 The neorealist bias according to which norms are imposed as constraints on social actors fails to recognize norms' "enabling" function. While actors are subject to norms, actors' practices alter the normative structures by which they "share meanings, communicate intentions, criticize claims and justify choices." Kratochwil, *supra* note 200, p. 61. On the other hand, many constructivist explanations might be also consistent with the conventional IR paradigms in terms of "chang[ing] the material incentive structure of their targets by raising the costs of existing practices." Brian C. Rathbun, "Uncertain about Uncertainty: Understanding the Multiple Meanings of a Crucial Concept in International Relations Theory," 51 (2007) *International Studies Quarterly* 533, 551.

204 See Ruggie and Kratochwil, *supra* note 41, pp. 35–6 (criticizing a narrow version of self-interest in international law based on rational choice theories).

205 See Ruggie, *supra* note 163, 338; see also March and Olsen, *supra* note 155 (arguing that a logic of appropriateness is fundamental to political action and that legitimacy often depends on appropriateness).

206 See Finnemore, *supra* note 140, 329. She also argues that this is the "entry point for culture" and that "the social values that support and legitimate some organizational forms and not others, some social activities and not others, are cultural values." *Ibid.*

Constructivism has recently brought a new dynamism to the study of IOs among IR scholars. For example, Catherine Weaver applies constructivism to the cultural-normative change within the World Bank. Weaver observes that various demands imposed on the World Bank in response to the ever-changing environment tend to create an inevitable gap between the Bank's word and action, which she describes as "hypocrisy."[207] Weaver considers the Bank as an actor on its own terms, adjusting itself vigorously to its environment for its survival, rather than a mere instrument subject to orders from member countries.[208]

In a similar vein, Phil Orchard adopts a constructivist approach in exploring the process of norm emergence in the area of protecting internally displaced persons. Rather than attempting to prove the ultimate efficacy of this particular international norm,[209] Orchard documents the internalization process in which a set of principles (soft law), not a treaty, nonetheless shapes behaviors of domestic actors in this area.[210]

In a path-breaking study on the post-conflict transition in Congo, Séverine Autesserre highlights a decisive role played by a discursive frame shared by main international actors. Autesserre concludes that the "post-conflict" label imposed by interventionists, such as the UN and NGOs, tends to neglect the root cause of the failed peace-building process, i.e., local conflict.[211] Autesserre's study justifies a constructivist approach, which captures a discursive frame, by critically observing that conventional theories focusing on vested interests and constraint could not explain the peace-building failure.[212]

Likewise, Nicole Deitelhoff demonstrates the formative power of discourse and persuasion within negotiations leading up to the creation of the International Criminal Court (ICC).[213] Deitelhoff argues that a coalition of NGOs and small powers succeeded in shifting the normative setting of negotiations in a way that could accommodate legitimate

[207] Catherine Weaver, *Hypocrisy Trap: The World Bank and the Poverty of Reform* (2008), p. 5.

[208] *Ibid.*, pp. 179–80.

[209] Phil Orchard, "Protection of Internally Displaced Persons: Soft Law as a Norm-Generating Mechanism," 36 (2010) *Review of International Studies* 281, 285.

[210] *Ibid.*, 287.

[211] Séverine Autesserre, "Hobbes and the Congo: Frames, Local Violence, and International Intervention," 63 (2009) *International Organization*, 249, 272–5.

[212] *Ibid.*, 261.

[213] Nicole Deitelhoff, "The Discursive Process of Legalization: Charting Islands of Persuasion in the ICC Case," 63 (2009) *International Organization*, 33, 45–60.

arguments mapping out possible outcomes.[214] Deitelhoff tends to challenge conventional rationalist models in that immediate sovereignty costs and risks of uncertainty accompanied by the Rome Statute could not avert the eventual advent of the ICC.[215]

In sum, constructivism provides a new theoretical frame that is capable of generating useful narratives complementary to preexisting IR theories such as neorealism and neoliberal institutionalism.[216] Constructivism can demonstrate, via various empirical confirmations, its analytical capability over modern developments of IOs.[217] In the next chapter, this book applies constructivism in analyzing the institutional evolution of the GATT/WTO.

C. *A community's legal personality*

A modern understating of public international law tends to substantiate the aforementioned social framework of an IO by according an IO legal personality. An IO's legal personality can be viewed as a legal conceptualization of social structure embedded in an IO. As social structure shapes actions of agencies, an IO, as a legal person, influences state behaviors.

The Westphalian tradition of public international law, built on the notion of state sovereignty, cannot fully embrace the constructivist logic of an IO's ontological independence because such logic would undermine the state's monopoly of power. From the traditional standpoint, the only restriction on sovereign power is self-restriction. Treaties based on the consent of sovereign states might regulate state behaviors not

214 *Ibid.*, 45.

215 Regarding other recent empirical studies applying constructivism, see e.g., Sabine Saurugger, "Constructivism and Public Policy Approaches in the EU: from Ideas to Power Games," 20 (2013) *Journal of European Public Policy* 888; Yong Wook Lee, "Synthesis and Reformulation of Foreign Policy Change: Japan and East Asian Financial Regionalism," 38 (2012) *Review of International Studies* 785; Joan DeBardeleben, "Applying Constructivism to Understanding EU–Russian Relations," 49 (2012) *International Policy* 418; Alice D. Ba, "Who's Socializing Whom?: Complex Engagement in Sino-ASEAN Relations," 19 (2006) *The Pacific Review* 157.

216 See Susan K. Sell and Aseem Prakash, "Using Ideas Strategically: the Contest between Business and NGO Networks in Intellectual Property Rights," 48 (2004) *International Studies Quarterly* 143, 145 (quoting Mayer N. Zald, "Culture, Ideology, and Cultural Framing," in *Comparative Perspectives on Social Movements* (1996), p. 262 (defining a "frame" as "specific metaphors, symbolic representations and cognitive clues used to render or cast behavior and events in an evaluative mode and to suggest alternative modes of actions")).

217 See Katzenstein *et al.*, *supra* note 23, 647–8 (viewing that research was generally more empirically oriented when analyzing social forces and political institutions).

because treaties constituted an autonomous organization of higher hierarchy than the contracting parties but because those states had given their word. However, after states witnessed the fatal flaw of this Hobbesian view of international relations, especially through two world wars, they decided to create legally independent international entities that would coordinate and govern states' behaviors in certain sector-specific areas, such as collective security (the UN) and international financial regulation (the IMF).

Reflecting this postwar trend, the modern tenets of public international law, in particular those related to IOs' legal personality, tend to provide useful insights on IOs' organizational autonomy.[218] The International Court of Justice (ICJ), in its *Reparation* case, ruled that an IO is "a subject of international law and capable of possessing international rights and duties."[219] Based on such legal capability, an IO holds the capacity to sue a state, regardless of its membership to the ICJ, for damage caused by a state's violation of one of its obligations toward the organization.[220] It is in this line that the International Law Commission (ILC) is working to create a draft governing the legal responsibility for damage that an IO may have towards states or other IOs.[221] Charters of most IOs confirm this position. For example, Article 104 of the UN Charter stipulates that "the Organization shall enjoy in the territory of each of its Members such legal capacity as may be necessary for the exercise of its functions and the fulfillment of its purposes."[222] Article 8:1 of the WTO Agreement also provides that "the WTO shall have legal personality, and shall be accorded by each of its Members such legal capacity as may be necessary for the exercise of its functions."[223]

Admittedly, the mere technical existence of an IO's legal personality should not necessarily be equated with a life of its own separate from the

[218] But see Giuseppe Marchegiano, "The Juristic Character of the International Commission of the Cape Spartel Lighthouse," 25 (1931) *American Journal of International Law* 339, 339 (finding the notion of international personalities as debatable).

[219] *Reparation for Injuries Suffered in the Service of the United Nations*, Advisory Opinion, 1949 ICJ 174, 179 (April 11).

[220] *Ibid.*

[221] International Law Commission, *Analytical Guide: Responsibility of International Organizations*, untreaty.un.org/ilc/guide/9_11.htm (last visited November 5, 2013).

[222] UN Charter, art. 104.

[223] Marrakesh Agreement Establishing the World Trade Organization, April 15, 1994, 1867 UNTS 154, art. 8; *Legal Instruments – Results of the Uruguay Round*, 33 ILM 1140, 1144–53 (1994).

wills of member states.[224] In other words, mere abstract legal capacity may not be a sufficient condition for genuine, practical autonomy. Varying institutional arrangements of IOs determine different patterns of governance and different degrees of autonomy. Although the UN holds its own legal personality, it is incapable of making any autonomous decisions over critical subjects, such as security, against the wills of a handful of powerful members who retain veto powers. Furthermore, even if an IO does enjoy a certain level of autonomy, sovereign states, which transfer part of their own autonomy to the IO, may want to retract the original delegation.[225]

Nonetheless, an IO's legal-institutional detachment from its members is still an important avenue for its socio-political autonomy in action. Approaching IOs' autonomy through a *legal* lens has a number of benefits. First, it is legal personality that mobilizes and institutes an indispensable set of bureaucratic resources and appliances necessary to sustain IOs' autonomous operation. For example, an IO's legal personhood enables us to employ legal principles and claims with which we investigate and study how IOs operate on a diurnal basis.[226] Those legal narratives offer unique perspectives in understanding IOs' autonomous operation. They not only explain but also generate a neutral, independent decision-making process based on reasons and principles, separate from political wills of powerful states.[227]

In particular, legal discourse informs two paramount issues which concern and shape the autonomy of IOs: *what* IOs produce and *how* they develop. First, some legal scholars have already highlighted various noticeable jurisgenerative phenomena in certain areas within sector-specific regulatory IOs.[228] These scholars often focus on vibrant government regulatory networks harbored by those IOs in which epistemic socialization among like-minded government officials and other professionals

224 David J. Bederman, "The Souls of International Organizations: Legal Personality and the Lighthouse at Cape Spartel," 36 (1995–1996) *Virginia Journal of International Law*, 275, 277.

225 See Anna Meijknecht, *Towards International Personality: The Position of Minorities and Indigenous Peoples in International Law* (2001), p. 38.

226 See Frederic L. Kirgis, Jr., *International Organizations in their Legal Setting* (2nd edn., 1993), pp. vii–viii.

227 See *ibid.*, p. viii.

228 Regarding the "jurisgenerative" nature of legal discourse, see Robert M. Cover, "Nomos and Narrative," in Martha Minow *et al.* (eds.), *Narrative, Violence, and the Law: The Articles of Robert Cover* (1992), p. 110.

crystallize into tangible normative products, such as guidelines and recommendations.[229]

Markedly, technically defined mandates flowing from IOs' particular legal personality tend to secure specialization and professional authority for these IOs. These regulatory IOs are represented not by government officials from the Department of State or the Ministry of Foreign Affairs but by transgovernmental regulators from sector-specific departments, such as the Department of Treasury or the Ministry of Finance, who, as professionals, tend to hold shared regulatory sensitivity and concern that transcends national boundaries.[230] An IO's legal personality tends to promote this epistemic bond by providing professional forums that enjoy a certain level of detachment from a culture of direct delegation from the headquarters.[231]

For example, the International Organization of Securities Commissions (IOSCO) harbors a transgovernmental network of securities regulators whose collective goals are articulated in a professional, not ambassadorial, fashion, i.e., to "establish standards and an effective surveillance of international securities transactions."[232] The IOSCO has issued a number of professional standards within its mandate, such as the "Risk Management and Control Guidance for Securities Firms and

[229] See notably Anne-Marie Slaughter, "Governing the Global Economy through Government Networks," in Michael Byers (ed.), *The Role of Law in International Politics: Articles in International Relations and International Law* (2000), p. 178; Anne-Marie Slaughter, *A New World Order* (2004); Sungjoon Cho, "Transgovernmentalism: A New Jurisgenerative Mechanism" (unpublished manuscript) (on file with the author). This idea of government (transgovernmental) networks dates back to the 1970s. See Robert O. Keohane and Joseph S. Nye, "Transgovernmental Relations and International Organizations," 27 (1974) *World Politics*, 39, 44; Raymond F. Hopkins, "Global Management Networks: The Internationalization of Domestic Bureaucracies," 30 (1978) *International Social Science Journal* 31, 31. Some scholars describe this term differently, but for more or less the same meaning. For instance, one scholar named the Basel Accord as a "gentlemen's agreement among central banks." Hal Scott, "The Competitive Implications of the Basel Capital Accord," 39 (1995) *St Louis University Law Journal* 885, 885. Another scholar termed the same work as "international soft law." Joseph Jude Norton, *Devising International Bank Supervisory Standards* (1995), pp. 176–7, 261–2.

[230] John E. Shockey, "Bank Regulatory Examination and Enforcement after Barings and Daiwa," 935 (1996) PLI / CORP. 681, 708 (1996).

[231] See notably Peter M. Haas, "Introduction: Epistemic Communities and International Policy Coordination," 46 (1992) *International Organization* 1 (discussing "epistemic communities" of elites with shared ideas).

[232] IOSCO, "General Information on IOSCO," www.iosco.org/about/ (last visited November 7, 2013).

their Supervisors."[233] Despite its non-binding nature, firms in each jurisdiction expect to implement these regulatory prototypes.[234] This normative authority, as it is repeated and reinforced, tends to equip these IOs with an aura of professional legitimacy, which in turn leads to a certain level of self-rule.

Second, the legal personality of an IO is also indicative of a dynamic understanding of its authentic institutional self. Since the juridical personhood warrants a certain level of permanence in its institutional existence, in particular *vis-à-vis* mere agreements (treaties), one can engage in a serious exploration of its unique pathway from creation through the subsequent institutional evolution as a legally distinct entity (person). This facilitates a panoramic comprehension of the IO's operational autonomy.

From a normative perspective, forming an IO's identity means establishing institutional criteria for behaviors or policies acceptable to the IO. Throughout its institutional lifetime, an IO embraces a different set of policies determined by its own understanding of its rationale (object and purpose). Importantly, this understanding is neither inalterable nor self-contained. An IO continuously defines and redefines such teleological realizations as it incessantly interacts with its environment. Just as an adolescent experiences an identity crisis in his or her interaction with peers, an IO may be exposed to confusion and stress as it adjusts its goals to external demands.[235]

D. *A paradigm shift?*

This book signifies a shift in paradigmatic emphasis, not an abandonment of the old framework due to its incurable defects. Note that the book does *not* argue here that the rationalist framework, such as neorealism or rational choice theory, is erroneous in and of itself. For the purpose of the book, a framework is not a matter of being right or wrong; rather, each framework is different. Every framework is premised on unique assumptions that are responsible for the kind of reality it constructs. This framework-specific reality, that is ontology, is inextricably linked to a corresponding way of knowing these things, namely, epistemology or

233 IOSCO, *Risk Management and Control Guidance for Securities Firms and their Supervisors: A Report of the Technical Committee of IOSCO*, May 1998, available at www.iosco.org/library/pubdocs/pdf/IOSCOPD78.pdf.

234 *Ibid.*, at p. 1.

235 See generally Sungjoon Cho, "An International Organization's Identity Crisis," 34 (forthcoming 2014) *Northwestern Journal of International Law and Business*.

theory.[236] Different methodologies tend to lead to different frameworks. Therefore, each framework is destined to leave behind certain blind spots. No framework can ever capture or explain everything.[237]

Paradoxically, however, we can only observe certain things by ignoring (bracketing) others.[238] In fact, this selectiveness is a hallmark of framework itself.[239] In this regard, the book observes that certain blind spots that rationalism inevitably leaves tend to obscure a more complete understanding of an IO, such as the WTO. The book therefore maintains that we need to identify those blind spots, and that an alternative framework, such as the one the book proposes here, could brighten those blind spots.

Rationalism denotes a structural theory to the extent that its main concern is to explain certain causal relations between the conditions of action and action itself.[240] Therefore, rationalism views that a state behavior is reduced to power (neorealism) or domestic preferences (neoliberalism). In other words, under rationalism, exogenous conditions (structure) both enable and constrain state actions in various ways.[241] Another epistemological characteristic of structural theory is reductionism.[242] According to Kenneth Waltz, a structure is an accidental arrangement that is generated by individual units differentiated by their properties or elements of domestic origin.[243] In this structure, international politics is an externalization of domestic politics (the "second image").[244] Thus, those interests of domestic

[236] See David Dessler, "What's at Stake in the Agent-Structure Debate?," 43 (1989) *International Organization*, 441, 448 (observing that an epistemological distinction between systemic and reductionist theories corresponds with the ontological distinction between the arrangement or structure of units in the international system and their interaction).

[237] See Jeffrey W. Legro and Andrew Moravcsik, "Is Anybody Still a Realist?," 24 (1999) *International Security* 5, 49 (aptly observing that "no single theory can or should claim to explain all of world politics").

[238] See notably Niklas Luhmann, "Operational Closure and Structural Coupling: The Differentiation of the Legal System," 13 (1992) *Cardozo Law Review* 1419.

[239] "All observation is theory-laden, dependent on background ideas, generally taken as given or unproblematic, about what kinds of things there are and how they are structured. We depend on these ontological assumptions particularly when the objects of our inquiry are not observable, as in IR [International Relations]." Wendt, *supra* note 23, p. 370.

[240] *Ibid.*, pp. 444, 461. [241] *Ibid.* [242] *Ibid.*, p. 448.

[243] See Kenneth N. Waltz, *Theory of International Politics* (1979), pp. 18, 39–40, 60, 91.

[244] *Ibid.*, pp. 39, 60; see Judith Goldstein and Lisa L. Martin, "Legalization, Trade Liberalization, Domestic Politics: A Cautionary Note," 54 (2000) *International Organization*, 219, 247 (observing that a trade policy depends on the domestic power balance between pro-trade and anti-trade groups).

elites or power groups tend to form an external policy position of that state, which is in fact the gist of the public choice theory.[245]

Therefore, rationalists locate their reality in individual states and their spontaneous interactions. Under rationalism, states are rational agents subject to, in a causal sense, material elements, such as power, utilities and interests. They know, and prove, *this* reality through certain empirical investigatory methodologies, such as those adopted by economists and political scientists. However, "the eye sees only what the mind is prepared to comprehend."[246] Rationalists are naturally incapable of observing what their assumptions originally leave out, such as the social structure. This bracketed reality remains unobservable under rationalism.[247] Their limited methodologies guided by their ontology cannot know or prove its existence. These are rationalism's paradigmatic blind spots. The book contends that we can remedy these blind spots only with a framework shift in the sense that ideational factors, such as culture and norms, are prioritized over material factors, such as power and interest.

At the same time, however, the framework shift is not so much that the new framework would completely replace the old one, but that we should seriously question the old framework's epistemological dogma. The paradigm shift should not translate into an unrealistic proposition that material factors, such as power and interest, are insignificant in understanding and analyzing the operation of an IO. States do, and will, pursue them. Rather, the paradigm shift concerns how state actors, as social actors, define and perceive those material factors as well as how the social structure shapes cultural perception of state actors.[248] Of course, the actual extent to which state actors in a particular IO are constituted by its social structure is an empirical question, which depends largely on the density of the structure.[249]

For example, the degree of social structuration (construction) tends to be quite salient in the WTO, where so many members have interacted with one another for an extended period of time (over six decades, including the GATT era), and more importantly, with a high level of performance. All in all, material factors alone do not determine the WTO system, although the WTO system still "supervenes" on those factors.[250] The reality around the

245 See Jack Snyder, *Myths of Empire: Domestic Politics and International Ambition* (1991).
246 Robertson Davies, *Tempest-Tost* (1951), p. 127.
247 See Wendt, *supra* note 23, p. 140. 248 *Ibid.*, p. 20. 249 *Ibid.*, p. 21.
250 Regarding "supervenience," see Alexander Wendt, "The State as Person in International Theory," 30 (2004) *Review of International Studies* 289, 300.

WTO is "multiply realizable" in the sense that both material factors (such as economic interest) and social factors (culture) may cause the same behavior of WTO members.[251]

In sum, insofar as the old framework is unbefitting for ideational factors in addressing new realities in the international field, a new perspectival endeavor, such as the one proposed in the book, should complement the conventional approach.[252] On balance, an IO's true reality may best manifest as a *double helix* structure[253] of the two frameworks, under which any single framework may not claim a disciplinary monopoly.[254] Neither rationalism nor constructivism may monopolize validity claims on IOs. Rationalism should not simply reject constructivism on the ground that the latter is wrong simply because the latter cannot be proven, or falsified, by the former's methodology.

251 *Ibid.*

252 See Peter J. Katzenstein *et al.*, "International Organization and the Study of World Politics," 52 (1998) *International Organization*, 645; James Fearon and Alexander Wendt, "Rationalism v. Constructivism: A Skeptical View," in Walter Carlsnaes *et al.* (eds.), *Handbook of International Relations* (2002), p. 53 (arguing that a "cross-paradigmatic" discourse between rationalism and constructivism can lead to a better understanding of world politics).

253 I owe this insight to Professor Joseph Weiler. See also Katzenstein *et al.*, *supra* note 23, 682 (emphasizing the complementarity between rationalism and constructivism).

254 The "structuration" theory may help elucidate this mutually complementary nature of rationalism and constructivism. See generally Anthony Giddens, *Central Problems in Social Theory: Action, Structure, and Contradiction in Social Analysis* (1979), p. 69. The structuration theory objects to structural determinism and emphasizes an ontological role of human agency. It "join[s] agents and structures in a 'dialectical synthesis' that overcomes the subordination of one to the other, which is characteristic of both individualism and structuralism." Wendt, *supra* note 23, p. 356. It also accommodates insights from historical institutionalism by arguing that "social structures are inseparable from spatial and temporal structures, and that time and space must therefore be incorporated directly and explicitly into theoretical and concrete social research." *Ibid.* Under the structuration theory, an IO as a social structure maintains the "duality" of structure. IO members (actors) and the IO (structure) are "mutually constitutive yet ontologically distinct" entities by "giving agents and structures equal ontological status." *Ibid.*, pp. 338–9, 360. They are "co-determined": an IO is the result of its members' intended actions and interactions, while these actions and interactions are at the same time mediated by the unique context of the IO's community, which is not necessarily reducible to its members. *Ibid.*, p. 360. For example, within the context of the European Union (EU), while members determine its original constitutional architecture (inter-governmentalism), the EU's supranational governance takes over once it is created by members and subsequently shapes members' culture and identities. See notably Joseph H. H. Weiler, *The Constitution of Europe: Do the New Clothes have an Emperor? And Other Essays on European Integration* (1999), p. 30 (observing that the original decision-making process had "strong supranational elements" and that the European Commission had "virtually exclusive proposal-making competence").

3

The world trade community

We should not underestimate the capacity of international discourses to transform mentalities ....

– Jürgen Habermas[1]

This chapter applies the social framework, in particular that informed by constructivism, as discussed in Chapter 2, to the WTO. For the purpose of this book, it is vital to locate the construction of the world trade community in a historically manifested process. The unprecedented evolution from the GATT to the WTO was a serious response by the GATT to the ever-intensifying global market integration and the challenges generated by such an altered environment. A plethora of legal and institutional changes borne of this evolution tend to justify a social framework as those changes represent the emergence of organic solidarity within the world trading system.

This chapter begins with an exploration of the GATT's contractarian origin. It then documents the GATT's organizational transformation that culminated in the launch of the WTO system. The chapter also addresses two distinct characteristics of the WTO, namely, its organizational autonomy and its egalitarian contents, which are inherent to the new approach.

I. The theory and legacy of the world trade contract

A. The theoretical foundation of the world trade contract

A treaty-based international organization, such as the WTO, is commonly deemed to be founded on a sovereign contract. *Contracting* parties stipulate their rights and obligations in an attempt to achieve

[1] Jürgen Habermas, *The Divided West* (Ciaran Cronin trans., 2006), p. 177.

certain regulatory goals. In this sense, the WTO Agreement may be seen as a multi-party pact by which member states pursue trade liberalization and global market integration. States negotiated and signed the GATT/WTO to maximize their joint, if not collective, gains from trade.[2] Thus, GATT/WTO obligations can be understood as "contractual commitments"[3] and the effect of their breach remains divisible and disposable.[4] WTO members engage in various types of bargains among themselves over various terms and conditions in the contract. Naturally, they vie to secure better terms and conditions than their fellow members.

This contractarian characterization of the world trading system is characteristic of rationalism.[5] States attempt to maximize their interests, such as enhanced market access, by using a rational device, the world trade contract.[6] This contract matters only to the extent that it could potentially facilitate interstate cooperation by providing information, reducing transaction costs, and monitoring compliance among WTO members.[7] The stability of this rational device indicates that conflicting domestic preferences have been somehow coordinated.[8] The so-called

[2] Warren F. Schwartz and Alan O. Sykes, "The Economic Structure of Renegotiation and Dispute Resolution in the World Trade Organization," 31 (2002) *Journal of Legal Studies*, S179, S180; Alan O. Sykes, "Protectionism as a 'Safeguard': A Positive Analysis of the GATT 'Escape Clause' with Normative Speculations," 58 (1991) *University of Chicago Law Review*, 255, 258.

[3] John W. Evans, "The General Agreement on Tariffs and Trade," 22 (1968) *International Organization*, 72, 72.

[4] See Joost Pauwelyn, "A Typology of Multilateral Treaty Obligations: Are WTO Obligations Bilateral or Collective in Nature?," 14 (2003) *European Journal of International Law*, 907, 931–2.

[5] See Gayl D. Ness and Steven R. Brechin, "Bridging the Gap: International Organizations as Organizations," 42 (1988) *International Organization* 245, 246; Harold K. Jacobson *et al.*, "National Entanglements in International Government Organizations," 80 (1986) *American Political Science Review*, 134, 141–59.

[6] Michael N. Barnett and Martha Finnemore, "The Politics, Power, and Pathologies of International Organizations," 53 *International Organization* 699, 702; Walter W. Powell and Paul J. DiMaggio (eds.), *The New Institutionalism in Organizational Analysis* (1991); Anna Grandori, "Notes on the Use of Power and Efficiency Constructs in the Economics and Sociology of International Organizations," in Siegwart Lindenberg and Hein Schreuder (eds.), *Interdisciplinary Perspectives on Organizational Studies* (1993), pp. 61–78.

[7] Robert O. Keohane, *After Hegemony: Cooperation and Discord in the World Political Economy* (1984) (viewing that international institutions facilitate decentralized cooperation among state actors).

[8] Andrew Moravcsik, "Taking Preferences Seriously: A Liberal Theory of International Politics," 51 (1997) *International Organization* 513, 537 (arguing that an international regime is stable when groups adjust so as to make domestic policy socially embedded and its reversal costly).

prisoners' dilemma might be avoided if the monitoring costs were sufficiently low and the actors' future discount rates not too high.[9]

As a logical corollary, the world trade contract could not claim its own independent ontology separate from its member states.[10] Even if the WTO may condition or structure state behaviors by controlling the information-decision flow between states, that alone might not grant the WTO any organizational autonomy.[11] In other words, the WTO as a contract exerts no independent impact on state behavior[12] since every single output generated by the WTO is in fact made *through* and *by* its members. After all, the world trade contract is an inorganic "empty shell."[13]

The appeal of the contractarian paradigm lies in its simplicity. Its commonsensical heuristic based on the basic principle of reciprocity appears to be indubitable. The history of trade negotiation is also rife with reciprocal bargains on tariff reduction. Moreover, its characteristic parsimony, namely, the limitation of employed variables, enables researchers to develop various models to offer compact explanations on trade relations. This economic modeling, such as the game theory and rational choice models, tends to satisfy a scientific urge to measure and prove.

Ironically, however, this theoretical superiority is a double-edged sword. Rationalism's characteristic propensity for parsimony[14] cannot fully capture non-material, ideational contents, such as culture and values.[15] Its methodological traits tend to marginalize the significance of social structure, such as the WTO itself *qua* organization, which is not reducible to atomistic agencies, such as states.[16]

[9] Robert Axelrod, *The Evolution of Cooperation* (1984), p. 182 (noting the importance of monitoring actual behavior so that players are able to observe and respond to each other's choices).

[10] Michael N. Barnett and Martha Finnemore, "The Politics, Power, and Pathologies of International Organizations," 53 (1999) *International Organization,* 699, 704.

[11] *Ibid.*

[12] John J. Mearsheimer, "The False Promise of International Institutions," 19 (1995) *International Security* 5, 7.

[13] See Kenneth A. Shepsle, "Studying Institutions: Some Lessons From the Rational Choice Approach," 1 (1989) *Journal of Theoretical Politics,* 131, 133.

[14] *Ibid.* ("the propensity to account for all appearances from as few principles as possible").

[15] Robert O. Keohane, "International Institutions: Two Approaches," 32 (1988) *International Studies Quarterly,* 379, 392.

[16] See Mark Gould, "Law and Sociology: Some Consequences for the Law of Employment Discrimination Deriving from the Sociological Reconstruction of Economic Theory," 13 (1992) *Cardozo Law Review* 1517, 1519; *cf.* Mark Granovetter, "Economic Action and Social Structure: The Problem of Embeddedness," 91 (1985) *American Journal of*

B. *The historical origin of the world trade contract*

The GATT as an archetype of the modern global trading system was created against the backdrop of a mutually destructive economic balkanization among trading nations in the interwar period. In a desperate attempt to escape the quagmire of the Great Depression at the expense of its trading partners, the United States under the Hoover administration commissioned one of the most egregious incarnations of protectionism in history, the Smoot-Hawley Tariffs Act of 1930.[17] This ill-conceived prescription provoked spontaneous retaliations from its trading partners.

This dismal phenomenon was quite a realist manifestation in that every country attempted to safeguard its own myopic national interest at the sacrifice of others. At the same time, it demonstrated an egocentric mindset in that those trading nations had totally failed to take into account their collective interests, let alone the interests of others. The consequent economic balkanization soon wreaked havoc on the global trading system, reducing the world trade volume by 70 percent and eventually contributing to the outbreak of the Second World War.[18]

The bitter Hobbesian experience brought to trading nations a rare Kantian moment of collective enlightenment. Bonding trading nations with a dense web of trade relations would be an effective way to prevent another tragic war.[19] The GATT's framers realized that they should promote open trade to achieve the Kantian aspiration of peace via collective prosperity,[20] engraved in the GATT's preamble as "raising

Sociology, 481, 504 (observing that economists' professional commitments to atomized actions theories lead to under-socialized views of human action).

17 See Judith Goldstein, "Ideas, Institutions, and American Trade Policy," 42 (1988) *International Organization*, 179, 187 (observing that the failure of the Smoot-Hawley Act to deal with economic decline led to the delegitimization of protectionism and created a policymaking crisis).

18 See Edward C. Luck, "American Exceptionalism and International Organization: Lessons from the 1990s," in Rosemary Foot *et al.* (eds.), *US Hegemony and International Organizations: The United States and Multilateral Institutions* (2003), pp. 25, 39 (quoting remarks by the former US Trade Representative Charlene Barshefsky on the US trade policy and the WTO on March 2, 2000).

19 See Sungjoon Cho, "A New Agenda for Peace: International Trade Law as a Practical Discourse," in Padideh Ala'i *et al.* (eds.), *Trade as the Guarantor of Peace, Liberty and Security?: Critical, Historical and Empirical Perspectives* (2006), p. 66 (observing that the cost of disputes increases when trading nations become tightly interlocked with one another).

20 Immanuel Kant, *Perpetual Peace: A Philosophical Essay* (Benjamin F. Trueblood trans., 1795), p. 33 ("it is necessary that *all together*, expressing the *collective unity* of their united will, should determine to bring about this condition... The society of citizens must act as a whole. Above the diversity of the particular wills of all a uniting cause must intervene.") (emphasis added).

standards of living, ensuring full employment and a large and steadily growing volume of real income and effective demand."[21] Thus, the community DNA already existed at the time the GATT was created. As Hersch Lauterpacht observed, it was the "Grotian tradition" that shaped the post-war Bretton Woods architecture: the framers of the GATT envisioned a new form of *jus gentium* inspired by human, in particular social, nature.[22]

Unfortunately, this Kantian aspiration was short-lived. The GATT framers had no option but to create a contract, not a community, at its inception. There was neither a lasting ethos of community among trading nations nor an adequate legal-institutional infrastructure to buttress the original lofty cause. Neither vibrant trade relationships nor collective trust existed among them. Under these circumstances, the most important mission was to promptly resuscitate anemic international trade and to staunch any further protectionism, i.e., the "substantial reduction of tariffs and other barriers to trade" and the "elimination of discriminatory treatment in international commerce."[23]

Against this unique historical background, the GATT started as a conventional contractarian entity that sovereign contracting parties established for the purpose of administering trade liberalization, in particular tariff reduction, and monitoring any cheating (protectionism) among contracting parties. The gist of this contract was to conduct reciprocal tariff reduction bargains and to preserve their outcomes (tariff concessions) via legally binding obligations. The GATT contract condemned discriminations that would counterbalance the delicate balance of concessions attained by previous tariff-cutting negotiations. As a contract, the GATT, and now the WTO that inherited the GATT's contractual legacy, naturally preserves the sanctity of reciprocal bargain based on the *quid pro quo* principle.[24] In the same vein, J. Michael Finger aptly observes that:

> The GATT was built on a mercantilist sense of economic welfare and a mercantilist sense that domestic producers had a higher claim than

[21] General Agreement on Tariffs and Trade, Oct. 30, 1947, 61 Stat. A-11, 55 UNTS 194, at pmbl.

[22] José E. Alvarez, "International Organizations: Then and Now," 100 (2006) *American Journal of International Law* 324, 326.

[23] *Ibid.*

[24] See Sungjoon Cho, "The Nature of Remedies in International Trade Law," 65 (2004) *University of Pittsburgh Law Review* 763, 766–7 (observing that GATT was mainly a reciprocal tariff reduction mechanism among contracting parties that was meant to preserve the "delicate balance of tariff concessions" or interests that "parties had labored to establish").

> foreign producers to the domestic market. The trade negotiations process did not attack this claim – it gave producers in each country an opportunity to increase the claim's value through mutually beneficial exchanges with producers in other countries.[25]

Importantly, the Lockean architecture – cooperative rivalry – embedded in the GATT contract betrayed the mercantilist relic of the past. The classic production model, under which any product would be harvested or manufactured entirely in one country (mono-location),[26] led naturally to a producer-oriented trade policy.[27] In turn, this producer-oriented trade policy nurtured a mercantilist myth that export would be a virtue and import a vice. A historically etched image of a sovereign country's power and its national interest naturally envisioned a mercantilist country amassing national wealth (foreign currencies) by promoting exports and discouraging imports. Imports, as concessions, were seen mostly as prices paid for better market access.

In this situation, domestic producers would be well positioned to lobby and capture their governments since their commercial interests are concentrated in this single-sourcing structure. Thus, competition between domestic and foreign producers would easily translate into competition between trading nations that endeavored to maximize their net exports (exports minus imports). This mercantilist structure explains a conventional trade negotiation model based on reciprocity: each trading nation acquires market access (export) from its trading partner only by offering corresponding concessions (import) to the latter. According to this framework, the GATT/WTO, as a global contract, exists to coordinate such reciprocal bargains whose ultimate purpose is to augment these material (commercial) values, which are equated with the titular national interests.[28]

[25] J. Michael Finger, "The GATT as an International Discipline over Trade Restrictions: A Public Choice Approach," in Ronald Vaubel and Thomas D. Willett (eds.), *The Political Economy of International Organizations: A Public Choice Approach* (1991), p. 137.

[26] See WTO, *Made in the World*, www.wto.org/english/res_e/statis_e/miwi_e/miwi_e.htm (last visited Feb. 20, 2012); see Paul R. Krugman, "The Move Towards Free Trade Zones," in *Policy Implications of Trade and Currency Zones*, available at www.kansascityfed.org/publicat/sympos/1991/S91krugm.pdf (as part of a symposium, sponsored by the Federal Reserve Bank of Kansas City, Jackson Hole, Wyoming on August 22–24, 1991).

[27] See John H. Jackson, *Sovereignty, the WTO and Changing Fundamentals of International Law* (2006), pp. 237–8.

[28] Concerning a similar line of thought problematizing a bargaining model of understanding the WTO, see Andrew T. F. Lang, *World Trade Law after Neoliberalism: Re-imagining the Global Economic Order* (2011).

Thus, one of the main functions of the GATT was to cut tariffs, as was seen in its very appellation, the General Agreement on Tariffs and Trade. Beware that the word "Tariffs" comes before "Trade." Cutting tariffs was the quintessential goal of a grand contract titled GATT. GATT framers prioritized a material, tangible term (Tariffs) over a cognitive, intangible term (Trade). Note that tariff reduction is basically a bilateral negotiation process,[29] which is run by a reciprocal bargain and culminates in a balance of mutual concessions, although benefits of these bilateral bargains are subsequently multilateralized. Under this *quid pro quo* structure, power and interest are the main currencies and languages of discourse; there is little room for ideational factors such as norms and values. Trade rules, such as the National Treatment principle, were originally designed to play only a secondary role of preserving the original balance of reciprocal concessions in trade negotiations, not for the sake of juridification of trade relations itself.[30]

As a sacrosanct concordat that contracting parties so laboriously produced, the parties themselves were eager to dictate the GATT's full operation. Trade diplomats were reluctant to let lawyers play a decisive role in interpreting what they had negotiated.[31] It was not until the early Eighties that the Office of Legal Affairs was created, on the quite paradoxical condition that its head should not be a lawyer![32] Contracting parties desired to maintain the identical balance of concessions, which naturally reflected the power-cum-interest configuration at the time of the GATT's creation. To them, law or legalism merely meant a tool to secure their words.

In a similar fashion, an earlier pattern of GATT jurisprudence attests to the aforementioned contractarian properties. For example, the

[29] See Joost Pauwelyn, "The Role of Public International Law in the WTO: How Far Can We Go?," 95 (2001) *American Journal of International Law* 535, 549 (arguing that most WTO treaty provisions can be reduced to bilateral state-to-state relationships); but see Chios Carmody, "A Theory of WTO Law," 11 (2008) *Journal of International Economic Law* 527 (contending that the WTO is based on a framework of collective obligations and individual rights, which promotes interdependence over time); Sungjoon Cho, "WTO's Identity Crisis," 5 (2006) *World Trade Review* 298 (book review) (observing that bilateralism "sacrifice[s] the autonomy of the WTO system," which has its own norms).

[30] See Sungjoon Cho, "GATT Non-Violation Issues in the WTO Framework: Are They the Achilles' Heel of the Dispute Settlement Process?," 39 (1998) *Harvard International Law Journal* 311.

[31] "Lamy Cites 'Very Broad Confidence' in WTO Dispute Settlement," WTO, June 28, 2012, available at www.wto.org/english/news_e/sppl_e/sppl240_e.htm.

[32] *Ibid.*

remedial prototype of the GATT was "nullification or impairment,"[33] which is equivalent to injuries or damages in the domestic law of contract. Once a contracting party inflicted any commercial loss (nullification or impairment) on another contracting party, the former was deemed to have undermined the subtle material balance of concessions made in the previous negotiation and thus became liable to the latter, regardless of whether the measure at issue conflicted with GATT provisions.[34] Therefore, early GATT panels often explored whether and how much a defendant's measure caused actual adverse commercial effects, such as the loss of exports, to the complainant.[35]

II. An organizational evolution into the world trade community

A. *The unsustainability of the world trade contract*

1. A new trade environment and trade anachronism

As discussed in Chapter 2, the contractarian framework of the GATT/WTO tends to neglect its historical properties. To rationalists, exogenous factors, such as power asymmetry, in the case of neorealism, or domestic politics, in the case of neoliberalism, determine state behaviors. As a central analytical unit, a state is just a state with a homogenous, default interest, such as the maximization of power and utilities. Therefore, to rationalists, a WTO member in 2013 is the same GATT

[33] GATT, *supra* note 21, art. XXIII.

[34] Since the contractarian nature of GATT 1947 prioritized contracting parties' original expectations on the balance of concessions struck in the tariff negotiation over any legal breach of GATT norms, GATT framers provided atypical remedies for those situations in which such expectations were unduly denied, i.e., when their potential benefits were nullified or impaired, even in the absence of any specific violation. GATT Article XXIII:1 (b) provides this special cause of action, labeled "non-violation" claims, which the WTO DSU also endorses. See generally Cho, *supra* note 30, 311 (discussing and critiquing non-violation provisions of GATT/WTO dispute settlement system).

[35] See e.g., Report of the Panel, *Italian Discrimination against Imported Agricultural Machinery*, ¶ 17, 20, October 23, 1958, GATT B.I.S.D. (7th Supp.), (1959), p. 60. In this early GATT case, the panel, after observing that the Italian measures violated GATT Article III (National Treatment), engaged in quite a thorough analysis as to "whether the operation of Law No. 949 had *caused injury to United Kingdom commercial interests*, and whether such an injury represented *an impairment of the benefits* accruing to the United Kingdom under the General Agreement." *Ibid.* ¶ 17 (emphasis added). The panel eventually recommended that Italy should remove the "adverse effects" which Law No. 949 had caused to the UK. *Ibid.* ¶ 20.

contracting party in 1947 that was mostly interested in the pursuit of more exports and better market access.

Importantly, however, the GATT/WTO system reflects the particular historical context of its time. Such context may be both ideological and material. As the GATT/WTO's environment changes, the old framework tends to lose its original traction as an analytical tool. In turn, this change in the milieu provoked the unprecedented organizational evolution within the GATT/WTO over the last six decades, which the old framework cannot fully capture.

First, from an ideological standpoint, the old GATT had operated under the dominant background of the East–West conflict. The GATT largely excluded the former Soviet bloc as well as Communist China during the Cold War era. This exclusion might have disqualified the GATT from being considered a genuine global trading system. Yet the sudden dissolution of the Soviet bloc and the rise of China as a major trading power during the last two decades have eloquently demonstrated the ever-intensifying trend of globalization-cum-interdependence. This sea change has invited more open, integrationist thoughts than ever, free from rigid statist, sovereignty-driven patterns of thought prevalent in the Cold War era.

From an economic perspective, technological innovations, in particular in the areas of transportation and telecommunication, have recently enabled businesses to pursue *trans*-national wealth and prosperity, challenging the sacrosanct notion of territoriality.[36] The contemporary revolution in production and trade, as seen in the GVC phenomenon, has seriously diminished territorial closure in international trade and challenged the relevancy of the traditional narrow, transaction-based notion of reciprocity, which might be dubbed "specific reciprocity."[37] Nowadays, more and more tradable goods are not just "made-here-sold-there" goods from the past.[38] GVCs and cross-border investments have blurred the hoary distinction between made-in-homeland and made-in-foreign land.[39] For example, made-in-China does not necessarily mean that every step of production is conducted in China, as a recent

[36] See John Gerard Ruggie, "Territoriality and Beyond: Problematizing Modernity in International Relations," 47 (1993) *International Organization* 139, 157.

[37] Robert O. Keohane, "Reciprocity in International Relations," 40 (1986) *International Organization* 1, 4.

[38] Richard Baldwin, "Multilateralizing 21st Century Regionalism," *Vox* (January 20, 2014), available at www.voxeu.org/article/multilateralising-21st-century-regionalism.

[39] *Ibid.*

study on the iPod manufacturing powerfully demonstrates.[40] Moreover, those factories manufacturing made-in-China products may even be owned by non-Chinese investors.[41] Under this sophisticated web of global sourcing networks, once parochially defined domestic trade interests have now expanded to every niche throughout the world.[42]

In sum, the prevailing concept of trade has shifted from a zero-sum (us *versus* them) image to that of positive-sum (us *and* them). Here, trading nations have become partners rather than rivals.[43] The rationalist framework cannot fully embrace this new trade reality. The mercantilist ethos, i.e., export as a virtue and import as a vice, revealed in the Doha Round negotiation is increasingly unsustainable against the backdrop of the new trade reality instantiated by GVCs and cross-border M&As.

2. Increasing normative challenges

In addition to the incomplete description of the new trade environment and internal institutional evolution, the contractarian framework, when it functions as a *modus operandi* for state behavior, is also subject to normative dilemmas. For example, a narrow functionalist agenda, such as trade liberalization, enshrined in the original GATT contract, cannot fully address an enhanced goal of the newly created WTO, such as an "integrated, more viable and durable multilateral trading system."[44] Only shared ideas and perceptions among WTO members can embrace such integration that often requires the mature, long-lasting reconciliation between trade and non-trade values.[45] In this

40 Hal R. Varian, "An iPod Has Global Value. Ask the (Many) Countries That Make It," *NY Times*, June 28, 2007; see also Pascal Lamy, WTO Director-General, *Speech to French Senate*, WTO (Oct. 15, 2010), available at www.wto.org/english/news_e/sppl_e/sppl174_e.htm (emphasizing the recent trend of "made-in-the-world").

41 Even as economic growth in China has reportedly slowed, 2011 was a record-breaking year with $103.8 billion in foreign direct investments in China. See Aileen Wang and Koh Gui Qing, "Foreign Investment in China Down First Time in 28 Months," *Reuters*, December 15, 2011.

42 Daniel Ikenson, "Made on Earth: How Global Economic Integration Renders Trade Policy Obsolete," 42 (2009) *Cato Institute Trade Policy Analysis* 1, 5.

43 See James Rice and Matthew Waller, "How to Make 'Made in China' Less Alarming," *Financial Times*, December 12, 2008, 9.

44 Marrakesh Agreement Establishing the World Trade Organization, April 15, 1994, 1876 UNTS 154, at pmbl. [hereinafter WTO Agreement].

45 See Thomas Cottier, "Limits to International Trade: The Constitutional Challenge," 94 (2000) *American Society of International Legal Proceedings* 220, 221 (observing that trade liberalization "inherently starts to require, rely upon and develop positive integration, i.e., it depends on common and shared standards and perceptions").

sense, integration is a serious normative project that requires socio-cultural dynamics beyond contractual inputs.

First of all, the contractarian nature of the GATT/WTO is naturally prone to positive narratives of power and economics,[46] as is often the case in a private contract.[47] For example, powerful WTO members, such as the United States and the European Union, may wield a unilateral veto power in the selection of the WTO Appellate Body members and may even refuse to comply with its decisions for domestic political reasons.[48] The power disparity within the global contract inevitably accords powerful members bargaining advantages.[49] Likewise, from an economic standpoint, some scholars apply a private contract model to WTO remedies and advocate an "efficient breach" thesis. They contend that WTO members should be allowed to pay monetary damages for their violations.[50] According to them, states *should* violate international

[46] While classical realists, such as Hans Morgenthau, did pay attention to normative factors, such as international law, which could restrain the exercise of power, the "turn" away from norms resulted from the wide adoption of an economic approach among political scientists in the late 1970s and 1980s. Obsessed with the propensity for "measurement," both realist and liberal scholars wanted to demonstrate, in an aura of scientific alacrity, that states pursue the maximization of "utilities" and that a coordinated "game" toward cooperation is possible even among these egocentric state actors. See Martha Finnemore and Kathryn Sikkink, "International Norm Dynamics and Political Change," 52 (1998) *International Organization* 887, 889–90.

[47] See e.g., Ian R. Macneil, "Power, Contract, and the Economic Model," 14 (1980) *Journal of Economic Issues* 909 (observing that there are two categories of power in contract and economics).

[48] See Richard H. Steinberg, "Judicial Lawmaking at the WTO: Discursive, Constitutional, and Political Constraints" 98 (2004) *American Journal of International Law* 247, 249 (contending that political constraints are difficult when powerful WTO members each have unilateral veto powers over Appellate Body member selections and can defy domestically unpopular political decisions by refusing to comply). In the *Gambling* dispute, the United States refused to comply with the Appellate Body decision and opted for renegotiations with affected WTO members. See WTO, *Dispute Settlement: Dispute DS 285 (Current Status), United States – Measures Affecting the Cross-Border Supply of Gambling and Betting Services*, www.wto.org/english/tratop_e/dispu_e/cases_e/ds285_e.htm (last visited November 4, 2013).

[49] See Keohane, *supra* note 15, 381, 387.

[50] Eric A. Posner and Alan O. Sykes, "Efficient Breach of International Law: Optimal Remedies, 'Legalized Noncompliance,' and Related Issues," 110 (2011) *Michigan Law Review*, 243; Alan O. Sykes, "The Remedy for Breach of Obligations under the WTO Dispute Settlement Understanding: Damages or Specific Performance?," in Marco Bronckers and Reinhard Quick (eds.), *New Direction in International Economic Law: Essays in Honor of John H. Jackson* (2000), p. 347.

law to preserve their national interests.[51] Under this logic, however, wealthy WTO members might be tempted to buy out their violations with impunity.

This power disparity tends to preserve the status quo in international relations[52] and thus marginalizes less powerful trading nations. Such marginalization, prone to create frustration and resentment from developing countries,[53] innately militates against the WTO's normative agenda, in particular its integrationist *telos*.[54] Shocking anecdotes abound. The United States currently collects more tariffs from Bangladesh than from France![55] While the EU's subsidy on every cow is $2 a day,[56] more than half of the world's human population lives with the same amount or less per day.[57] Most problematically, rich countries' protectionism falls on poor countries' only lifeline products, such as African cotton,[58] Moldovan fruits,[59] and Cambodian garments.[60] Yet enhancing market access for poor countries' main exports is not to accord those countries a special favor, but is merely to play by free

[51] Oona A. Hathaway and Ariel N. Lavinbuk, "Rationalism and Revisionism in International Law," 119 (2006) *Harvard Law Review*, 1404, 1405 (reviewing Jack L. Goldsmith and Eric A. Posner, *The Limits of International Law* (2005)).

[52] Alexander Wendt, *Social Theory of International Politics* (1999), p. 377.

[53] See B. S. Chimni, "International Institutions Today: An Imperial Global State in the Making," 15 (2004) *European Journal of International Law* 1 (arguing that a "transnational capitalist class" (TCC) has recently shaped international economic norms and institutions to its advantage and that these imperial developments deepened the North–South divide); B. S. Chimni, "Co-option and Resistance: Two Faces of Global Administrative Law," 37 (2005) *New York University Journal of International Law & Politics*, 799, 806 (2005) (observing that an emerging notion of global administrative law is an essential character of imperial international laws and institutions).

[54] Andrew Emmerson, "Conceptualizing Security Exceptions: Legal Doctrine or Political Excuse?," 11 (2008) *Journal of International Economic Law* 135, 146, 150 (arguing that realism assumes a pre-established order reflecting powerful state interests and that this concern with maintaining the status quo is irreconcilable with the WTO's economic integration objective).

[55] Dustin Smith, "The Truth About Industrial Country Tariffs," 39 (2002) *Finance and Development*, available at www.imf.org/external/pubs/ft/fandd/2002/09/smith.htm.

[56] James Lamont, "Doha Deal 'Close to Conclusion,'" *Financial Times*, September 3, 2009, 4 (quoting Dhruv Sawhney, a past president of the Confederation of Indian Industry).

[57] Population Reference Bureau, www.prb.org/Journalists/PressReleases/2005/MoreThanHalftheWorldLivesonLessThan2aDayAugust2005.aspx (last visited Feb. 20, 2012).

[58] See "Stitched Up: African Irritation at Rich Countries' Cotton Subsidies," 368 *Economist*, July 26, 2003, 71.

[59] See "Moldova's Poverty: Outsiders Aren't Helping," 366 *Economist*, February 15, 2003, 48.

[60] See David Woods, "Two Queries – and Same Answer – for U.S. Textile Lobbyists," *Financial Times*, December 22, 2005, 12.

trade principles.[61] Many government subsidies in rich countries violate both the spirit and the letter of trade rules. Nonetheless, rich countries, under the frustrating logic of mercantilist *quid pro quo* (reciprocity), repeatedly find fault with the lack of concessions from poor countries even in the current development round.[62]

Power politics also disadvantage developing countries in the regulatory bargain. For example, by linking the intellectual property rights (IPR) to development assistance programs such as the Generalized System of Preferences (GSP), rich countries pressured developing countries into accepting the IPR protection regime.[63] While this realpolitik discourse may explain how and why the TRIPS regime came to light in the WTO, it nonetheless overlooks critical socio-legal debates as to whether the TRIPS' existence within the WTO is normatively justified[64] and how WTO members perceive, and will eventually reform, this new regime, as revealed in certain contentious issues, such as AIDS drugs and human health.[65]

At the same time, the rationalist framework is inherently vulnerable to capture. Domestic politics, engineered by interest groups, shape[66] or constrain[67] the formation of trade policies. The rationalist framework

[61] Sixth WTO Ministerial Conference, December 13, 2005, "Day 1: Conference Opens Formally and Ministers Consult on Industrial Goods," available at www.wto.org/english/thewto_e/minist_e/min05_e/min05_13dec_e.htm.

[62] See Oxfam Press Release, "Responsibility on EU and US to Deliver Fair Trade Rules for 2006," December 20, 2005, available at www.oxfam.org/en/news/pressreleases2005/pr051220_hongkong.

[63] Anu Bradford, "When the WTO Works, and How it Fails," 51 (2010) *Virginia Journal of International Law*, 1, 15.

[64] *Ibid.*, 3.

[65] The patent protections accorded to AIDS drugs under the WTO Agreement on Trade-Related Aspects of Intellectual Property Rights is a contentious issue with several African WTO members. See e.g., Ben Sihanya, "Patents, Parallel Importation and Compulsory Licensing of HIV/AIDS Drugs: The Experience of Kenya," in *Managing the Challenges of WTO Participation: 45 Case Studies* (2005). Regarding the relationship between WTO Agreements and various contentious health policies such as tobacco, drugs, and intellectual property rights, see "WTO Agreements and Public Health: A Joint Study by the WHO and the WTO Secretariat" (2002), available at www.wto.org/english/res_e/booksp_e/who_wto_e.pdf.

[66] Bradford, *supra* note 63, 19–21 (arguing that strong lobbies from developed countries' domestic interest groups, such as big pharmaceutical companies, pushed forth the launch of the TRIPS Agreement in the Uruguay Round).

[67] See Timothy J. McKeown, "Firms and Tariff Regime Change: Explaining the Demand for Protection," 36 (1984) *World Politics*, 215, 216 (observing that the civil society's demands put constraints on the government's tariff policies since ignoring such demands incur high political costs in the competitive political system).

tends to naturalize protectionism-cum-mercantilism,[68] which is symptomatic of the normative encroachment of the GATT/WTO system. This dyad has in fact become trade ontology. In the global contract, the parochial domestic politics of powerful trading nations directly control trade negotiations. Captured domestic governments, which are largely unresponsive to the general public (both domestic *and* global) welfare gains from open markets, repeat the same old protectionism seen in the interwar era.[69] For example, powerful domestic lobby groups, such as the American Farm Bureau and the National Association of Manufacturers, tailed the US negotiators all the way to Geneva not only to monitor the negotiation but also to give direct instructions to negotiators.[70] It is this die-hard mercantilist bargaining driven by a myopic obsession with exports as utilities and imports as disutilities which has deadlocked the Doha Round negotiation for the past decade.[71]

Consider the Doha Round deadlock. Interestingly, the old and the new frameworks present a "diagnostic struggle"[72] over the recent Doha debacle. Under the rationalist framework, the debacle is yet another botched deal due to the failure of negotiators to discover a balanced bargain. Yet, the rationalist framework is oblivious to the fact that the Doha Round was originally meant to be a development round. Major

[68] Robert Gilpin, *US Power and the Multinational Corporation: The Political Economy of Foreign Direct Investment* (1975) (arguing that the US needs a trade-dominated mercantilist strategy and should impose selective controls and taxation).

[69] Ikenson, *supra* note 42, 10 ("Mercantilist negotiating strategies or trade barriers may temporarily benefit some producers, but they invariably hurt consumers, wholesalers, retailers, importers, truck drivers, warehouse operators, designers, engineers, accountants, marketers, financiers, and globally integrated producers who rely on imports and who have great stakes in an open world economy").

[70] Paul Blustein, "The Nine-Day Misadventure of the Most Favored Nations: How the WTO's Doha Round Negotiations Went Awry in July 2008," *Brookings Institute*, December 5, 2008, p. 11, available at www.brookings.edu/articles/2008/1205_trade_blustein.aspx.

[71] Of course, the South itself may not be free from the accusation of mercantilism. Developing countries are also eager to protect their own champion industries by means of tariffs and other trade barriers. Although some protection, such as certain agricultural protection for the food security or rural livelihood concern, may be justified, others, such as high industrial tariffs, may not. See generally Sungjoon Cho, "A Bridge Too Far: The Fall of the Fifth WTO Ministerial Conference in Cancún and the Future of Trade Constitution," 7 (2004) *Journal of International Economic Law* 219; Jagdish Bhagwati, "Wanted: Jubilee 2010 (Dismantling Protection)," June 26, 2002, available at www.oecdobserver.org/news/fullstory.php/aid/713/Wanted:_Jubilee_2010.html.

[72] Terrence C. Halliday, "Recursivity of Global Normmaking: A Sociolegal Agenda," 5 (2009) *Annual Review of Law and Social Science*, 16.1, 16.16.

WTO members largely failed to factor development into their interest matrices. Development values were hardly fused to the WTO's social structure based on which WTO members self-evaluate their particular behaviors as appropriate or not. While powerful members' externalization of domestic interests may appear natural from a realist standpoint, it seldom addresses the solemn consequence that the Doha failure takes an enormous toll on the world's poor.[73] Ominously, the recent financial crisis only highlights this normative deficiency of the rationalist model, as the Hobbesian struggle might precipitate an entropic vision of the world.[74]

Furthermore, the rationalist framework is largely ill-equipped to address new types of trade restrictions such as "non-tariff barriers" (NTBs). After rounds of trade talks, conventional trade barriers, such as tariffs and quotas, were dismantled dramatically. In contrast, domestic regulations have begun to emerge as new trade barriers that rapidly replace tariffs and quotas.[75] Concomitantly, as the era of the welfare state dawned, modern governments began to multiply domestic regulations in response to novel regulatory demands in such areas as the environment and human health. Left largely uncoordinated, these diverging domestic regulations themselves function as trade barriers even without protectionist intent.[76] Of course, these domestic regulations, shrouded in legitimate policy objectives, often cater to protectionist needs.[77] Hard to measure, these administrative barriers cannot be simply bargained away.

This is a serious challenge to the WTO *qua* organization. Should a trade organization tolerate non-protectionist, yet still trade-restrictive, measures? If so, how far? How can the world trading system reconcile trade and non-trade (societal) values? This is a structural problem whose solution requires more than a conventional bargain based on routine

[73] See generally Sungjoon Cho, "The Demise of Development in the Doha Round Negotiations," 45 (2010) *Texas International Law Journal* 573.

[74] See Gideon Rachman, "Welcome to a Zero-Sum World," *The Economist*, November 22, 2010.

[75] See Daniel Y. Kono, "Optimal Obfuscation: Democracy and Trade Policy Transparency," 100 (2006) *The American Political Science Review* 369, 371 (viewing that democracy reduces incentives to employ tariffs while increasing incentives to employ less transparent NTBs).

[76] See generally Sungjoon Cho, *Free Markets and Social Regulation: A Reform Agenda of the Global Trading System* (2003).

[77] See notably Kono, *supra* note 75 (contending that core NTBs are clearly protectionist by restricting import supply).

strategic cost-benefit analysis under each member's trade balance sheet.[78] Rather, it necessitates much collective thinking and soul-searching dialogue among trading nations, and their nationals (traders), on such normative issues as values, goals, and the collective identity of the world trading system.

For example, the old framework might ascribe the failure to reach an international antitrust agreement in the WTO to the power conflict between the United States and the EU.[79] As seen in high-profile cases such as *GE/Honeywell* and *Microsoft*, these two jurisdictions cannot form a firm consensus on how much the government should intervene to rectify the market dominance of powerful firms.[80] Under the neo-realist logic, powerful members such as the United States and the EU might not readily compromise.[81] The rationalist model is insufficient to prescribe how in the future such a clash could be avoided and instead a consensus formed. It would not pay attention to the lack of genuine regulatory dialogue between these two jurisdictions on this subject: two parties are simply *not talking*. Behavioral changes necessary to global antitrust cooperation may ensue only after much collective thinking and discourse among regulators on critical issues such as the nature of market, the definition of fair competition, and the ultimate role of the government in a free market economy.[82]

Although the Kantian enlightenment pursuing collective prosperity via free trade inspired the launch of the GATT prototype, power politics still fuels, and is fueled by, the aforementioned mercantilist trend. This depressing pattern is confirmed by the recent protectionist trends in the aftermath of the global financial crisis[83] as well as the deadlock of the Doha Round talks. If WTO members discontinue sharing information

[78] See generally Sungjoon Cho, "Linkage of Free Trade and Social Regulation: Moving beyond the Entropic Dilemma," 5 (2005) *Chicago Journal of International Law* 625 (approaching the linkage ("trade and . . .") issues from a constitutional perspective).

[79] Bradford, *supra* note 63, 17. [80] *Ibid.*

[81] See David J. Gerber, *Global Competition: Law, Markets and Globalization* (2010).

[82] *Ibid.*

[83] See Simon Evenett, "Managed Exports and the Recovery of World Trade: The 7th GTA Report," *Center for Economic Policy Research*, September 16, 2010, www.globaltradealert.org/sites/default/files/GTA7.pdf; Christian Henn and Brad McDonald, "Crisis Protectionism: The Observed Trade Impact," *Vox*, December 22, 2010, www.voxeu.org/index.php?q=node/5960 (emphasizing that new protectionist measures, such as bailouts and buy national policies, are not suitable for conventional modeling frameworks (partial or general equilibrium models) and therefore might not render a full picture of crisis protectionism).

with one another, their understanding toward each other could easily turn into a "they-relation," rather than a "we-relation."[84] In the they-relation, the content of their relation tends to become anonymous and relatively empty. The they-relation may be anonymous in that WTO members stop perspective-taking. The delegate from another WTO member is just one of them: a contemporary rather than a fellow member. He or she would be an object to be handled for my rational purpose. The content of the relation may be empty in the sense that it is abstract and devoid of particular details, such as unique developmental challenges faced by some developing countries. In the absence of the we-relation, a WTO member would find few confirmations in its own understanding of the Doha situation with those of other members.

Under this cognitive framework, WTO members' primary goal in their trade policies remains the maximization of the alleged national economic interests, even at the expense of their trading partners' welfare. As long as WTO members perceive and construct international trade basically as a mercantilist enterprise, this shrinks the civilizing power of legal discourse in international trade relations.[85] To that extent, the world trading system is never immune to the old Hobbesian economic balkanization.[86] This structural dilemma confronted by the WTO calls for a new paradigm in perceiving the world trading system, which will be discussed below.

B. *The social foundations of world trade*

As discussed above, the contractarian view does not exhaust plausible explanations as to why the world trading system exists and operates. Indeed, this highly integrated, synchronized, and spontaneous web of trade relations, if sustainable, requires a more stable and predictable foundation than is provided by a patch of contingent reciprocal transactions. In particular, the ever-sophisticated division of labor transpiring

[84] Alfred Schutz and Thomas Luckmann, *The Structures of the Life-World 2* (Richard M. Zaner & David J. Parent trans., 1989), pp. 83–5.

[85] See Cho, *supra* note 19, p. 66 (noting that "a legal vacuum resulting from a lack of discourse tends to push international commercial relations and dynamics beyond the realm of law").

[86] See, e.g., Ernesto Zedillo, "The Multilateral Trading System: A Response to Its Challengers," in Richard Baldwin and Simon J. Evenett (eds.), *The Collapse of Global Trade, Murky Protectionism, and the Crisis: Recommendations for the G20* (2009), p. 15 (observing the economic balkanization of the post-crisis protectionism now appears to be more a "possible scenario" than a mere "historical reminiscence").

in every niche of GVCs has enhanced the level of "organic solidarity" among trading states and individuals alike.[87] Not only co-existence but also cooperation is embedded in this heightened level of connection.[88] This unprecedented material transformation has made trade relations more susceptible to sociological inquiries than in the past, when the mono-location production-trade system was simple enough to be analyzed under the mechanical solidarity.

Here, the traditional notion of narrow, specific reciprocity should be diffuse enough to connote a general level of expectation of standard behavior toward another. This "diffuse reciprocity" inevitably involves a normative element, such as duty, since logically it requires the existence of a unilateral, unrequited sense of cooperation.[89] (Note that such voluntarism may be deemed absurd, or irrational, under specific reciprocity).[90] After all, diffuse reciprocity is not of calculation in a static sense, but of trust in a dynamic sense, that is in the "shadow of the future."[91] Indeed, one can locate a deep-seated notion of trust in various WTO provisions. First of all, the preamble of the WTO Charter declares the paramount goal of the WTO system, i.e., "an integrated, more viable and durable multilateral trading system," which would be impossible to materialize without trust among WTO members. Also, Article 3.2 of the DSU stipulates the goal of the WTO dispute resolution mechanism is to provide "security and predictability," which is an obverse side of trust in the WTO system.

Against the backdrop of the rediscovered notion of reciprocity and trust, the WTO can be defined as the world trade community that emerges, rather than being created by its members, based on endogenous factors, such as ideas, values, and norms,[92] *vis-à-vis* exogenous factors

[87] *Cf.* Emile Durkheim, *The Division of Labor in Society* (George Simpson trans. 1933, 1964).

[88] See notably Wolfgang Friedmann, *The Changing Structure of International Law* (1964).

[89] See notably Robert Sugden, "Reciprocity: The Supply of Public Goods through Voluntary Contributions," 94 (1984) *Economic Journal*, 775–6.

[90] Keohane, *supra* note 37, 8.

[91] See Robert Axelrod, *The Evolution of Cooperation* (1984), p. 13.

[92] See Philip M. Nichols, "Forgotten Linkages – Historical Institutionalism and Sociological Institutionalism and Analysis of the World Trade Organization," 19 (1998) *University of Pennsylvania Journal of International Economic Law* 461, 504; Gardner Patterson and Eliza Patterson, "The Road from GATT to WTO," 3 (1994) *Minnesota Journal of Global Trade* 35, 41–2 (documenting how Professor John Jackson's study led to the creation of the WTO).

such as power, interest, or domestic politics.[93] The contract model informed by rationalism has largely bracketed the critical social process as it perpetuated its calculative methodology as ontology.[94]

This community view of the WTO features a collective identity of WTO membership as a whole, which is formulated against a social backdrop, rather than in an egocentric player image from an individual WTO member.[95] Here, collective identity may be defined as a deeply internalized structure made up of trade norms emerging from social interactions among WTO members for the past six decades.[96] This social, collective identity shapes WTO members' behaviors in given situations and thus defines their collective interests.[97]

This collective identity can develop into a strong empathy, which is a "cognitive extension of the self," among trading partners.[98] Based on diffuse reciprocity, WTO members may be discouraged from uncooperative behaviors such as free-riding and become more inclined to tolerate short-term costs out of long-term trade relations.[99] Notably, such observation is empirically proven in areas other than trade.[100] Admittedly,

93 See *infra* Section I.

94 Wendt, *supra* note 52, pp. 367–8 (observing that rationalism "isolates an important moment in the social process, a moment of perfect subjectivity when actors choose actions on the basis of identities and interests which are for an instant given").

95 "The resolutely positivist . . . approach of international law . . . has been replaced by an objective conception of international law, a law more readily seeking to reflect a collective juridical conscience and respond to the social necessities of States organized as a community." *Legality of the Threat or Use of Nuclear Weapons*, Advisory Opinion, 1996 ICJ. 226, 270–71 (July 8), ¶ 13 (Declaration of President Bedjaoui).

96 John Gerard Ruggie, "What Makes the World Hang Together?: Neo-Utilitarianism and the Social Constructivist Challenge," 52 (1998) *International Organization*, 855, 868.

97 See Alexander Wendt, "Collective Identity Formation and the International State," 88 (1994) *The American Political Science Review* 384, 385. This line of framework, often dubbed "constructivism," in fact dates back to the 1950s when Karl Deutsch "highlighted the importance of identity formation measured by social transactions and communications." Jutta Brunnée and Stephen J. Toope, "International Law and Constructivism: Elements of an Interactional Theory of International Law," 39 (2000) *Columbia Journal of Transnational Law* 19, 26 (quoting Peter J. Katzenstein *et al.*, "International Organization and the Study of World Politics," 52 (1998) *International Organization*, 645, 654). There are many different forms of constructivism. In this book, I draw mainly on a modest form of constructivism that Alexander Wendt developed along the line of "structurationist and symbolic interactionist sociology." Wendt, *supra* note 52.

98 See Wendt, *supra* note 97, 385.

99 *Ibid.* at 386.

100 See Linnda R. Caporael *et al.*, "Selfishness Examined: Cooperation in the Absence of Egoistic Incentives," 12 (1989) *Behavioral and Brain Sciences*, 683; Robyn M. Dawes *et al.*, "Clinical Versus Actuarial Judgment," 243 (1989) *Science*, 1669.

these intersubjective qualities of social identities are not necessarily cooperative; they may be conflictual, as was seen in the Cold War.[101] Likewise, trade wars may happen. Nonetheless, this intersubjective meaning structure[102] still *enables* certain types of international authority, such as the world trade community, whose elements include not only power but also appropriate causes, such as trade norms.[103]

It is these trade norms that bring to terms these social behavioral patterns among WTO members.[104] As discussed in Chapter 2, the WTO practices and jurisprudence share similar operational patterns with a language in that the structure of norms is basically self-referential.[105] Through norms *qua* medium, WTO members' communicative competence transforms into an administrative power that can effectively coordinate their trade-related behaviors by "put[ting] ourselves in the place of any other man."[106]

Suppose that a WTO member claims that its measure is consistent with WTO norms. The eventual reception of this particular member's validity claim, or legal interpretation, by other WTO members hinges on the contextualized exercise of reasons.[107] That is to say, that WTO

[101] Wendt, *supra* note 97, 386. In this sense, constructivist thinking has been around ever since Karl Deutsch envisioned "security communities" in which social interactions among members led to unique *identity* formation. See Brunnée and Toope, *supra* note 97, 26; Karl W. Deutsch *et al., Political Community in the North Atlantic Area: International Organization in the Light of Historical Experience* (1957).

[102] John Gerard Ruggie, "International Regimes, Transactions, and Change: Embedded Liberalism in the Postwar Economic Order," 36 (1982) *International Organization* 379, 380.

[103] *Ibid.*, 382. Ruggie's use of the term "social purpose" seems ambivalent. On the one hand, it seems to signify a *domestic* social purpose (such as smooth adjustment), which inevitably compromises the goal of the multilateral trading system, i.e., free trade. On the other hand, however, it also appears to indicate the GATT's institutional purpose itself, which tends to construct its institutional identity and states' interest.

[104] According to Jutta Brunnée and Stephen J. Toope, a strong sociological tradition, in particular Anthony Giddens' "structuration theory," shaped the development of constructivism. Structurationists view that agents' self-understandings of their behaviors are inseparably linked to social structures and that agents and social structures constitute each other via interaction. Brunnée and Toope, *supra* note 97, 27; see also Anthony Giddens, *The Constitution of Society: Outline of the Theory of Structuration* (1984), pp. 281–4.

[105] See generally José E. Alvarez, *International Organizations as Law-Makers* (2005) (arguing that the age of IOs has given rise to international norms, which alter the mechanisms behind the making, implementation, and enforcement of international law).

[106] Jürgen Habermas, *Between Facts and Norms: Contributions to a Discourse Theory of Law and Democracy* (William Rehg trans., 1992), p. 150 (quoting Immanuel Kant, *Critique of Judgment* (John Henry Bernard trans., 1951), §40).

[107] *Ibid.*, 36.

member's claim originates from its own perspective, which may be sustained unless challenged by another WTO member. Another WTO member may challenge the measure at issue by exposing it to better arguments based on its own interpretation of WTO norms.[108] Thus, WTO norms channel its members' behaviors as WTO members interact with each other guided by an operative blending of generalizable rules and discursive merits.[109] In this sense, a violation committed by a WTO member can be self-corrective by referring to WTO norms.[110] This rhetorical role of WTO norms does not necessarily translate into a utilitarian function or a sovereign command. Rather, as sociologists observed, norms prescribe a discursive validity claim mediated by language.[111]

In sum, under the community framework the WTO exists not solely because it is efficient but because as a social good it is perceived to be appropriate and thus legitimate.[112] This is how the community model also allows us to grapple with the cultural traits of the WTO *qua* independent entity.[113]

C. *Defining the world trade community*

Defining a community is a difficult task in social science due to its conceptual fluidity. One of the classical definitions originates from the celebrated dichotomy created by Ferdinand Tönnies, *Gemeinschaft* and

[108] *Ibid.*

[109] Friedrich V. Kratochwil, *Rules, Norms, and Decisions: On the Conditions of Practices and Legal Reasoning in International Relations and Domestic Affairs* (1991), p. 43 (arguing that rules and norm guide choices via deliberation and discourse on the merits and "cast in terms of universalizable rules").

[110] Keohane, *supra* note 15, 384.

[111] Lauren B. Edelman *et al.*, "The Endogeneity of Legal Regulation: Grievance Procedures as Rational Myth," 105 (1999) *American Journal of Sociology* 406, 406–7 (arguing that "the content and meaning of law is determined within the social field that it is designed to regulate"); see also Robin Stryker, "Rules, Resources, and Legitimacy Processes: Some Implications for Social Conflict, Order, and Change," 99 (1994) *American Journal of Sociology* 847; Kratochwil, *supra* note 109, p. 97.

[112] Martha Finnemore, "Norms, Culture, and World Politics: Insights from Sociology's Institutionalism," 50 (1996) *International Organization* 325, 329. She also argues that this is the "entry point for culture" and that "the social values that support and legitimate some organizational forms and not others, some social activities and not others, are cultural values."

[113] Christian Reus-Smit, "The Constitutional Structure of International Society and the Nature of Fundamental Institutions," 51 (1997) *International Organization*, 555, 585.

Gesellschaft. While *Gemeinschaft* represents a community based on kinship in a traditional agrarian society, *Gesellschaft* denotes a contractarian association based on interest in a modern industrial society.[114] The main operative mechanism of the traditional community (*Gemeinschaft*) is habituated norms or customs widely shared and taken for granted among members of the community.

Interestingly, Tönnies did not necessarily equate *Gemeinschaft* with obsolescence in a modern world. On the contrary, based on its aspirational appeal, Tönnies advanced the notion of the "*Gemeinschaft* of the Mind" as an inoculating tool for the degenerating *Gesellschaft*.[115] Following this tradition, Steven Brint modernized the notion of *Gemeinschaft*. He defined a community (*Gemeinschaft*) as a set of certain salient attributes in human relations, rather than an actual physical locus, such as a rural town.[116]

This modern reincarnation of community can also be found in the notion of "security communities" in IR literature. IR scholars explain a stable and peaceful relationship based on trust among members of certain security organizations, such as the North Atlantic Treaty Organization (NATO), through the lens of community. According to those scholars, members of security communities share certain practices, beliefs, and values, which are often institutionalized in the form of norms.[117]

In a similar vein, the WTO can be reframed as a world trade community based on shared ideas and values regarding international trade.[118] Without such intersubjective meanings on trade, the existence of WTO norms would remain unfathomable.[119] In fact, the enhanced visibility of shared goals, such as global market integration and sustainable development, is increasingly manifest in the WTO text and its recent jurisprudence. This teleological prominence helps WTO members converge their normative expectations, which is a prerequisite for building a collective identity of the world trade community.[120]

114 Ferdinand Tönnies, *Community and Society (Gemeinschaft und Gesellschaft)* (Charles P. Loomis trans. & ed., 1957), pp. 223–1 reprinted in Marcello Truzzi, *Sociology: The Classic Statements* (1971), pp. 145–54.

115 *Ibid.*; see Steven Brint, "Gemeinschaft Revisited: A Critique and Reconstruction of the Community Concept," 19 (2001) *Sociological Theory* 1.

116 Brint, *supra* note 115, 1–2.

117 See generally Emmanuel Adler and Michael Barnett, *Security Communities* (1998).

118 See Brint, *supra* note 115, 3–4.

119 *Cf.* Anthony Clark Arend, *Legal Rules and International Society* (1999), p. 138.

120 See Chios Carmody, "A Theory of WTO Law," 11 (2008) *Journal of International Economic Law* 527, 535 (2008) (characterizing the WTO as a "constitutional"

Importantly, WTO norms are a *language* that denotes the world trade community in that those norms are used to transmit intentional claims and arguments of WTO members, and at the same time, they reproduce themselves and become taken for granted among their users.[121] Certain "semantic regularities," as seen in case law and precedents, administer the WTO's community in that this WTO jurisprudence features grammatical aspects of the WTO and thus shapes meanings of the WTO text within the WTO's own socio-cultural context.[122] For example, WTO members can make their domestic regulations understood in trade relations by invoking the notion of "like products." Under the like products case law, a ban on the importation of carcinogenic products may be consonant with no such ban on harmless substitutes of those products. It guides trading nations to communicate among each other. The "like products" case law was not thrust upon WTO members. It gradually crystallized into its current form as a result of numerous discourses, such as those in the adjudicative setting, conducted by various participants of the world trade community for the past six decades.

In sum, the linguistic properties of GATT/WTO norms reflect members' social interactions.[123] From this standpoint, trade norms are no longer exogenously given as mere records of a sovereign contract. Instead, trade norms are now endogenously self-generating via intersubjective, communicative, and cultural discourses among participants of the world trade community, which connotes not only trading nations but also individual economic players, such as producers, investors, importers, consumers, and even scholars and policymakers.[124]

instrument which "seeks to protect the distribution of expectations concerning the trade-related behavior of governments").

[121] *Cf.* Roy Bhaskar, *The Possibility of Naturalism* (3rd edn, 1998), pp. 38, 43–4 (observing that norms, as a language, form a "duality of praxis" where they are employed to transmit ideas).

[122] See Peter Goodrich, *Legal Discourse: Studies in Linguistics, Rhetoric and Legal Analysis* (1987), pp. 134, 139, 177.

[123] Gerald Postema describes this sociological aspect of norms as a "congruence thesis." Postema argues that "legal norms and authoritative directives can guide self-directed social interaction only if they are broadly congruent with the practices and patterns of interaction extant in the society generally." Gerald J. Postema, "Implicit Law," 13 (1994) *Law and Philosophy* 265, 273–4.

[124] *Cf.* Gregory C. Shaffer, *Defending Interests: Public-Private Partnerships in WTO Litigation* (2003) (highlighting private parties' influences in the WTO dispute resolution process).

D. *The emerging world trade community*

As discussed above, under the contemporary multi-origin manufacturing structure, more trading nations *and* individual economic players can benefit from global commerce than under the old monolocation structure. Diversified and diffused configurations of trading nations and individual traders care more about stability at the systematic level, which secures their footloose transnational business activities, than vested domestic rent-seekers. Indeed, the world trade contract has adjusted itself to this altered trade reality by rearticulating its norms. For example, the *Section 301* panel held that:

> The security and predictability in question are of the multilateral trading system. The multilateral trading system is, per force, composed not only of States but also, indeed mostly, of individual economic operators. The lack of security and predictability affects mostly these individual operators.[125]

Importantly, the new trade environment has facilitated the juridification of the GATT/WTO system. While the rationalist legacy is still at large, the institutional development of the GATT/WTO for the last six decades has nonetheless demonstrated emerging ideational elements in constructing the GATT/WTO.[126]

For example, what is vital in a global contract is that it maintains an overall balance of *quid pro quo* across issue areas. From the reciprocal bargain perspective, the meaning of certain legal provisions would not matter much if they were bargained for other provisions in different issue areas.[127] The conventional negotiation style, such as single-undertaking, reflects this cross-bargaining. Subsequently, however, discourses on those rules develop in various discursive forums, such as in the committee meetings or WTO dispute settlement proceedings. These discourses transpire not necessarily within the context of an original

[125] Panel Report, *United States – Sections 301–310 of the Trade Act of 1974*, ¶ 7.76, WT/DS152/R (January 27, 2000).

[126] See Andrew T. F. Lang, "Reconstructing Embedded Liberalism: John Gerard Ruggie and Constructivist Approaches to the Study of the International Trade Regime," 9 (2006) *Journal of International Economic Law*, 81, 85.

[127] Robert Howse, "Do the World Trade Organization Disciplines on Domestic Subsidies Make Sense?: The Case for Legalizing Some Subsidies," in Kyle W. Bagwell *et al.* (eds.), *Law and Economics of Contingent Protection in International Trade* (2010) (submitting that a political bargain perspective of the WTO views legal constraints on subsidies as a desirable cost of a bargain that curbs CVDs [countervailing duties] used against subsidies).

political bargain but more likely against the teleological backdrop of the WTO legal system. In fact, this critical mismatch between selfish positions from certain members and normative interpretations of the WTO often generates tensions.[128]

Perhaps these tensions are a natural consequence of juridification in sync with the construction of the world trade community. Decades of institutional evolution under the GATT began to form a new legal dynamic.[129] The GATT slowly evolved into a unique system that original contracting parties could not simply dissolve for political inconveniences.[130] Naturally, the earlier remedial requirement of nullification or impairment was fossilized as it was simply presumed whenever a panel detected a violation, which as a normative element became more important to the community of law than its material consequences (nullification or impairment), such as the decrease of export.[131] Now, any violation would ipso facto constitute a nullification or impairment.[132]

Overall, a successful institutionalization, in particular, the juridification of the GATT/WTO – substantive (such as jurisprudence) and procedural (such as the DSU) – attests to the emerging presence of trade norms *qua* language of the world trade community. As discussed earlier, these norms not only mediate communication among WTO members but also construct their behaviors, identities, and social realities around them, just as a language does.

The growing prominence of international trade law, both in academia and in practice, helps this *lingua franca* of the world trade community circulate farther.[133] For example, Professor John Jackson, a leading

[128] See Sungjoon Cho, "Global Constitutional Lawmaking," 31 (2010) *University of Pennsylvania Journal of International Law*, 621 (contrasting the US' sovereignty-maximizing interpretation of its zeroing practice with the majority of WTO members' institution-preserving construction of the same practice).

[129] John Gerard Ruggie describes this as "communicative dynamics." Ruggie, *supra* note 96, 868; see also Peter Goodrich, *Legal Discourse: Studies in Linguistics, Rhetoric and Legal Analysis* (1987), p. 134 (defining discourse as a historical "unit of meaning").

[130] Debra P. Steger, "Afterword: The 'Trade and . . .' Conundrum – A Commentary," 96 (2002) *American Journal of International Law* 135, 137.

[131] Understanding Regarding Notification, Consultation, Dispute Settlement and Surveillance, Nov. 28, 1979, GATT BISD (26th Supp.), 210 (1980) [WTO Doc. Symbol L/4907].

[132] See *United States – Taxes on Petroleum and Certain Imported Substances*, January 17, 1987, GATT BISD (34th Supp.) at 136, §§ 5.1.3–5.1.12 (1988) [WTO Doc. Symbol L/6175].

[133] See Jackson, *supra* note 27, p. 46 (observing that international economic law (IEL) might be the most "populated" subject of international law in terms of the "numbers of persons and hours spent working on IEL, as well as the amount of practice").

international trade law scholar whose influence played a critical role in building the current form of the WTO system, launched the "*Journal of International Economic Law*" in 1998 to lead and develop academic discourse on international trade law issues.[134] A few years later, none but the WTO Secretariat itself embarked on the publication of the "*World Trade Review*" for a similar purpose.[135] Importantly, these academic initiatives have helped spread international trade law discourses beyond scholars to policymakers, business circles, and the general public.

These WTO Secretariat staff, WTO tribunal members, trade lawyers, and trade law scholars may be labeled "discursive agents"[136] in that they collectively preserve and develop trade law ideas and discourses in the carefully coordinated policy sphere.[137] As sentient agents,[138] they do not mechanically apply preexisting legal texts but instead creatively criticize, deliberate, and construct policies and norms. Granted, those discursive agents may initially confront each other with different terms of discourse since their original meaning structures channeling their thoughts and actions diverge.[139] Yet the dialectical interactions tend to approximate the discourse toward a converging point. Notably, discourses within the WTO by those discursive agents do not only concern particular policies or programs; they may also touch upon a deeper philosophy that often remains unarticulated to most actors in the WTO.[140] Therefore, when these discursive agents, such as the WTO

[134] See 1 (1998) *Journal of International Economic Law* 1.
[135] See 1 (2002) *World Trade Review*, 3.
[136] A number of scholars have identified this phenomenon under various labels. See generally Vivien A. Schmidt, "Discursive Institutionalism: The Explanatory Power of Ideas and Discourse," 11 (2008) *Annual Review of Political Science*, 303; see also Peter M. Haas, "Introduction: Epistemic Communities and International Policy Coordination," 46 (1992) *International Organization*, 1 ("epistemic communities" of elites with shared ideas); Paul A. Sabatier and Hank C. Jenkins-Smith (eds.), *Policy Change and Learning: An Advocacy Coalition Approach* (1993) ("advocacy coalitions" of elites with shared ideas and policy access); Margaret E. Keck and Kathryn Sikkink, *Activists Beyond Borders: Advocacy Networks in International Politics* (1998) ("advocacy networks" of activists contesting ideas in international politics); Neil Fligstein and Iona Mara-Drita, "How to Make a Market: Reflections on the European Union's Single Market Program," 102 (1996) *American Journal of Sociology, 1* ("entrepreneurs"); Bruno Jobert, "The Normative Frameworks of Public Policy," 37 (1989) *Political Studies*, 376, 376–86 ("mediators").
[137] See Schmidt, *supra* note 136, 2. [138] *Ibid.*, 3.
[139] See *ibid.*, 303–9; William E. Connolly, *The Terms of Political Discourse* (1993).
[140] See Schmidt, *supra* note 136, 308.

Appellate Body members, reconstruct trade norms via constitutional adjudication against parochial interests, they explicitly or implicitly engage in a discourse on the very *telos* of the WTO.[141]

III. Main properties of the world trade community

A. *Autonomy*

As discussed in Chapter 2, the rationalist model rejects the ontological independence of the WTO. From a rationalist perspective, the WTO as a contract is nothing but a vehicle for its organizing members. Thus, it basically adopts the typical reductionist view. According to reductionism, even if the WTO is said to have its own intention in a metaphoric way, it is simply an aggregation of individual member intentions.[142] The reductionist logic is as follows: "we-intentions are *nothing but* interlocking I-intentions toward a group;"[143] a contract should be reduced to those contracting *parties*; a contract cannot have a life on its own. In this approach, the operation of the WTO contract, including adjudication, could not follow its own internal (autonomous) logic and procedures. Instead, a set of external parameters, such as political contingencies and payoff matrices,[144] most of which are attributable to parties, determine the WTO's operation. Under the rationalist model, the WTO is basically a tool for its members, not an independent teleological entity.

However, this reductionist proposition raises some serious doubts when applied to the WTO.[145] First, within the context of the WTO, a WTO member is not a mere contracting party, but a *member*. Being a member presupposes the existence of a membership organization (here, the WTO). Therefore, the reductionist logic seems to be circular. Second, the WTO as a whole can intend a certain goal (such as development) even though some individual members do not intend such a thing. In this

[141] See *ibid.*, 12; Sungjoon Cho, "Global Constitutional Lawmaking," 31 (2010) *University of Pennsylvania Journal of International Law* 621 (viewing that the WTO was able to reconstruct trade norms regarding antidumping practices despite the United States' sovereignty-maximizing interpretation of its zeroing practice).

[142] See Alexander Wendt, "The State as Person in International Theory," 30 (2004) *Review of International Studies* 289, 298.

[143] *Ibid.*, 299.

[144] See Richard Münch, "The Law as a Medium of Communication," 13 (1992) *Cardozo Law Review*, 1655, 1662.

[145] Here, I draw on Alexander Wendt's criticism on the reductionist construct on the state-individuals relationship. Wendt, *supra* note 142, 299.

regard, the main reason why the Doha Round negotiation is still under way despite multiple death knells rung by so many individual members is that the Doha "Development" Round was originally launched under the auspices of the WTO. It was *not* a casual project based on a coalition of the willing. Regardless of diverging calculations of individual members that have deadlocked the negotiation, its institutionalized goal (development) remains intact. Finally, the WTO can perform certain functions that individual members cannot. For example, the WTO system prohibits any unilateral retaliation against an alleged violating member. As stipulated in the DSU, only the WTO (the Dispute Settlement Body) can authorize an official enforcement measure after it exhausts certain procedural steps.

One can clear these doubts by embracing a social perspective in which the WTO's autonomy is an ontological prerequisite for the WTO's community. The WTO is as *real* as its members. It is beyond a matter of metaphor. Admittedly, it was the WTO members that created the WTO in the first place. Still, however, the WTO's intention does not rest on any particular members.[146] The WTO's quasi-supranational structure envisions its own intentions that are not necessarily reduced to those of its members. Thus, the WTO's autonomy is critical since it enables us to understand and predict the WTO's organizational operation (and evolution) in a reliable manner with very little information about individual members.[147]

B. *Intersubjectivity*

Why does a defending party respond to a complaining party's consultation request? Under the rationalist model, it is in the defending party's interest to do so; otherwise, it must bear various unpleasant consequences, including losing the dispute. In this regard, the defending party's material consideration might be said to cause its compliant behavior. Yet, this explanation does not offer a holistic picture on the disputants' interaction under the WTO dispute settlement mechanism, in particular, and the WTO's operation, in general. What do we mean by "interest"? Would this interest only concern winning or losing a particular case at hand or something else? How would the defendant's interest form in the first place?

[146] See *ibid.*, 300 (discussing "supervenience"). [147] See *ibid.*, 297.

The social framework adopts a different perspective. It focuses on the socio-normative structure of the WTO and attempts to comprehend the WTO operation based on the structure. For example, a complainant's role in raising an issue with a defendant's measure is not only typified as a WTO action (complaining) by the defendant, but it also works as a critical factor constituting the defendant's own role.[148] Suppose that the defendant's response initially originated from a selfish reason, as discussed above. Despite its undisclosed motivation, the defendant's response, as a default pattern of cooperation within the context of the WTO system, manifests itself "as if" it values the complainant's concern.[149] Here, the defendant sends a strong signal of trust to the complainant: "I am doing this because I *believe* you will do the same."[150] This nuanced role expectation as a cooperator ("altercasting") is based on a diffused sense of reciprocal recursivity.[151]

This mutuality or interdependency between WTO members is what makes the WTO community social. For example, a complaining party (Country X) knows that its behavior will be given a certain meaning as it is interpreted by a defending party (Country Y). Country X also knows that Country Y knows that Country X knows this exact point! The structure of this meaning attribution is institutionalized in the WTO in the form of various normative patterns, which might be written or unwritten, formal or informal, soft or hard. Suppose that Country Y argues that its recent ban on the importation of cloned beef products from Country X was based on scientific justification. Here, Country Y's intentional choice of a term (scientific justification) is not random in the sense that Country Y did not invent it from scratch. In fact, such a choice is shaped deliberately by preexisting normative patterns in this kind of situation (sanitary regulation), which can be found in Articles 2 and 5 of the SPS Agreement and related case law, such as *Hormones* and *Hormones II*. In doing so, Country Y is conscious that Country X would interpret Country Y's ban based on the same normative schemas. Country Y is also cognizant that Country X knows that Country Y knows Country X's such meaning-attribution.

Rationalism might render a different narrative as to the aforementioned hypothetical situation. Rationalism views that these two countries are placed in an adversarial, competitive situation. They would want to

[148] *Cf.* Peter L. Berger and Thomas Luckmann, *The Social Construction of Reality* (1967), p. 56.

[149] See Wendt, *supra* note 52, p. 346. [150] See *ibid.*, pp. 342, 346. [151] See *ibid.*

prevail over each other in their arguments. For this purpose, they are likely to manipulate whatever normative patterns exist to their own strategic advantage. Here, subjective motivation ("I have to win this case!") prevails over any collective imagination. The other party is an object to defeat, not one to work with to form a mutual understanding.

In contrast, a social approach proposed in this book highlights a general thesis of intersubjectivity.[152] In the aforementioned hypothetical case, Country Y, an importing country, would assume Country X's perspective. Then, would Country Y still adhere to the same explication that it obtained before this perspective-taking? Of course, this may happen to Country X as well. In combination, this mutual perspective-taking opens a window for each party to experience, and thus explicate, things detached from its own biographical contexts. Through such self-distancing and de-contextualization, both parties may narrow the gap of their original disagreement. They could think and act *as if* they were placed in the same situation. This is how their experiences can be socialized. In sum, this "reciprocal mirroring" is key to the process of socialization as it constitutes any subjective experience through an intersubjective experience.[153] Country Y formulates its claim or measure as it anticipates responses from its fellow WTO members. Likewise, responses from those WTO members are also conditioned upon a likely response from Country Y.

This intersubjectivity is susceptible to mutual understanding via regulatory dialogue. The SPS Agreement offers a good illustration of this dialectic process. Mutual understanding becomes possible when such dialogue changes either party or both parties participating in the dialogue. This dialectic is not about one party forcing the other party to accept the former's original position. Rather, hermeneutical convergence may occur when a dialogue induces the modification of an original position of either or both parties in the form of mutual understanding. The following table demonstrates this dialectical change under the stylized settings of regulatory dialogue.[154]

In the aforementioned hypothesis, X0 is X's original position on risk science according to which Y's sanitary measure is without scientific justification. Y0 is Y's original position on risk science according to which its measure is scientifically justified. Under the first scenario,

[152] See Schutz and Luckmann, *supra* note 84, pp. 60–1. [153] See *ibid.*, p. 67.

[154] Sungjoon Cho, "From Control to Communication: Science, Philosophy, and World Trade Law," 44 (2011) *Cornell International Law Journal* 249, 271–2.

Table 3.1 *Two possible routes for regulatory convergence*

1.	X0 → (Y0 → Y1) → X0 → (Y1→ Y2) → . . .
2.	X0→ Y0 → (X0→ X1) → (Y0→ Y1) → . . .

X demands from Y the scientific justification behind Y's measure. In the course of preparing for answers to X's inquiry, Y may seek to discover the context of X's inquiry, such as X's motivation, background, culture, and interest. Such discovery tends to help Y better understand X0. Then, Y may want to voluntarily modify its original position (Y0→Y1) to accommodate X0. This process may continue multiple times until Y's policy change truly fuses with X's original position (X0).

In the second scenario, the modification of original positions is reciprocal. In the course of reason-giving and reason-receiving both parties embrace opportunities to change their original positions (X0→X1 and Y0→Y1). After multiple loops of such regulatory dialogue the parties may reach a mutual understanding based on their mutually changed positions. In other words, as the number of loops or interactions (n) increase, the hermeneutical discrepancy (Yn-Xn) tends to shrink toward zero. Between these two highly simplified yet non-exhausted scenarios, one might reasonably speculate that the second scenario might signify a better chance for mutual understanding because the probability of closing the hermeneutical gap (Yn-Xn) appears higher here than the first scenario.

Admittedly, the rationalist model, to some extent, may accommodate the existence of the WTO's socio-normative structure. For example, a defending party's failure in response may eventually lead to its defeat in the WTO dispute that would involve various material consequences. In this sense, the WTO's socio-normative structure does constrain, or regulate, the defendant's behaviors. Yet, under the rationalist model the structure is still not constitutive in that it would not change the properties, such as interests and identities, of the defendant as a social actor.[155] Under the old framework, the defendant would behave according to the logic of (material) interest, not the logic of appropriateness. Thus, the defendant might elect to behave differently next time if

[155] See Wendt, *supra* note 52, p. 27.

material conditions change. Here, the WTO norms would not construct the defendant's motivation (interest) in its response to the complaint.

Nonetheless, the defendant might simply feel obliged to respond to the complaint and to participate in the dispute settlement proceeding, even if doing so would not necessarily meet its own rationalist calculus of whatever interest. If you ask the delegation of the defending party why his or her country responded to the complaint, he or she might reply that they *believe* it is a right thing to do. Or he or she might reply that it is in their interest in doing so, while not articulating exactly what kind of interest she is talking about. The point here is that this unarticulated interest is not the same type as the one narrowly defined by a rationalist calculation. In fact, being a WTO member constitutes the properties of *that* interest, which naturally converge into the WTO's own institutional, or social, interest.

C. *Egalitarianism*

Critically, the ultimate destination of this cognitive-communicative construction of international trade law is a long-forgotten egalitarianism embedded in law in general.[156] Legal discourse retains its egalitarian nature with inclusiveness and perspective-taking.[157] As a social actor, one WTO member's individual action may affect another member's well-being in a constitutive manner, in particular in the contemporary trade reality characterized by GVCs.[158] This is an inevitable ethical implication of every social relationship.

The current WTO system has at least demonstrated some possibilities for egalitarian legal discourse. For example, the WTO case law highlights the vitality of taking into account the predicaments faced by other trading partners in implementing one's own domestic policies when such policies exert negative externalities on those trading partners, as eloquently demonstrated in *Gasoline* and *Shrimp-Turtle*.[159] The WTO case law mandates a regulating country to reach out to its trading partners and to establish some cooperative arrangements to avoid

156 Regarding the egalitarian content of law, see notably Habermas, *supra* note 1, p. 131.

157 See *ibid.*, p. 185.

158 See Humberto R. Maturana and Francisco J. Varela, *Autopoiesis and Cognition: The Realization of the Living*, xxvi (1980).

159 See Appellate Report, *United States – Standards for Reformulated and Conventional Gasoline*, WT/DS2/9 (May 20, 1996); Appellate Report, *United States – Import Prohibition of Certain Shrimp and Shrimp Products*, WT/DS58 (November 6, 1998).

these negative (trade-restrictive) impacts.[160] Cooperation, which may be defined as one party's behavioral change depending on that of others, is a benign, albeit not inevitable, consequence of discourse.[161] Likewise, the WTO's side agreements, such as the SPS and the TBT Agreement, impose on WTO members a plethora of procedural disciplines, including notification, transparency, and reason-giving. These disciplines intend to facilitate regulatory dialogue and cooperation between regulating countries and those affected by the regulation.[162] In short, these legal – both textual and interpretive – changes under the new WTO system signify a paradigmatic shift from control to communication.[163]

The aforementioned egalitarian trade discourse symbolizes an institutional maturity under which the WTO can grow out of its narrow-minded pro-trade bias and embrace a trade constitution within the WTO system. On account of this emerging communicative framework, a new form of cognitive connection tends to emerge between exporting and importing (regulating) countries that enhances trade sensitivity in the latter's regulatory process. With such trade sensitivity, the importing (regulating) country is more willing to consider any negative trade impact that its regulation may exert on the exporting country. Here, various avenues of legal discourse under the WTO system, such as the notification, enquiry and reason-giving functions under the SPS/TBT Agreement, help both importing and exporting countries stay tuned to the same cognitive radar. Eventually, such a cognitive bond between importing and exporting countries empowers the WTO to overcome an original pro-trade bias under the old GATT by contributing to a more effective reconciliation between trade and non-trade values. This

160 Regarding the detailed discussion on this case law, see Chapter 4 ("The Basic Law of International Trade").

161 See Keohane *supra* note 15, 380 (arguing that cooperation is a deliberate, not automatic, process where individuals change their behavior contingent on changes in the other's behavior).

162 Regarding similar proceduralist views, see Andrew Lang and Joanne Scott, "The Hidden World of WTO Governance," 20 (2009) *European Journal of International Law*, 575, 596 (observing that the SPS Agreement monitoring process "serves as a catalyst for dialogue," which allows for the exchange of information and situates the committee as "an interlocutor in the process of international harmonization"); Rosie Cooney and Andrew T. F. Lang, "Taking Uncertainty Seriously: Adaptive Governance and International Trade," 18 (2007) *European Journal of International Law* 523, 544; Joanne Scott, "International Trade and Environmental Governance: Relating Rules (and Standards) in the EU and the WTO," 15 (2004) *European Journal of International Law* 307.

163 See generally Cho, *supra* note 154.

normative dimension of a trade constitution cannot be fully captured by contractarian properties, such as interest and bargain.

Concededly, the presence of global norms does not automatically translate into an immediate revision of a state's strategic balance sheet. Political gravitational force is always at large: short-term election cycles may interfere with or delay certain socio-cognitive transformations within an IO.[164] As the former GATT official Jan Tumlir aptly observed, states might be tempted to discard any new way of thinking in the face of protectionist pressure from their home fronts in a "cycle of learning and unlearning."[165] In this regard, constructivism might not claim a disciplinary monopoly in understanding the WTO. A communitarian bond in the WTO might be loose enough to yield occasionally to parochial considerations. One should not equate a new framework with the empiricalness.[166] There may still be some gaps between the idealist structure envisioned by the new framework and a certain type of reality that the conventional framework may better explain.

Nonetheless, the new framework does provide us with creative pathways toward a better future. The constructivist narrative of the WTO's community based on legal discourse offers a powerful avenue in reconstructing the WTO's *nomos* in a way that can effectively transform the conventional mercantilist politics. The WTO's community could raise the cost of maintaining mercantilism-protectionism by altering the nature of national interests in trade relations. In the WTO community of law, a wide array of individual economic players, such as importers, transporters, insurers, bankers, wholesalers, retailers, and consumers, could benefit from an orderly and stable legal environment, while politically well-connected domestic producers might still prefer lobbying politicians for special interests. Therefore, in the WTO's community, where both trading nations and individual economic players interact and communicate with one another via a language of (international trade) law, mercantilism–protectionism results in an enormous decrease in the collective welfare – both domestically and internationally – only to serve a handful of special interests.

[164] See Audie Klotz, *Norms in International Relations: The Struggle against Apartheid* (1995).

[165] Kent Jones, *The Doha Blues: Institutional Crisis and Reform in the WTO* (2010), p. 16 (quoting Jan Tumlir).

[166] In fact, this constructivist thinking can be traced back to Grotius, Kant, Hegel, and more recently to Karl Deutsch, Ernst Haas, and Hedley Bell. See Wendt, *supra* note 52, p. 3.

In sum, the WTO's community as a community of *law* could help modify the rationalist nature of power and utility. Then, it can serve a broader circle of economic participants within the world trading system by envisaging an expanded horizon of collective gains from trade that used to be eclipsed by the old mercantilist–protectionist perspective.[167] This is the egalitarian law of international trade.

[167] See Brian C. Rathbun, "Uncertain about Uncertainty: Understanding the Multiple Meanings of a Crucial Concept in International Relations Theory," 51 (2007) *International Studies Quarterly*, 533, 551.

4

Norms and discourse: the internal operation of the world trade community

Life is not only . . . choice but also interpretation.
James G. March & Johan P. Olsen[1]

Based on the new conceptualization of the WTO as a community of law, this chapter illuminates the internal operation of the world trade community based on legal discourse. The chapter first defines WTO norms as the *lingua franca* of the world trade community that enables various forms of discourse among members of the community. It then introduces three main institutionalized forms of WTO discourse – adjudication, peer review and negotiation (consultation). These three forms of WTO discourse are mainly responsible for the diurnal operation of the world trade community. Finally, in an attempt to provide the world trade community with an effective heuristic on the WTO language, the chapter formulates the "Basic Law of International Trade" extrapolated from rich discursive practices developed within the GATT/WTO.

I. WTO norms as a language of the world trade community

As discussed above, the new social framework views the WTO as a community of law and thus highlights its normative properties.[2] In this regard, what is happening within the world trade community can be understood through legal principles and legal reasoning. The WTO's consistent and systematic operation based on norms engenders

[1] *Rediscovering Institutions: The Organizational Basis of Politics* (1989), p. 51.

[2] For purposes of this book, norms are defined as "collective expectations about proper behavior for a given identity." Ronald L. Jepperson *et al.*, "Norms, Identity, and Culture in National Security," in Peter J. Katzenstein (ed.), *The Culture of National Security: Norms and Identity in World Politics* (1996), p. 54; see also Charles Taylor, "Interpretation and the Sciences of Man," 25 (1971) *The Review of Metaphysics* 3.

principled arguments that are predictable based on similar situations.[3] This norm-based operation furnishes the WTO with a firm communal bond, which remains largely unfathomable by the contract model alone. Given this repeated, collective and self-referential nature, one can reasonably conceptualize WTO norms as a common language (*lingua franca*) within the world trade community. Note that "norms" are defined broadly for the purpose of this book: they include not only codified rules (black letter law) but also various interpretive practices – administrative and judicial – emerging from within the community.

WTO norms, *qua* language, serve as the storehouse of historically accumulated collective meaning and experience throughout the GATT/WTO era.[4] Since language is a sign system comprised of typifications, it can turn a concrete social fact, such as an adjudicated dispute, into an abstract, and thus duplicable, pattern. This way, a particular dispute between the United States and the EU regarding the latter's import ban on the former's hormone-treated beef is seamlessly subsumed under the (whole) WTO case law. From now on, any WTO member will reference this *Hormones* case law when it faces an SPS issue. Sociologically speaking, the normative meaning of the *Hormones* case law is real both objectively (as a social fact) and subjectively (as perceived so by an individual WTO member). In other words, the *Hormones* case law is real not only in Geneva but also in Washington D.C. Even US politicians take this WTO reality into account when they debate on domestic policies, such as farm subsidies.[5] To this extent, the WTO reality is integrated into the US reality by making its own enclave within the latter. For that matter, the span of the US reality is now extended and shares the same social sphere with the rest of the WTO members.

Importantly, the meaning of language adopted in this book does not merely denote a medium for conveying information. Such a narrow definition of action coordination via language would be limited to a strategic, instrumental use of language.[6] In contrast, the true import of

[3] See Frederic L. Kirgis, *International Organizations in their Legal Setting* (2nd edn, 1993), p. viii.

[4] For this part, *cf.* Peter L. Berger and Thomas Luckmann, *The Social Construction of Reality* (1967), pp. 37–40.

[5] See e.g., "US Senate Debates Potential for WTO Challenge to 2013 Farm Bill," 17 *Bridges Weekly Trade News Digest*, May 23, 2013 (quoting the US Senator Pat Roberts, who observed that the "Adverse Market Payments (AMP)" included in the recent farm bill might violate the WTO norms).

[6] See Jürgen Habermas, *Between Facts and Norms: Contributions to a Discourse Theory of Law and Democracy* (William Rehg trans., 1996), p. 18.

language in legal discourse, as used in the WTO context, is a communicative one, which concerns an interlocking dimension, such as argumentation, persuasion, and perspective-taking.[7] This communicative understanding of language is oriented toward action coordination and social integration. Therefore, legal discourse is a communicative *action*, which establishes certain stabilized standards or expectations.[8]

First of all, WTO norms *qua* social knowledge provide WTO members with typified schemata through which to understand specific WTO situations, such as a dispute.[9] Suppose that Country X exports beef to Country Y. Country Y bans the beef import from Country X on the grounds that the imported beef was administered with growth-promotion hormones. Country X would grasp the situation through the lens of relevant preexisting WTO norms, such as the SPS Agreement and the *Hormones* case law. Here, the high degree of typicality, that is, the degree to which the factual pattern in question resembles the preexisting stock of social knowledge (WTO norms), tends to accord Country X an immediate familiarity with these WTO norms and satisfies Country X with its own interpretation of the situation at hand. Then, Country X would communicate its own interpretation with Country Y, as the former would anticipate possible responses from the latter also drawn from the same stock of social knowledge based on WTO norms.

Importantly, both Country X and Country Y's clinical use of social knowledge is basically selective, reflecting each nation's motivation in a particular situation. Country X's utilization of WTO norms as an *importing*, not exporting, country would feature a completely different vector from the current hypothetical situation. In fact, one might reasonably speculate that Country X's invocation of WTO norms as an importing country in another dispute would be quite similar to that of Country Y in the current situation. This idealized nature of WTO norms sustains itself as a stable stock of social knowledge.

7 *Cf.* Rajeev Bhargava, *Individualism in Social Science* (1992), p. 147.

8 See Habermas, *supra* note 6, p. 21. Scholars discuss "legal discourse" beyond the realm of IR theories (e.g., constructivism), such as in legal philosophy. See notably Peter Goodrich, *Legal Discourse* (1987), p. 2 (regarding law as a "system of communication"). This book draws on, and benefits from, rich discussions from a broad range of literatures whenever relevant.

9 For this part of discussion on typicality and social knowledge, I draw on Alfred Schutz and Thomas Luckmann, *The Structures of the Life-World* (Richard M. Zaner & David J. Parent trans., 1989), pp. 144–6.

Although the high typicality allows WTO members to rely on their prior knowledge of WTO norms, some situations could lead them to adjust the prior knowledge. Suppose that Country Y bans the cloned beef imported from Country X. In its protest to Country Y, Country X would attempt to identify any relevant schemata from the preexisting stock of WTO norms. First, it might not locate any WTO case law that would immediately satisfy the level of typification it needs. It might still find some useful patterns or typifications in the related SPS case law, such as *Hormones* and *Biotech Products*.[10] Then, it would revert to the next directly relevant stock of knowledge, such as the SPS Agreement itself. It might attempt to apply certain plausible schemata stipulated in Annex A of the Agreement, such as disease-causing organisms or contaminants. Of course, this new typification might trigger a different typification from Country Y that would better serve Country Y's own situation in the same dispute.

The WTO tribunal would eventually accept, reject, or modify such new typifications from both countries. Note that as far as the WTO discourse is concerned, WTO panelists or Appellate Body members are not passive umpires, but active interlocutors. They do not merely pick a better rhetoric between two disputing parties: they often reconstruct their rhetoric and create a new one as guided by the WTO's normative goals.[11] The outcome of this whole set of discourse, including both countries' claims (typifications) and the WTO tribunal's own interpretation (re-typifications), could alter the preexisting stock of WTO norms.

The objectified nature of WTO norms *qua* social knowledge detached from subjective stock of knowledge characterizes them as a language.[12] Social norms, such as WTO norms, are comprised of predetermined sets of meaning patterns that are idealized from episodic, situation-specific sets of knowledge. It is the unique faculty of language as a medium of communication, characterized by syntactic regularities and connectional possibilities, which enables social actors to learn, confirm, transfer, and even generate knowledge about realities. As a language, WTO norms can even provide knowledge that WTO members cannot immediately experience.

[10] Panel Report, *European Communities – Measures Affecting the Approval and Marketing of Biotech Products*, WT/DS291, WT/DS292, WT/DS293, (circulated on September 29, 2006).

[11] See text accompanying *infra* note 55.

[12] *Cf.* Schutz and Luckmann, *supra* note 9, pp. 233–5.

As a common referential structure, WTO norms function as a set of commonly accepted ideas that shape both trading nations' and private businesses' sense of what is socially real within the meaning-context of the world trade community.[13] For example, Mexico would not question, and thus would take for granted, the US's commitment under the latter's tariff schedules that the latter would impose no tariffs on tequila exports from the former. Likewise, a Texan liquor retailer may plan to market Mexican tequila without worrying that she might suddenly be compelled to pay tariffs for tequila imports in the future.

Analogous to a language, WTO norms feature three main attributes: sharedness, rhetoric, and reproduction. First, narratives shared by those who use the same language define a community where those narratives emerge alongside the language's historical pathway. As Robert Cover aptly observed, any legal entity or community cannot be separated from the "narratives that locate it and give it meaning."[14] These narratives are nothing but a collective representation of shared ideas and experiences among the GATT/WTO members through six decades of uninterrupted discursive practices.[15] These narratives are more stable than any anecdotal, individual sensations since they have been collectively formulated and elaborated for decades.[16]

One cannot understand the WTO without appreciating those collective behavioral patterns in various institutionalized forms, for example a panel proceeding or a peer review session under the TBT Committee.[17] They are non-trivial social facts that enable us to agree intersubjectively on the social reality called the WTO.[18] With these social facts, social actors constitute epistemological bases for understanding the WTO.[19] Such "intersubjective sedimentation" becomes truly *social* only when it is

[13] *Cf.* John W. Meyer *et al.*, *Institutional Structure* (G. Thomas *et al.* eds., 1987), pp. 12–37 ("ontology and rationalization in the Western cultural account"); Paul Schiff Berman, "Global Legal Pluralism," 80 (2007) *Southern California Law Review*, 1155, 1173, n.81; Paul Schiff Berman, "Seeing Beyond the Limits of International Law," 84 (2006) *Texas Law Review* 1265.

[14] Robert M. Cover, "Foreword: Nomos and Narrative," 97 (1983) *Harvard Law Review* 4, 4.

[15] *Cf.* Émile Durkheim, *Elementary Forms of Religious Life* (Joseph Ward Swain trans., 1915), pp. 434–7.

[16] *Ibid.*, pp. 434–5.

[17] *Cf.* Alexander Wendt, *Social Theory of International Politics* (1999), p. 163.

[18] *Cf.* Vincent Pouliot, "'Sobjectivism': Toward a Constructivist Methodology," 51 (2007) *International Studies Quarterly* 359, 362–3.

[19] Emanuel Adler, *Communitarian International Relations: The Epistemic Foundations of International Relations* (2005).

somehow objectified in the form of WTO norms (language).[20] Speaking the same language may not solve all the problems, but it can certainly initiate a dialogue and be a first step to problem-solving; more importantly, it may change the nature of the problem by rebuilding social reality around the WTO.[21]

This sharedness of the WTO language is characteristic of its *public* nature. Any language is public in that it is a product of the cultural representation of a given community.[22] A language would lose its rationale if it could be privatized. In contrast, a contractarian model of the WTO would accord, based on the notion of party autonomy, the dispositive power to a bargain struck by negotiating members. From a contractarian standpoint, parties should be allowed to settle in whatever terms that they would entertain between themselves. Admittedly, under the current WTO Dispute Settlement Understanding (DSU), complainants and defendants do settle on their own terms. Nonetheless, from the standpoint of the world trade community, even this settlement might not be completely dispositive. In other words, those *terms* of settlement must still be within the acceptable purview of WTO norms because the settlement may affect other parties. The language used by any two parties, no matter how convenient to themselves, cannot change the grammar and syntax of the *lingua franca* commonly used in the community.

For example, after a heated negotiation followed by an epic WTO dispute on cotton subsidies,[23] the United States, the defendant, and Brazil, the complainant, struck a deal. Under the deal euphemistically labeled the "framework agreement," the United States (the Commodity Conservation Corporation) agreed to subsidize the Brazilian cotton farmers (the Brazilian Cotton Institute) up to $147 million annually in the name of technical assistance.[24] However, this payment would not absolve the United States from its WTO obligation as long as it maintained its cotton subsidies that had been found to be inconsistent with the WTO subsidy norms. In fact, other cotton producing countries, in

[20] *Cf.* Berger and Luckmann, *supra* note 4, p. 67.

[21] *Cf.* Brian C. Rathbun, "Uncertain about Uncertainty: Understanding the Multiple Meanings of a Crucial Concept in International Relations Theory," 51 (2007) *International Studies Quarterly*, 533, 551.

[22] Ludwig Wittgenstein, *Philosophical Investigations* (1953), §§ 244–271 (G. E. M. Anscombe trans., 3rd edn. 1967).

[23] Appellate Body Report, *United States – Subsidies on Upland Cotton*, WT/DS267/AB/R (March 3, 2005).

[24] "Congress Votes to Preserve US Subsidies for Brazilian Cotton Farmers," 15 *Bridges Weekly Trade News Digest* (February 24, 2011), ictsd.org/i/news/bridgesweekly/101379/.

particular a group of African, Caribbean, and Pacific (ACP) countries, complained that such buying out of violations hurt cotton producers in poor countries and aggravated inequality in treatment.[25] To the extent that these countries could initiate a new adjudication on the same issue and that they would prevail against the United States, the previous negotiation between the United States and Brazil might not be dispositive in its genuine sense.

Second, WTO narratives originate from various rhetorical practices, such as discussing, arguing, debating, persuading, deliberating, and learning,[26] within the WTO's socio-legal context. These rhetorical practices distinguish the WTO's discourse from a pure bargaining process. While the bargaining plays a strategic role, the discursive practice serves an interpretive function. Here, interpretation is more than a literal reduction of legal text to law.[27] Instead, it is an intersubjective process of "mirroring" or "reflected appraisals."[28] Each member's own interpretation of both facts and norms in a particular dispute setting may or may not converge with that of another member.[29] Parties in the dispute may address such hermeneutical divergence through ritualized forms of dialogue, such as the establishment of a panel, surveillance of parties' compliance and even enforcement consultation, under DSU. These rituals not only glue WTO members together by imbuing a deep-seated sense of relatedness but also create collective meanings in members' normative interactions within the

[25] "ACP Countries Call For 'Immediate Action' on Cotton Subsidies," 15 *Bridges Weekly Trade News Digest* (February 2, 2011), ictsd.org/i/news/bridgesweekly/99981/.

[26] Regarding the discussion of rhetorical practices, see Friedrich V. Kratochwil, *Rules, Norms, and Decisions* (1991), p. 209; Jutta Brunnée and Stephen J. Toope, "International Law and Constructivism: Elements of an Interactional Theory of International Law," 39 (2000) *Columbia Journal of Transnational Law*, 19, 40, n.82. Participants in the rhetorical practice "first assent to the language and values of the text itself, and use the language and values to inform their relations with one another." A. H. Kastely, "Unification and Community: A Rhetorical Analysis of the United Nations Sales Convention," 8 (1988) *Northwestern Journal of International Law and Business* 574, 574; see also Bruno Zeller, "The Language of International Trade Law: Problems or Salvation?," 10 (2003) *International Trade and Business Review* 179, 183 (discussing a "rhetorical community" involving the United Nations Convention on the International Sales of Goods (CISG)).

[27] Joseph Vining, "Fuller and Language," in Willem J. Witteveen and Wibren van der Burg (eds.), *Rediscovering Fuller* (1999), pp. 453, 457.

[28] Wendt, *supra* note 17, p. 327.

[29] *Cf.* Hans-Georg Gadamer, *Truth and Method* (Joel Weinsheimer & Donald G. Marshall trans., 2nd rev. 1989), p. 306 (viewing understanding as "fusion of horizons of the interpreter and interpretandum").

mechanism, such as consultations, argumentations, persuasion, settlement, and compliance.[30]

If parties' dialogue cannot create a dialectical closure between them, institutional interlocutors, such as panelists or the Appellate Body members, may intervene in an adjudicative mode and seal this interpretive gap. Once issued and publicized, an end-product of the foregoing dialogue or trilogue, such as a panel or the Appellate Body decision, immediately constitutes an interpretive foundation for another case in the future. This process of hermeneutical convergence tends to set in motion a virtuous circle since it generates the so-called "elicitative" trust by communicating the expectation for cooperation from the other party.[31] To enhance their communicative power, institutional interlocutors often frame esoteric legal doctrines into generally accessible principles, such as good faith.[32]

Third, WTO norms are not only transmitted but also preserved and reproduced through routinized patterns of certain sequential actions.[33] They travel around from the first point of utterance to other occasions of use with their basic meanings intact.[34] Peter Goodrich's linguistic–discursive understanding of law helps capture these reproductive aspects of the WTO norms. Peter Goodrich identified certain linguistic–discursive elements in law, such as organized appropriation of norms, prioritization over widely recognized meanings, and selective rejection of alternative meanings.[35]

The WTO norms also exhibit these elements. First of all, the existence of common law-type precedents bespeaks organized appropriation of rules. The WTO Agreement provides that "the WTO shall be guided by the decisions, procedures and customary practices followed by the Contracting Parties to GATT 1947 and the bodies established in the

[30] Regarding this "relatedness," see Kratochwil, *supra* note 26, p. 123.

[31] Wendt, *supra* note 17, p. 347; Roderick Kramer *et al.*, "Collective Trust and Collective Action," in R. Kramer and T. Tyler (eds.), *Trust in Organizations* (1995), p. 357.

[32] David A. Snow *et al.*, "Frame Alignment Processes, Micromobilization, and Movement Participation," 51 (1986) *American Sociology Review*, 464.

[33] *Cf.* Walter W. Powell, "The New Institutionalism," in *The International Encyclopedia of Organization Studies* (2007); Ronald L. Jepperson, "Institutions, Institutional Effects, and Institutionalization," in Walter W. Powell and Paul J. DiMaggio (eds.), *The New Institutionalism in Organizational Analysis* (1991), pp. 144–5.

[34] *Cf.* Lynne G. Zucker, "The Role of Institutionalization in Cultural Persistence," 42 (1977) *American Sociology Review*, 726, 728.

[35] Peter Goodrich, *Legal Discourse: Studies in Linguistics, Rhetoric and Legal Analysis* (1987), p. 3.

framework of GATT 1947."[36] Likewise, the Appellate Body in *Shochu II* highlighted this very point. It ruled that:

> Adopted panel reports are an important part of the GATT *acquis*. They are often considered by subsequent panels. They create legitimate expectations among WTO Members, and, therefore, should be taken into account where they are relevant to any dispute. . . . We agree that a panel could nevertheless find useful guidance in the reasoning of an unadopted panel report that it considered to be relevant.[37]

In other words, regardless of technical formality (adopted or unadopted), panel reports are meant to be systematically appropriated by WTO members as useful precedents. Therefore, any given panel report may remain usable not only between the parties concerned. It will be used, that is, cited, quoted and referenced, even by third parties and future WTO tribunals, such as panels and the Appellate Body, that desire to make, and reinforce, their own arguments and reasoning by means of invoking interpretations of the original reports.

Next, the jurisprudential use of certain legal precepts, such as due process,[38] as recurrent referential points is tantamount to the utilization of widely recognized meanings. The WTO court frequently invokes interstitial norms, namely general principles of law,[39] not necessarily because they are binding in and of themselves but more because they are

[36] Marrakesh Agreement Establishing the World Trade Organization, Apr. 15, 1994, 1867 UNTS 154, art. XVI, ¶ 1.

[37] Appellate Body Report, *Japan – Taxes on Alcoholic Beverages*, WT/DS8/AB/R, WT/DS10/AB/R, WT/DS11/AB/R (adopted November 1, 1996).

[38] See, e.g., Appellate Body Report, *Mexico – Anti-Dumping Investigation of High Fructose Corn Syrup (HFCS) from United States*, WT/DS132/AB/RW (adopted November 21, 2001).

107. In our view, the duty of panels under Article 12.7 of the DSU to provide a "basic rationale" reflects and conforms with the *principles of fundamental fairness and due process* that underlie and inform the provisions of the DSU. . . . Article 12.7 also furthers the objectives, expressed in Article 3.2 of the DSU, of *promoting security and predictability in the multilateral trading system* and of clarifying the existing provisions of the covered agreements, because the requirement to provide "basic" reasons contributes to other WTO Members' understanding of the nature and scope of the rights and obligations in the covered agreements (emphasis added).

[39] *Cf.* Daniel A. Farber, "The Supreme Court, the Law of Nations, and Citations of Foreign Law: The Lessons of History," 95 (2007) *California Law Review*, 1335, 1336 (2007) (discussing "background legal principles"); Andrew D. Mitchell, *Legal Principles in WTO Disputes* (2008); Marion Panizzon, "Good Faith, Fairness, and Due Process in WTO Dispute Settlement Practice," in Julian Chaisse and Tiziano Balmelli (eds.), *Essays on the Future of the World Trade Organization* (vol. 2): *The WTO Judicial System: Contributions and Challenges* (2008).

essential to process legal reasoning.[40] Thus, the use of these general principles of law tends to facilitate legal communication not only between the court and disputing parties but also between the court and the rest of the WTO members. This way, any particular decision of the WTO court potentially constitutes an important element of the broader WTO jurisprudence. It is one effective way to augment the intersubjective nature of the court's reasoning in that such fundamental principles are widely shared and accepted in any community of law, such as the WTO's community.

Finally, a certain mechanism must exist to screen out meanings that do not conform to norms. Utterances that contradict the grammar and syntax of a given language are to be rejected. From a sociological standpoint, any radical departure from the objectified social knowledge (norms) is deemed as deviance from reality and therefore invalid.[41] This authoritative selectivity is a key factor in securing the coherence that any kind of judicially reproductive system may require. For example, the Appellate Body, as a cardinal interlocutor of the WTO, has unequivocally rejected an alternative, pro-zeroing interpretation of the Antidumping Code, to which a minority of WTO members, such as the United States, refers, and yet is inconsistent with the well-established WTO jurisprudence. The Appellate Body also criticized a panel's rebellious departure from the well-established anti-zeroing jurisprudence as it emphasized that only the Appellate Body can "uphold, modify or reverse" panels' legal interpretations.[42]

Of course, this stability does not necessarily translate to non-adaptability. As the grammar and syntax of a language may change over time, so do the WTO norms. In fact, the GATT/WTO's gradual yet undeniable path toward juridification lends credence to such evolution. Specific meanings of various GATT/WTO vocabularies, ranging from "nullification or impairment" to "like products," have been subject to interpretive change,[43] particularly as the initial GATT contract transformed into a community.[44]

[40] Vaughan Lowe, "The Politics of Law-Making: Are the Method and Character of Norm Creation Changing?," in M. Byers (ed.), *The Role of Law in Politics: Essays in International Relations and International Law* (2000), pp. 207, 212–21.

[41] *Cf.* Berger and Luckmann, *supra* note 4, p. 66.

[42] Appellate Body Report, *United States – Final Anti-Dumping Measures on Stainless Steel from Mexico*, WT/DS344/AB/R (April 30, 2008), ¶ 161.

[43] *Cf.* John W. Mohr and Marc J. Ventresca, "Archival Research Methods," in Joel A. C. Baum (ed.), *The Blackwell Companion to Organizations* (2002), pp. 805–28.

[44] See Chapter 3 of this book.

II. Rediscovering the WTO operation: three modes of WTO discourse

WTO norms as a language of WTO discourse are not monolithic. Different institutionalized forms may channel different kinds of socially meaningful patterns of practice, which are eventually crystallized into socially acceptable norms. From this perspective, three conventional institutionalized forms of the WTO operation, i.e., adjudication, peer review, and negotiation–consultation, can be rediscovered as three different modes of WTO discourse. Each mode provides a distinctive avenue in which various actors interact and communicate as they use and at the same time develop shared WTO norms.[45] Importantly, these different forms of WTO discourse subsequently engender numerous derivative discourses. That is, numerous communications and interactions in trade and trade-related areas of everyday life are based on various types of social knowledge, such as panel reports, minutes of committee meetings, working party reports, and negotiation history.[46] It is through such derivative discourse that various micro-participants of the WTO community, such as producers, importers and NGOs,[47] engage in, and ultimately sponsor, WTO discourse. Derivative discourse may even reduce the relative significance of primary institutionalized forms of WTO discourse. For example, WTO members have recently become less litigious, which may attest to the enhanced level of understanding and routinization of WTO norms in their everyday lives.[48]

A. Adjudication

Adjudication is a distinctive form of WTO discourse, *vis-à-vis* peer review and negotiation–consultation, in that it involves an arbiter,

[45] *Cf.* Susan Park, "Norm Diffusion within International Organizations: A Case Study of the World Bank," 8 (2005) *Journal of International Relations and Development*, 111, 113.

[46] See Moshe Hirsch, "The Sociology of International Economic Law: Sociological Analysis of the Regulation of Regional Agreements in the World Trading System," 19 (2008) *European Journal of International Law*, 277, 281 (observing that "international trade spreads knowledge, norms and values, through traders who often cross boundaries and settle in new communities").

[47] *Cf.* Park, *supra* note 45, 111, 115–19 (2005) (emphasizing NGO's active participation in the legal discourse within international organizations via "transnational advocacy networks").

[48] See Progressive Policy Institute, "The WTO Has Handled 391 Disputes Since 1995," April 22, 2009.

such as a panel or the Appellate Body, which manages the discourse in a hierarchical, not horizontal, sense. The primary role of this impartial interlocutor is to resolve a dispute by rendering an independent decision that is binding on both disputants. Sophisticated procedural rules under the DSU symbolize the characteristically serious nature of this mode of discourse. All participants of adjudicative discourse, such as complaining parties, defending parties, the WTO Secretariat and even panelists (or the Appellate Body members), share rich and well-established communicative foundations offered by the WTO language, namely substantive norms based on various WTO legal documents and jurisprudence as well as procedural norms grounded in DSU and its supplementary rules. In accordance with such communicative foundations, those participants complain, respond, argue, counter-argue, refute, prove, reason, interpret and judge. Even after a panel or the Appellate Body renders a decision, the discourse continues if a losing party refuses to comply and a winning party challenges such non-compliance under Articles 21 and 22 of the DSU.

Note that WTO adjudication as a full-blown mode of legal discourse was not programmed at the outset of the GATT. In fact, it has emerged over a long period of time. As discussed above,[49] the GATT in its origin was biased in favor of dispositive settlement of disputes, rather than full adjudication. Its contractarian nature led GATT contracting parties to be obsessed with the restoration of any breach of a delicate balance of tariff concessions established after laborious tariff negotiations. The legal barometer for such balance was the nullification or impairment under GATT Article XXIII. Therefore, in the early days of the GATT (1958), when the United Kingdom complained that an Italian statute discriminated against the former's exporters by providing special credit facilities exclusively to purchasers of Italian tractors, the GATT panel focused on the issue of whether the Italian measure had caused the British exporters any actual commercial damages.[50]

Interestingly, this original preoccupation with the restoration of commercial balance created a special cause of action without even requiring the existence of violations ("non-violation" claims). For example, a 1950 GATT working party ruled that Australia had nullified or impaired Chile's benefits by maintaining subsidies on the purchase of domestic

[49] See Chapter 3.

[50] Panel Report, *Italy – Discrimination against Imported Agricultural Machinery*, L/833 B.I.S.D. 7S/60 (adopted on October 23, 1958), ¶ 12.

ammonium sulphate fertilizers while suddenly discontinuing those on the purchase of Chilean sodium nitrate fertilizers. According to the working party, Chile had reason to believe that benefits, including those from Australian subsidies, derived from Australian tariff concessions on sodium nitrate fertilizers in 1947 would have continued.[51]

However, the subsequent accumulation of cases generated a set of jurisprudence that reconfigured the GATT dispute settlement system from private arbitration to public litigation. The once quintessential requirement of nullification or impairment, which was a hallmark of GATT remedies, was marginalized.[52] A violation itself, rather than its commercial consequences, has become what really matters. In terms of *legal*, not necessarily dispositive, discourse, any particular outcome of litigation, be it a panel ruling or an Appellate Body ruling, is now part of a coherent set of discourse in the form of precedent. Technically speaking, such a ruling binds only disputants to that particular case, which demonstrates a strong semblance to arbitration. Nonetheless, these rulings as past units of discourse effectively guide subsequent WTO rulings. After rounds of these guided rulings, the original "informal normativity" turns into a more established "legal normativity," in the form of case law or jurisprudence.[53]

John Jackson demonstrates a stronger, and more direct, position on this reproductive effect of precedents. He views that a WTO panel or the Appellate Body decision, once adopted, in general obligates *all* WTO members to change their policies in order to conform to the decision.[54] Likewise, even a settlement between WTO members is made in the shadow of the WTO jurisprudence. In this sense, a settlement is also a discursive outcome informed by precedents.

Importantly, the social dimension of adjudicative discourse is distinct from the conventional triadic dispute resolution, which some scholars criticize as potentially representing a "sociologically impoverished universe."[55] Owen Fiss contends that individualistic party structure

[51] Working Party Report, "The Australian Subsidy on Ammonium Sulphate," GATT B.I. S.D. 2S/188 (adopted on April 3, 1950).

[52] Panel Report, *United States – Taxes on Petroleum and Certain Imported Substances*, BISD 34S/136 (adopted on June 17, 1987).

[53] See Brunnée and Toope, *supra* note 26, 48.

[54] John Jackson, *The Jurisprudence of GATT and the WTO: Insight on Treaty Law and Economic Relations* (2000), p. 163.

[55] Owen M. Fiss, "The Social and Political Foundations of Adjudication," 6 (1982) *Law and Human Behavior*, 121, 122–4.

equates a judge with a passive referee. According to him, such a passive role deprives the judge of a broader sociological–structural dynamic behind any given dispute that potentially affects multiple parties. In contrast, WTO adjudication can be depicted as a constitutional adjudication whose remedy requires the elimination of threats to the WTO's fundamental values, rather than focusing entirely on individual compensation.[56] Here, a judge may transcend private interests, such as the restoration of the status quo, and instead enunciate norms in a prospective sense.[57] Therefore, theorized as a form of discourse, WTO adjudication does not necessarily translate into an adversarial mechanism. Instead, the WTO adjudication depends on assumed general duties to cooperate among adjudicative participants.[58] In this regard, the *locus standi* ("legal interest") in the WTO dispute settlement mechanism is more liberal than in a typical domestic litigation. Participating in a WTO discourse (adjudication) benefits the world trade community as a whole, which confirms the hypothesis of a "communitization" of WTO norms.[59]

Indeed, the WTO's unique "third party" intervention policy attests to the social dimension of adjudicative discourse. In stark contrast to an ordinary domestic adversarial litigation structure, the WTO dispute resolution system is quite lenient in allowing non-disputants (third parties) to participate in the panel and the Appellate Body proceedings. For example, Article 4.11 facilitates third parties' access to consultation through a permissive *locus standi* requirement,[60] while Article 10.2 allows third parties with a substantial interest to submit their comments to the panel.

Note the innate *public* nature of adjudicative discourse substantiated by the WTO's liberal third party policy. Granted, third parties may be incentivized to intervene since a particular adjudicative outcome affects

[56] See generally Sungjoon Cho, "Global Constitutional Lawmaking," 31 (2010) *University of Pennsylvania Journal of International Law*, 621.

[57] See Harold Hongju Koh, "Transnational Public Law Litigation," 100 (1991) *Yale Law Journal* 2347, 2348–9, 2368.

[58] See Anne Peters, "International Dispute Settlement: A Network of Cooperational Duties," 14 (2003) *European Journal of International Law*, 1, 2, 9, 15–16.

[59] See Pascal Lamy, "The Place of the WTO and Its Law in the International Legal Order," 17 (2006) *European Journal of International Law* 969.

[60] Marc L. Busch and Eric Reinhardt, "Three's a Crowd: Third Parties and WTO Dispute Settlement," 58 (2006) *World Politics*, 446, 451 (observing that the WTO panels seldom reject third parties' requests to join the consultations).

them in an economic sense.[61] However, even without direct commercial interests involved, a third party may engage in a WTO discourse initiated by other WTO members for the sake of public, systemic interests.[62] Such access tends to offer third parties an opportunity to contribute to the shaping of the very discourse in which they participate.[63] Naturally, this institutionalized channel for third parties both broadens and deepens the WTO discourse among its members.

Therefore, third party interventions play a critical norm-sponsoring role in the world trade community. Not only are third parties entitled to exchange submissions with the parties of the dispute, but also the WTO tribunal should reflect third parties' submissions in its decision.[64] Here, WTO members can effectively expand what would have otherwise been a bilateral discourse into a multilateral one. The WTO tribunal can establish a valuable discursive connection to the enlarged WTO membership beyond the parties directly concerned in a particular dispute.[65] Those interventions may even help legitimize a panel or the Appellate Body's finding that references them. In sum, third parties as norm sponsors help preserve the normative integrity of the WTO's community. They convert

[61] Chad P. Bown, "MFN and the Third Party Economic Interests of Developing Countries in GATT/WTO Dispute Settlement," in Chantal Thomas and Joel P. Trachtman (eds.), *Developing Countries in the WTO Legal System*, (2009), p. 265.

[62] United States – Section 306 of the Trade Act of 1974 and Amendments Thereto, Request to Join Consultation (Communication from Canada), WT/DS200/8 (June 27, 2000). Admittedly, commercial interests may still influence third party interventions. See Kyle Bagwell and Robert W. Staiger, "Multilateral Trade Negotiations, Bilateral Opportunism, and the Rules of GATT/WTO," 1 (2004) *Journal of International Economics*, 63 (implying that third parties aim to preserve their "own share of the dispute market" through interventions); Chad Bown, "Participation in WTO Dispute Settlement: Complainants, Interested Parties and Free Riders," 2 (2005) *World Bank Economic Review*, 19 (observing that those countries having a considerable "market share" in the disputed market tend to become third parties).

[63] *Cf.* Lorand Bartels, "Procedural Aspects of Shared Responsibility in the WTO Dispute Settlement System" (University of Cambridge Faculty of Law Research Paper No.27-2012, 2012), available at papers.ssrn.com/sol3/papers.cfm?abstract_id=2181526## (raising various situations in which third parties may share elements of a primary actor's responsibility).

[64] Understanding on Rules and Procedures Governing the Settlement of Disputes art. 10-2, 10-3, April 15, 1994, Marrakesh Agreement Establishing the World Trade Organization, Annex 2, 1869 UNTS 401 [hereinafter "DSU"].

[65] James McCall Smith, "WTO Dispute Settlement: The Politics of Procedure in Appellate Body Rulings," 2 (2003) *World Trade Review* 75, 85; see also Chi Carmody, "Of Substantial Interest: Third Parties under GATT," 18 (1997) *Michigan Journal of International Law*, 18.

an otherwise private exchange between a complaining and defending party into a genuine public discourse.[66]

Perhaps the public (multilateral) nature of WTO adjudication may also explain why the ratio of settlement in the WTO setting is far lower than in the domestic setting.[67] In the WTO dispute settlement system, commercial stakes as well as long-term normative considerations motivate an adjudicative discourse. Governments themselves often initiate certain disputes to establish legal precedents even without serious commercial considerations.[68]

B. Peer review

While adjudication remains a judicial, hierarchical form of WTO discourse, peer review in various avenues, such as WTO Committees and the Trade Policy Review Mechanism (TPRM), represents an administrative, horizontal type of discourse. It is administrative, or trans-governmental, in that administrative agencies, rather than trade diplomats, are directly involved in the discourse. It is horizontal in that no higher authority, such as the WTO Appellate Body, directs parties' discourse. One of the most salient features of the WTO system created in the Uruguay Round is the institutionalization of such peer review, as seen in the TBT Agreement, the SPS Agreement, and the TPRM Agreement. These side agreements require WTO members to engage in "justificatory discourse"[69] through various discursive platforms, such as notifications, inquiries, and reason-giving. By framing their inquiries and responses within the context and terms of WTO norms, both an inquirer and a respondent transmit WTO norms to each other.

[66] Abram Chayes famously attributed this "demise of the bipolar structure" to one of the characteristics of *public* law litigation as opposed to private law litigation. Abram Chayes, "The Role of the Judge in Public Law Litigation," 89 (1976) *Harvard Law Review*, 1281, 1289; see also Henry P. Monaghan, "Constitutional Litigation: The Who and When," 82 (1973) *Yale Law Journal*, 1363, 1371 (observing that constitutional litigation as "public actions" might not involve private rights).

[67] According to Amelia Porges, about a half of formal complaints launched in the WTO dispute settlement system reached a panel stage from 1996–2000, and only 35 percent of these complaints resulted in a panel ruling. In the domestic setting, only 10 percent of all suits reach a trial. Amelia Porges, "Settling WTO Disputes: What Do Litigation Models Tell Us?," 19 (2003) *Ohio State Journal on Dispute Resolution*, 142.

[68] *Ibid.*, 154.

[69] *Cf.* Abram Chayes and Antonia Handler Chayes, *The New Sovereignty: Compliance with International Regulatory Agreements* (1995), p. 27.

For example, the TPRM Agreement provides a regular peer review forum where WTO members collectively monitor whether an individual member's trade policies and practices are consistent with WTO norms. In each trade policy review, a policy statement written by the monitored WTO member and the WTO Secretariat's independent report are available to WTO members. Based on these documents, WTO members hold several meetings under the auspices of the Trade Policy Review Body, where WTO members discuss a wide range of trade and trade-related measures by the monitored WTO member. As the monitored WTO member responds to other WTO members' inquiries in those meetings, it justifies its measures for being in compliance with WTO norms.[70]

Justificatory discourse enables WTO members to generate "regulatory learning and adaptation," concepts which might not be fully captured by rationalist narratives.[71] This social element of regulatory dialogue tends to sensitize regulating (importing) states as to the external (trade) impact of their regulations on affected (exporting) members, and thus make regulating states susceptible to regulatory cooperation.[72] Notably, clarification on the meaning of some SPS provisions often results from informal discussions among working-level government officials, rather than from the Appellate Body reports.[73] This endogenous nature of social interaction among like-minded regulators explains the "normative self-understanding" among them, which eventually forms their collective identity.[74]

The recently initiated "SPS Information Management System" (SPS IMS) may serve as an empirical confirmation for the aforementioned social thesis of peer review. The SPS IMS is an inclusive source that enables users, both governments and the public, to locate and obtain information on notified measures, specific trade concerns, the SPS Committee documents, domestic enquiry points and the authorities

[70] WTO, "Trade Policy Reviews: Ensuring Transparency," www.wto.org/english/thewto_e/whatis_e/tif_e/agrm11_e.htm (last visited March 6, 2014).

[71] See Joanne Scott, *The WTO Agreement on Sanitary and Phytosanitary Measures: A Commentary* (2007), p. 4.

[72] *Ibid.*, p. 57.

[73] Robert Wolfe, "See You in Geneva? Legal (Mis)Representations of the Trading System," 11 (2005) *European Journal of International Relations* 339.

[74] John Gerard Ruggie, "What Makes the World Hang Together?: Neo-Utilitarianism and the Social Constructivist Challenge," 52 (1998) *International Organization*, 855, 860; see generally Max Weber, *The Methodology of the Social Sciences* (Edward A. Shils & Henry A. Finch eds. and trans., 1949).

that handle notification.[75] This database helps not only WTO members but also private businesses locate various SPS information in a way that serves their particular needs. It is a user-friendly system that provides a variety of search criteria such as "geographical groupings, product codes, comment periods, and keywords, etc."

This type of innovative institutionalization greatly facilitates an administrative discourse among regulators from WTO member countries by broadening the base of shared information on members' SPS measures. Any WTO member can now easily identify any questionable SPS measure from another member which may affect the former's exporters. Then, the former may designate it as a "specific trade concern (STC)" which is numerically coded for identification purposes, such as "STC 229." Within the SPS Committee, members discuss and debate these STCs, with some members challenging them and other members defending them. Under certain circumstances, WTO members can easily defuse trade disputes via dialogue before they are escalated to full-blown complaints for adjudication.

Granted, peer review might not necessarily deliver the desired outcome, such as enhanced compliance. A number of potential obstacles may hinder its full manifestation. Due to its soft, non-binding nature, peer review may end up with the titular cheap talks. Furthermore, developing countries' participation in these meetings is limited due to the lack of their technical and financial capacities.[76] These obstacles lead to questions on the legitimacy of WTO discourse.[77] Nonetheless, various empirical studies point out that social actors are more likely to change their behaviors when they are regularly given an opportunity to examine and defend their original position in the face of new information.[78] This is especially so when members of committees manage to produce "secondary law,"[79] such as decisions and recommendations, as a result of their deliberations.

75 WTO, "SPS Information Management System, spsims.wto.org/ (last visited November 8, 2013).

76 B. S. Chimni, "Co-Option and Resistance: Two Faces of Global Administrative Law," 37 (2005) *New York University Journal of International Law and Politics* 799, 806, 813–14.

77 For a thorough discussion on this issue, see Chapter 6.

78 See, e.g., James L. Gibson, "A Sober Second Thought: An Experiment in Persuading Russians to Tolerate," 42 (1998) *American Journal of Political Science*, 819.

79 See Petros C. Mavroidis, "No Outsourcing of Law?: WTO Law as Practiced by WTO Courts," 102 (2008) *American Journal of International Law*, 1, 9.

Ironically, however, this informal and provisional nature of peer review tends to "open up space for less powerful actors to articulate their position."[80] As Nico Krisch aptly observes, a formal, concentrated regulatory decision-making setting is likely to be exposed to power disparities and thus vulnerable to regulatory capture. In contrast, peer review enables less powerful actors, such as developing countries, to contest dominant regulatory positions and thus maintain a pluralist structure of regulatory governance.

Finally, it is imperative to grasp a cloaked meaning of responsibility underlying peer review. More often than not, this type of discourse is deemed a right that a concerned WTO member exercises, in the form of inquiry, over another member's measure that appears to affect the former's trade interest. However, such dispute awareness would not exhaust the institutional nature and purpose of peer review. Indeed, any WTO member, albeit not directly affected by a measure in question, *should* actively participate in such surveillance mechanisms to ensure that the measure is consistent with WTO norms. As Max Scheler passionately argued, solidarity flowing from the notion of community connotes a "co-responsibility" that every member bears for the action of others.[81] Applying Scheler's notion of solidarity and co-responsibility to the world trade community, one could plausibly maintain that a WTO member should always remain vigilant against any possible violation of its fellow members and endeavor to prevent it via peer review.

In this regard, the embedded regularity, and therefore generativity, of regulatory discourse, in the form of inquiries, reason-giving, exchanges of information, and learning, tends to turn WTO members into "sociological citizens."[82] Sociological citizens can devise unscripted yet creative solutions to their common regulatory challenges in the areas of public health, public safety, or the environment within the context of the SPS and the TBT Agreements. Rather than simply implementing the

80 Nico Krisch, "The Pluralism of Global Administrative Law," 17 (2006) *European Journal of International Law,* 247, 276–7; but see Gregory Shaffer, "A Structural Theory of WTO Dispute Settlement: Why Institutional Choice Lies at the Center of the GMO Case," 41 (2008) *New York University Journal of International Law and Politics,* 1, 64–5 (warning that pluralist approaches may allow powerful actors to "manipulate processes to give the appearance of consideration of affected foreigners without in any way modifying a predetermined outcome").

81 Max Scheler, *Stanford Encyclopedia of Philosophy* (December 8, 2011), available at plato.stanford.edu/entries/scheler/.

82 See generally Susan S. Silbey *et al.* (eds.), *The Sociological Citizen: Recognizing Relational Interdependence in Law and Organizations* (2009).

preprogrammed set of obligations under those Agreements, WTO members can develop pragmatic regulatory solutions that fit particular circumstances.[83]

C. *Negotiation–Consultation*

In a conventional sense, negotiation may be synonymous with bargain. Bargaining tends to be strategic: it reflects market logic[84] and involves economic exchanges between parties.[85] Ministerial meetings where tariff reduction deals take place may best suit this conventional definition of negotiation. At the same time, however, negotiation may serve other purposes, such as fact-finding and persuasion. By juxtaposing and debating over contested facts, members may turn a negotiation into a consultation, which enables an impartial assessment of the situation and therefore narrows down the members' original differences.[86] For this reason, WTO norms not only encourage[87] but also mandate[88] the parties concerned to engage in a consultation when they encounter any disputes. In fact, a majority of disputes have been resolved in the consultation stage.[89] At the same time, however, parties might not engage in genuine discourse in the consultation stage if they have already decided to move to a next stage, adjudication. They might attempt to

[83] Some scholars describe these *ad hoc*, experimental regulatory solutions based on social interactions in a local, practical setting as "relational regulation." See Ruthanne Huising and Susan S. Silbey, "Governing the Gap: Forging Safe Science through Relational Regulation," 5 (2011) *Regulation and Governance*, 14.

[84] Thomas Risse, "Let's Argue!: Communicative Action in World Politics," 54 (2000) *International Organization*, 1, 8 (citing Jon Elster, "The Market and the Forum: Three Varieties of Political Theory," in Jon Elster and Aanund Hylland (eds.), *Foundations of Social Choice Theory* (1986), pp. 1–18).

[85] Andrew T. Guzman and Beth A. Simmons, "To Settle or Empanel?: An Empirical Analysis of Litigation and Settlement at the World Trade Organization," 31 (2002) *Journal of Legal Studies*, S205, S206 (arguing that WTO members are more likely to settle on such subjects as make transfer payments between parties easier than those ones that leave little room to compromise).

[86] Robert Echandi, "How to Successfully Manage Conflicts and Prevent Dispute Adjudication in International Trade" 26 (ICTSD Issue Paper No. 11, 2013).

[87] See, e.g., General Agreement on Tariffs and Trade, October 30, 1947, 61 Stat. A-11, 55 UNTS 194, art. 22 [hereinafter "GATT"].

[88] See, e.g., DSU, *supra* note 64, art. 4.2, 4.6.

[89] WTO, "Dispute Settlement System Training Module: Chapter 6, The Process – Stages in a Typical WTO Dispute Settlement Case," available at www.wto.org/english/tratop_e/dispu_e/disp_settlement_cbt_e/c6s2p1_e.htm.

minimize any substantial discussion on a given dispute as they heed a subsequent panel procedure.[90]

Notably, negotiation–consultation is by far less formal than other modes of WTO discourse, such as adjudication or peer review. Although flexibility may be a virtue, negotiation–consultation is still prone to an innate risk of inequity. To induce the counterpart to accept its position, a more politically powerful party may mobilize various kinds of threats against a less powerful one.[91] Superpowers, such as the United States and the EU, enjoy enormous advantages in drafting WTO rules since they can deploy unsurpassed resources.[92] Considering an average of ten meetings per working day in the WTO,[93] how could poor countries effectively follow up all those meetings and reflect their positions in final policy drafts? These negotiation–consultation leverages held structurally by rich countries are easily captured and exploited in turn by powerful domestic constituencies in those countries.[94] This explains, in part, why so many protectionist policies, ranging from agricultural subsidies to antidumping rules, claim their place in the WTO despite their departure from the spirit of free trade.

Importantly, however, the conventional dimension of negotiation represented by reciprocal bargain has increasingly become anachronistic, and even misleading.[95] Under the old, mono-location production model, it was clear where an imported product originated.[96] Thus, a domestic producer would easily target an exporting country and lobby his or her importing country into imposing trade barriers, such as tariffs, against the foreign product from *that* exporting state. As most trading nations were prone to this mercantilist politics, the conventional *modus operandi* of trade negotiation was mutual tariff reduction based on

90 See William J. Davey and Amelia Porges, "Performance of the System I: Consultations & Deterrence," 32 (1998) *International Lawyer* 695, 705.

91 Jon Elster, *Arguing and Bargaining* (1991), p. 3.

92 John Braithwaite and Peter Drahos, *Global Business Regulation* (2000), p. 196.

93 Gregory Shaffer, "Power, Governance, and the WTO: A Comparative Institutional Approach," in Michael Barnett and Raymond Duvall (eds.), *Power of Global Governance* (2005), pp. 130–4.

94 *Ibid.*

95 Pascal Lamy, Director-General, WTO, "Changes in Trade Challenge How We Manage Trade Policies," *WTO News* (March 16, 2012), available at www.wto.org/english/news_e/sppl_e/sppl221_e.htm.

96 Regis McKenna, "Technology, Enterprise, and Freedom," in David V. Gibson *et al.* (eds.), *The Technopolis Phenomenon: Smart Cities, Fast Systems, Global Networks* (1992), pp. 19, 22.

reciprocal bargain.[97] The quantifiable nature of tariffs was also instrumental to this operation.

Under the new trade reality, however, more than half of global exports in manufactured products are in fact inputs (parts and components) to other unfinished goods.[98] In the altered situation befitting global sourcing, not only has it become difficult to locate the origin of a particular product, but also consuming industries' interest has increasingly countered domestic producers' lobbying power. At the same time, one should also take the changing nature of trade barriers seriously. Administrative barriers, such as domestic regulations, have recently replaced the traditional mode of trade barriers, such as tariffs, which are generally in decline after a series of trade rounds in the past.[99] Trading nations cannot simply bargain away these new non-tariff barriers. To tackle these barriers, they should first understand the nature of each other's regulation and learn to broaden their common regulatory grounds through discursive practices, such as argumentation, persuasion, and deliberation.

Once WTO members disabuse themselves of anachronistic mercantilism and embrace the new reality of economic interdependency, the nature of negotiation shifts from reciprocal bargain to consultation or cooperative dialogue. The recent success of the WTO "Information Technology Agreement" (ITA) provides a case in point, particularly in stark contrast to the epic failure of the Doha Round talks. Global production chains are represented by IT products, ranging from semiconductors to flat panel displays (FPDs) to wireless internet equipment. Their production is divided into multiple stages in multiple countries in a way which minimizes transaction costs.

This contemporary reincarnation of the classical division of labor among participating countries benefits both developed and developing countries that contribute different production factors, be they labor, capital, or technology, to manufacture one single product. Moreover,

97 J. Michael Finger *et al.*, "Market Access Bargaining in the Uruguay Round: Rigid or Relaxed Reciprocity?" (World Bank, Policy Research Working Paper No. 2258, 1999), pp. 2–4.

98 Pascal Lamy, Director-General, WTO, "Trade Improves the Lives of People," *WTO News* (April 12, 2012), available at www.wto.org/english/news_e/sppl_e/sppl224_e.htm.

99 See Daniel Y. Kono, "Optimal Obfuscation: Democracy and Trade Policy Transparency," 100 (2006) *The American Political Science Review* 369, 371 (viewing that democracy reduces incentives to employ tariffs while increasing incentives to employ less transparent NTBs).

IT products tend to generate enormous derivative trades in services, such as software development and online travel reservation.[100] Sparked by a rare moment of collective enlightenment, a selected group of WTO members launched the ITA in 1996 to facilitate the global stream of IT products by eliminating their tariffs. This initiative has proved to be one of the greatest successes in WTO history. The original twenty-eight members have grown into the current seventy-four members; the total world exports of IT products have tripled since its inception.

The ITA Committee circumspectly incubated the cooperation-inducing shift from negotiation to consultation. Under the auspices of the ITA, the Committee provides a discursive forum for ITA participants to resolve their specific concerns arising under the ITA. For example, in 2000 the United States and the EU consulted with Thailand under the Committee regarding the latter's origin certificates requirement imposed on certain IT imports. The United States' and the EU's interpretation of the ITA eventually persuaded Thailand to undo the old requirement.[101]

All told, negotiation as a mode of WTO discourse, for the purposes of this book, is defined rather broadly, connoting not only the conventional reciprocal bargain but also discursive properties of consultation.[102] In reality, the latter dimension of negotiation often overshadows the former. The latter may shape the former from a normative perspective[103] because a bargain is not likely to emerge from a pure normative vacuum. In fact, it transpires in the shadow of WTO norms.[104] Even bilateral settlements still remain in the public sphere: they may be subject to further surveillance and monitoring by the world trade community. The DSB must be notified of all mutually acceptable solutions so that those solutions can be subjected to potential intervention from the rest of WTO members.[105] It is in this context that WTO norms provide

[100] See generally WTO, *15 Years of the Information Technology Agreement: Trade, Innovation and Global Production Networks* (2012).

[101] *Ibid.*, p. 27.

[102] See Sungjoon Cho and Claire R. Kelly, "Promises and Perils of New Global Governance: A Case of the G20," 12 (2012) *Chicago Journal of International Law*, 491.

[103] *Cf.* Habermas, *supra* note 6, p. 166.

[104] See Richard H. Steinberg, "In the Shadow of Law or Power?: Consensus-Based Bargaining and Outcomes in the GATT/WTO," 56 (2002) *International Organization* 339; *cf.* Robert H. Mnookin and Lewis Kornhauser, "Bargaining in the Shadow of Law: The Case of Divorce," 88 (1979) *Yale Law Journal*, 950.

[105] DSU, *supra* note 64, art. 3.7; Emanuela Ceva and Andrea Fracasso, "Seeking Mutual Understanding: A Discourse-Theoretical Analysis of the WTO Dispute Settlement System," 9 (2010) *World Trade Review*, 457, 476.

"institutional power" to parties in negotiation, which can effectively check "compulsory power."[106]

In the same vein, negotiation need not be a zero-sum game. Negotiating parties can continuously adjust their different interpretations and eventually expand their shared grounds. In this sense, negotiation may be understood as cross-persuasion: one party's persuasion is contingent on that of the other party.[107] The dynamic outcome of such negotiation as cross-persuasion holds the potential for a positive-sum in the form of regulatory convergence. After all, negotiation as a mode of discourse adopted in this book bears a public nature where WTO members sustain the discourse in a collective sense.[108]

D. *The intermodal dynamic of the WTO discourse*

Distinctive as these three modes of WTO discourse may be, one should not understand each of them in isolation. In fact, each mode is somehow interrelated with another. Such a dynamic may be positive or negative.

1. Adjudication v. peer review

Peer review may redress a certain limitation intrinsic to adjudication. For example, peer review may prevent adjudication from generating undesirable circumstances due to one of the adjudication's structural attributes, such as adversarial finality. In some highly controversial issues, such as food regulation, both importing and exporting countries are often sharply divided by ostensibly irreconcilable dogmatic positions. These issues involve diverging, and often conflicting, socio-cultural positions in different regulatory jurisdictions.[109] Entwined with vested commercial interests and seasonal politics, disputes around those issues are often emotionally escalated.

In this situation, disputants are likely to fashion their claims into flamboyant rhetoric to produce self-serving narratives, rather than

[106] *Cf.* Michael Barnett and Raymond Duvall, "Power in Global Governance," in Michael Barnett and Raymond Duvall (eds.), *Power in Global Governance* (2005), pp. 13–17.

[107] See Cho and Kelly, *supra* note 102, 509.

[108] *Cf.* Charles Taylor, "Interpretation and the Sciences of Man," 25 (1971) *Review of Metaphysics* 60.

[109] See generally Sungjoon Cho, "Of the World Trade Court's Burden," 20 (2009) *European Journal of International Law* 675.

engaging in a workman-like discourse.[110] The *Hormones* dispute between the United States and the EU is a case in point. This dispute, whose origin dates back to the GATT era in the Eighties, was adjudicated under the WTO twice, once in 1998 and once in 2008. It still remains unresolved. Here, the US position, which supports the safety of hormone-treated beef for human consumption, and the EU position, which questions the safety of the same product, are diametrically opposed. What we often witness in this kind of dispute is a vicious circle of non-compliance and subsequent re-litigation.[111]

In dealing with those disputes resulting from fundamental socio-cultural differences, adjudication should yield to regulatory dialogue via peer review or consultation. Here, the 2001 breakthrough between Canada and Brazil over the mad cow disease (BSE) dispute provides an excellent example. The Canadian import ban on Brazilian beef for the fear of mad cow disease (BSE) in February 2001 invited fierce protest from Brazil, which threatened to sue Canada before the WTO tribunal.[112] Soon, however, parties elected to address the issue in the SPS Committee instead of pursuing adjudication. In the course of deliberation under the SPS Committee, Brazil proposed a new mandate for developed countries to notify the WTO of the introduction of SPS measures that may negatively affect trade opportunities of developing countries.[113]

The SPS Committee eventually adopted this proposal in the form of a revised "Recommended Procedures for Implementing the Transparency Obligations of the SPS Agreement (Article 7)."[114] Both Brazil and Canada agreed that the dispute was resolved with the adoption of the revised recommendation. The aforementioned example is not an isolated anecdote. In fact, an increasing number of SPS concerns have been resolved through regulatory discourse through the SPS Committee

[110] Vivien A. Schmidt, *The Futures of European Capitalism* (2002).

[111] See Sungjoon Cho, "United States – Continued Suspension of Obligations in the EC – Hormones," 103 (2009) *American Journal of International Law* 299.

[112] International Center for Trade and Sustainable Development, "Canadian Ban on Brazilian Beef Imports Escalates Trade Battle," *Bridges Weekly Trade News Digest*, February 13, 2001.

[113] WTO Committee on Sanitary and Phytosanitary Measures, "Implementation Proposal under Paragraph 21: Proposal by Brazil," G/SPS/W/108, June 22, 2001.

[114] WTO Committee on Sanitary and Phytosanitary Measures, "Recommended Procedures for Implementing the Transparency Obligations of the SPS Agreement (Article 7): Revision," G/SPS/7/Rev.2, April 2, 2002.

instead of by WTO adjudication.[115] Nearly 30 percent of the "specific trade concerns" reported to the SPS Committee were addressed by discussions and consultations under the Committee.[116]

Admittedly, such soul-searching regulatory dialogue should not be taken for granted. It requires trust-building and thus takes time. Any outcome of regulatory dialogue, if fully implemented, requires both parties concerned to engage in serious risk communication efforts within their own domestic jurisdictions.[117] These efforts are seldom visible and appreciable. Politicians subject to short-term election cycles are often impatient with this vague, long-term vision. Pressured by interest groups, they are often tempted to have recourse to a quicker, more direct strategy, such as litigation. Given this situation, once an exporting country requests a consultation with an importing country, such a consultation may be a preparatory step for a subsequent full litigation, rather than a genuine effort toward reconciliation.

Also, peer review might not always prevent a dispute from full adjudication. For example, not all IT disputes are resolved in the ITA Committee. The Committee failed to resolve a recent dispute over the EU's refusal to accord certain IT products, such as flat panel displays and set top boxes, duty-free treatment under the ITA. A WTO panel eventually struck down the EU's tariff treatment on these IT products.[118] This panel report is significant in that it upheld the evolutionary nature of technology by prioritizing functionality over product properties of IT products. One might reasonably speculate that such a finding will reinforce discursive power of those who advocate the expansion of the ITA.[119]

2. Adjudication v. Negotiation–consultation

First of all, adjudication has a unique faculty to negotiation. For example, when trade negotiators struggle to draft a decision or agreement, they

[115] See generally Sungjoon Cho, "From Control to Communication," 44 (2010) *Cornell Journal of International Law* 249.

[116] WTO Committee on Sanitary and Phytosanitary Measures, "Review of the Operation and Implementation of the Agreement on the Application of Sanitary and Phytosanitary Measures," G/SPS/36, July 11, 2005.

[117] See generally WHO, "Food Safety: Risk Communication," www.who.int/foodsafety/micro/riskcommunication/en/ (last visited March 6, 2014).

[118] Panel Report, *European Communities and its Member States – Tariff Treatment of Certain Information Technology Products*, WT/DS375/R, (August 16, 2010).

[119] See, e.g., WTO, "Information Technology: Progress Reported on Expanding Product Coverage," *WTO News* (November 1, 2012), available at www.wto.org/english/news_e/news12_e/ita_01nov12_e.htm.

seldom create new meanings for each provision from scratch. Their discourse (negotiation) is mediated by, and at the same time based on, the outcome of previously established discourses, be it adjudication or peer review, which collectively constitute the GATT *acquis*.[120] Note that a number of DSU provisions are simply codifications of past GATT practices. Trade negotiators in the Uruguay Round did not invent the panel proceeding under Articles 6–16 of the DSU for the first time. In fact, they imported this time-honored practice from the past discourse under the old GATT. In particular, the *Superfund* decision in 1987[121] shaped the principle of "presumption of nullification or impairment" with the demonstration of violations, as stipulated in Article 3 of the DSU. Also, one might easily notice that a number of key precepts under the SPS Agreement, such as "less trade-restrictive" means (Article 5.6), originate from the old GATT jurisprudence, such as the *Section 337* decision in 1989.[122]

In contrast, adjudication and negotiation may often cancel each other out. To settle or to litigate is always a difficult decision for disputing parties. WTO norms are basically structured so that consultation toward settlement is a precondition to full adjudication. GATT Article XXII:1 provides that each contracting party shall accord an "adequate consideration for consultation to another contracting party with respect to any dispute arising under the GATT." The WTO DSU even prefers settlement through consultation to adjudication. DSU Article 3.7 stipulates that "a solution mutually acceptable to the parties to a dispute and consistent with the covered agreements is clearly to be preferred."

Those scholars who adopt a rationalist approach might not take this primacy of consultation seriously. According to them, settlement through consultation and adjudication is simply a matter of rational choice informed by strategic calculations. For example, Andrew Guzman and Beth Simmons argue that WTO members elect to settle in those disputes where transfer payments are relatively easy (such as disputes involving tariff rates) and adjudicate in other disputes where such transfer payments are difficult (such as disputes involving health and safety

120 See Fiona Smith, "Law, Language and International Trade Regulation in the WTO," in George Letsas and Colm O'Cinneide (eds.), 63 *Current Legal Problems 2010*, 458 (2010).

121 Panel Report, *United States – Taxes on Petroleum and Certain Imported Substances*, BISD 34S/136 (adopted on June 17, 1987).

122 Panel Report, *United States – Section 337 of the Tariff Act of 1930*, BISD 36S/386, para. 5.11 (adopted on November 7, 1989).

issues).[123] As long as the choice between settlement and adjudication is dictated by rational calculation, one cannot fully explain the structural primacy of consultation.

From the social framework proposed in this book, however, such primacy of consultation can be easily understood. The operative nature of adjudication is adversarial and therefore inevitably accompanies a certain social cost, such as escalation of antagonism, in its course. This confrontational structure of litigation may increase the level of hostility among trading nations and thus poison the atmosphere for subsequent negotiation. In this context, the former WTO Director-General Pascal Lamy warned that replacing negotiations with litigation could undermine the delicate balance between interpretation of existing texts and the creation of new ones.[124] In the same vein, DSU Article 3.7 warns that "before bringing a case, a Member shall exercise its judgement as to whether action under these procedures would be fruitful." Therefore, from a normative standpoint consultative discourse should precede adjudicative discourse.

Moreover, once disputants enter into an adjudicative mode, certain factors beyond their control might further complicate settlement. In this regard, the institutionalization of third parties' liberal access to the WTO dispute settlement mechanism may be a mixed blessing. Currently, third parties participate in about 60 percent of all WTO disputes.[125] As William Davey warns, such prominence of third party interventions could be a disservice to the WTO dispute settlement mechanism since third parties often hold very different views from the disputants.[126] Even when third parties raise systemic legal issues that might matter to the whole WTO membership, complicating the original dispute tends to inevitably shrink room for settlement between the disputants.[127] Therefore, third party participation in general is likely to hamper early settlement and instead provoke a full adjudication.[128] While such full adjudication exhibits a law-generating function of WTO discourse, it may also suppress another form of discourse that may contribute to conflict resolution in a more amicable way.

[123] Andrew T. Guzman and Beth A. Simmons, "To Settle or Empanel? An Empirical Analysis of Litigation and Settlement at the WTO," 31 (2002) *Journal of Legal Studies*, S205.

[124] "Governments Exploring How to Restart Doha Round Talks," 10 *Bridges Weekly Trade News Digest*, August 2, 2006, ictsd.org/i/news/bridgesweekly/7547/.

[125] Busch and Reinhardt, *supra* note 60, 446.

[126] William J. Davey, "The WTO Dispute Settlement Mechanism" (Illinois Public Law and Legal Theory Research Papers Series, No. 03–08, University of Illinois 2003), p. 15.

[127] Busch and Reinhardt, *supra* note 60, 457. [128] *Ibid.*, 448.

On the other hand, however, a deadlock in the consultation–negotiation mode of discourse may spur an adjudicative mode of discourse, thereby generating the risk of over-litigation. As the negotiation track closes with the collapse of Doha Round talks, more WTO members venture to litigate their way to enhanced access to foreign markets.[129] In particular, some WTO members may be determined to resolve those issues unaddressed in the Doha negotiations via the WTO dispute settlement mechanism. This litigation drive appears inevitable for now. Since the failure of the Doha deal, Brazil has plans to sue the United States for the latter's cotton subsidies and tariffs on Brazilian ethanol.[130] Brazil originally expected that the United States would reduce its subsidies on a wide range of farm products such as cotton and ethanol; however, the failure of the negotiation has led Brazil to have recourse to WTO litigation instead.[131] In sum, while the abundance of litigation may be an auspicious sign of rule of law in the WTO system, overburdening the WTO dispute settlement system with more and harder cases will soon fatigue the system and test its integrity.[132]

3. Peer review v. Negotiation–consultation

As discussed above, the nature of negotiation has recently shifted from a traditional bargain to consultation or a cooperative dialogue. To an extent, negotiation increasingly resembles peer review. Indeed, this new perspective merits considering the very nature of the WTO's future agendas, such as services, food security, and non-tariff barriers. The remaining hardest nuts to crack seem to hinge not on episodic, big time bargains but more on workman-like, diurnal regulatory dialogue that could widen shared grounds among members; not overnight by negotiations, but incrementally by mutual understanding.

In this regard, ramifications of the recent Bali package, in particular the Trade Facilitation Agreement, which rekindled the moribund Doha

[129] See Sungjoon Cho, "Doha's Development," 25 (2007) *Berkeley Journal of International Law* 165.

[130] Jonathan Wheatley, "Brazil to Dispute US Subsidies," *Financial Times*, August 3, 2008.

[131] *Ibid.*

[132] See William J. Davey, "WTO Dispute Settlement: Segregating the Useful Political Aspects and Avoiding 'Over-Legalization,'" in Marco Bronckers and Reinhard Quick (eds.), *New Directions in International Economic Law: Essays in Honor of John H. Jackson* (2000), pp. 295–6 (prioritizing "consultation" over adjudication in resolving politically sensitive disputes).

Round trade negotiations, are non-trivial, although disappointing to some in the scope of the Agreement.[133] For a moment, WTO members suspended a tacit commitment to the taken-for-granted mercantilist attitude.[134] Ironically, WTO delegates in Bali could deliver the deal only by stopping bargaining. For that moment, at least, they appeared to realize that the old bargaining model based on an instant *quid pro quo* mentality might not always work. They subscribed to the critical proposition that trade is not a game of winning or losing and that a trading nation might not always need to outsmart its trading partner to get a better deal.

Once WTO members refocus their negotiation under this social framework, they will soon realize that each trade negotiation on a certain subject must be guided by a peer review process under a corresponding WTO committee on the same subject. For example, negotiations on agricultural subsidies must be in parallel with simultaneous peer review processes in the Agriculture Committee, the Cotton Sub-Committee and the Committee on Subsidies and Countervailing Measures. Accordingly, negotiations must not be driven by a rigid, on–off *deal* mentality, as eloquently demonstrated in the notion of "single-undertaking." Instead, they must be flexible and incremental.

This sober recognition of the vital operational flexibility, which leaves room for talk, and therefore learning, among WTO members, is the true accomplishment of the Bali deal.[135] The Trade Facilitation Agreement certainly departs from the legalistic rigidity symbolized by the single-undertaking principle. As a framework agreement, its implementation requires WTO members to fill in a number of unknown details. This room for talk is essential under the social framework proposed in this book. Learning about, and subsequently better understanding of, each

133 See Richard Baldwin, "WTO Agreement: The Bali Ribbon," *Vox* (December 12, 2013), www.voxeu.org/article/wto-agreement-bali-ribbon.

134 The WTO Director-General Roberto Azevêdo also attributed the Bali success to a "collective awareness" among WTO members that: "(1) the agreement being pursued was desirable for everyone and, above all, doable for everyone; (2) a positive outcome would not produce winners and losers, nor a north–south divide (both developed and developing countries would need to work for the agreement); (3) the multilateral trading system needs to be reinvigorated to benefit everyone, particularly the smallest countries and those with least capacity to manage the intricacies of large-scale trade negotiations." WTO, "Bali Is Just the Start" – *Azevêdo, WTO News* (January 6, 2014), available at www.wto.org/english/news_e/spra_e/spra4_e.htm.

135 See Uri Dadush, "How Can the World Trade Organization Stay Relevant?," *World Economic Forum* (January 14, 2014), available at forumblog.org/2014/01/how-can-the-world-trade-organization-stay-relevant/.

other's system and situation, not bargaining, is key to overcoming new barriers borne not of protectionism but of differences in both administrative culture and the level of economic development.

E. *A proceduralist turn*

One persistent problem in the WTO discourse is that the very nature of adjudication, namely, picking a winner (and a loser as well), is ill-suited to address the deep-seated regulatory chasm. Given the aforementioned inadequate level of pre-litigation discourse between parties, a losing party would find it difficult to accept such a binary (win or lose) decision. Any definite answer-giving from adjudicators might further complicate communication between already dogmatic parties. The only way out of this negative loop is to shift to different modes of discourse, that is, away from adjudication. Thus, it is vital for the WTO tribunal to shape its own discursive pattern (interpretation) in a way which may incentivize disputants to engage in non-adjudicative discourse, such as peer review or consultation.

For this purpose, the WTO court could reconfigure its hermeneutical focus on procedural obligations, such as notification and reason-giving, provided in various WTO Agreements so as to mandate dialogue between parties concerned.[136] These procedural obligations would enable regulating states to address neglected concerns, such as those of foreign governments and producers, and gain access to the latter's regulatory horizon.[137] In fact, this duty to engage is not an entirely new concept. The WTO Appellate Body has emphasized in various cases, such as *Gasoline* and *Shrimp-Turtle*, that a WTO member should take into account its trading partner's concerns when the former adopts and applies a measure that potentially affects the latter.[138]

[136] Regarding a similar position, see Shaffer, *supra* note 80, 61–7 (observing that the WTO panel in *EU – Biotech Products* took a "proceduralist turn" by focusing on whether the EU's *de facto* moratorium on genetically modified organisms (GMOs) violated procedural disciplines under the SPS Agreement and therefore avoiding determining the *de facto* moratorium's violation of substantial obligations); see also Andrew T. Guzman, "Food Fears: Health and Safety at the WTO," 45 (2004) *Virginia Journal of International Law,* 1, 4.

[137] See Jonathan Baert Wiener and John D. Graham, "Resolving Risk Tradeoffs," in John D. Graham and Jonathan Baert Wiener (eds.), *Risk Versus Risk: Tradeoffs in Protecting Health and the Environment* (1995), pp. 226, 230.

[138] Appellate Body and Panel Report, *United States – Standards for Reformulated and Conventional Gasoline*, WT/DS2/9 (adopted May 20, 1996); Appellate Body Report,

In an effort to facilitate this regulatory dialogue between regulating states and those affected by such regulations, the WTO court may accord certain probative value to the regulating state's undertaking of these procedural obligations. In other words, whether the regulating state has discharged its burden of proof on certain substantive requirements, such as the existence of a rational relationship between a risk assessment and the final regulation, may depend on whether the regulating state performed relevant procedural obligations.[139] The underlying logic of this probative incentive is that risk regulations adopted without regulatory dialogue tend to lack a rational basis. Indeed, such flawed regulations could derive from disguised protectionism. This idea of a procedural–substantive nexus is not new: courts often link certain procedural deficiencies to substantive violations.[140]

Suppose that under the SPS Agreement a regulating state promulgates a regulation that deviates from an international standard. In this case, the regulating state must notify other WTO members of those products covered by the regulation with an explanation of the purpose of the regulation.[141] If the regulating state fails or neglects to release a notification, such failure or neglect may generate a plausible suspicion that the regulating state in fact lacks a rational justification for the regulation in question. At this juncture, the burden of proving that the regulation nonetheless complies with the risk assessment requirement (SPS Article 5.1) shifts to the defendant (regulating state). Under the SPS Agreement, one may locate several examples of such a nexus between procedural and substantive obligations, the most significant of which are identified in Table 4.1. In each nexus, a regulating state's failure to fulfill a certain procedural obligation may militate against discharging the state's burden of proving that it complied with a corresponding substantive obligation.

United States – Import Prohibition of Certain Shrimp and Shrimp Products, WT/DS58/AB/R (October 12, 1998).

139 Cho, *supra* note 109, 717–18 (discussing a "Copernican turn" of shifting from "substantive finality" to "procedural legitimacy").

140 Under some jurisdictions, a procedural failure, such as the absence of notification, may lead to disapplication of an underlying (substantive) measure. See, e.g., Case C-194/94, *CIA Security International SA* v. *Signalson SA and Securitel SPRL*, 1996 ECR I-2201 (1996) (ruling that a domestic court should disapply a technical regulation if that member has failed to notify the European Commission of such regulation under Directive 83/189).

141 Agreement on the Application of Sanitary and Phytosanitary Measures, 1867 UNTS 493 (1995), Annex B, ¶ 5(b).

Table 4.1 *Matching procedural obligations with substantive obligations under the SPS Agreement*

Procedural obligations	Substantive obligations
Article 3.4 (requiring members to engage in serious dialogue on international standards); **Article 5.8** (requiring a member deviating from international standards to answer an exporting country's inquiries)	**Article 3.1** (requiring members to base their SPS measures on relevant international standards)
Article 5.8 (requiring a member deviating from international standards to answer an exporting country's inquiries); **Article 7** (requiring members to provide information on their SPS measures)	**Article 5.1** (requiring the existence of a rational relationship between a risk assessment and an SPS measure)
Article 5.8 (requiring a member deviating from international standards to answer an exporting country's inquiries); **Article 7** (requiring members to provide information on their SPS measures)	**Article 5.4** (requiring members to take into account the goal of minimizing negative trade effects); **Article 5.5** (requiring members to maintain consistency in determining the appropriate level of regulatory protection)
Article 5.7 (the 3rd and 4th prong) (requiring members to explore additional information for an objective risk assessment when imposing a provisional measure and to review the measure within a reasonable period of time)	**Article 5.7 (the 1st and 2nd prong)** (allowing members to adopt a provisional measure when there is insufficient scientific information, provided that it is on the basis of any pertinent available information)

III. Toward the basic law of international trade

A. The concept of the basic law

The WTO discourse is mediated by WTO norms that embody the tripartite *telos* of the world trading community, that is, free trade, market integration, and development. What best serves the world trade community constitutes what best serves its members in general, although it might not coincide with what best serves particular members in the short run. While individual WTO members' rights still matter, their often underlying communal duties, such as the duty to cooperate,[142] tend to shape operative terms of those particular rights. As a language, WTO norms convey, and at the same time reify, these communal duties. Thus, this communicative construction of international trade law evokes a long-forgotten global empathy that echoes through the current debate on trade and development.

As discussed in Chapter 3, egalitarian trade discourse matures the world trade community so that exporting and importing countries develop trade sensitivity in the latter's regulatory process. Note that this sensitivity should not be equated with vague altruism. It is a practical awareness of interdependence among participants of the world trade community. As a matter of fact, such interdependence is best witnessed among individual economic players, such as importers, transporters, insurers, bankers, wholesalers, retailers, and consumers, in terms of de-territorialized GVCs. In this new trade reality, the old mercantilist characterization of trade relations is unsustainable. The WTO discourse mediated by WTO norms could disabuse WTO members of false promises of mercantilist politics by altering the nature of national interests.

However, as witnessed in the current debacle of the Doha Round talks, the empirical manifestation of the WTO discourse has not been powerful enough to fulfill its normative ideal. The WTO discourse still suffers from distracting background noise generated by protectionist politics. The less audible the WTO language is, the less effective the WTO norms will become. Unfortunately, WTO norms as a language still remain esoteric to most of us. They are technical, complicated, and often unintelligible, in particular to everyday people. Inaudible and unarticulated, the WTO language self-limits its value.

Therefore, if the WTO language is to be shared broadly and the legal gravitational force of WTO norms expanded, it should become more audible, articulated, and therefore exoteric to the world. For this purpose, one might recapitulate the normative quintessence of international trade law and formulate the "Basic Law of International Trade" so that both state and private actors can more easily identify and become more

[142] Many thinkers, old and new, have acknowledged this notion of duty to assist. See Emmerich de Vattel, *The Law of Nations* (1758); John Rawls, *The Law of Peoples* (1999).

willing to *speak* its language. The main goal of the Basic Law here is not to advance any universal, dogmatic tenets of international trade law; rather, it aims to offer a representative heuristic on WTO norms. It will visualize what has already been normatively shared among WTO members and further expand the horizon of a common law of international trade.[143]

In this regard, the cardinal function of the Basic Law parallels that of the Restatement in the United States or Commentaries in Europe. Although the Basic Law does not constitute a primary source of WTO law in a formal sense,[144] this essential set of core trade law principles may nonetheless be a testable reference for persuasive authority. As a carefully articulated heuristic of major WTO norms, the Basic Law can facilitate the WTO discourse by guiding interlocutors of the WTO language, ranging from jurists to judges, to develop a consistent and coherent way of communication.[145] Thus, the Basic Law will help the WTO members express a collective thought and speak a common language.[146] It will eventually interconnect WTO members' ideas and beliefs[147] and thereby enlarge the realm of their interpretive community.[148]

If the Basic Law does convey the world trade community's collective voice, it might be said to reflect the intention of the world trade community.[149] Note that the notion of intention is distinguishable from the consent of individual WTO members in that consent may manifest itself in various avenues of decision-making, such as consensus or majority voting. Instead, this collective intentionality[150] is not instantaneous: it

143 See notably Joseph H. H. Weiler, "Cain and Abel – Convergence and Divergence in International Trade Law," in Joseph H. H. Weiler (ed.), *The EU, the WTO and the NAFTA: Towards a Common Law of International Trade* (2000), pp. 1, 2.

144 Public international law also recognizes a scholarly contribution to the WTO discourse. See Article 38 of the Statute of the International Court of Justice. *Cf.* James F. Byrne, Jr., "Reevaluation of the Restatement as a Source of Law in Arizona," 15 (1973) *Arizona Law Review*, 1021, 1021 (observing that "the Restatement principles do not represent law in the sense of final judicial decisions or legislative enactments").

145 *Cf.* Joseph Dainow, "The Civil Law and the Common Law: Some Points of Comparison," 15 (1967) *American Journal of Comparative Law*, 419, 428.

146 Benjamin N. Cardozo, *The Growth of the Law* (1924), p. 9.

147 *Cf.* Rajeev Bhargava, *Individualism in Social Science* (1992), p. 147.

148 Stanley Fish, *Is There a Text in this Class?: The Authority of Interpretive Communities* (1982).

149 *Cf.* Gennady M. Danilenko, "International Jus Cogens: Issues of Law-Making," 2 (1991) *European Journal of International Law*, 42, 51–2.

150 Regarding the notion of collective intentionality in general, see Jennifer Mitzen, *Power in Concert: The Nineteenth-Century Origins of Global Governance* (2013), pp. 5–7.

gradually materializes over a considerable period of time. It is in this sense that the nature of the Basic Law turns constitutive, rather than merely regulative.[151] A particular WTO Appellate Body decision is regulative in that it may directly cause a losing member's specific behavioral change. Nonetheless, such regulative effect may also result from an instrumental consideration: the losing party may elect to comply *even if* it does not actually believe in the legitimacy of that decision. The losing party may simply want to avoid any negative consequences from noncompliance, such as retaliation.

In contrast, the Basic Law as a set of fundamental legal precepts distilled from the WTO rules and jurisprudence is constitutive in that it operates in the cultural dimension of WTO members. The Basic Law embodies those core WTO principles that most WTO members deem appropriate because its contents reflect rich narratives developed and shared within the world trade community for the past six decades. In this sense, compliance with the Basic Law might be deemed a default pattern.[152]

Ultimately, the Basic Law maintains the structural integrity of the world trade community. As a community of law, it is vital that the world trade community sustains, through a dense web composed of individual discourses, stability and predictability, which is one of the main properties of a legal system. For example, every adjudicative discourse is supposed to produce a dispositive remedy in the end that binds, in a technical sense, only participants of that particular discourse. Nonetheless, even this episodic remedy should be in sync with a communal remedy that denotes the Basic Law.[153] After all, every WTO discourse, even though some might be executed in a bilateral setting, is inherently a public discourse that is to be shared, actually or potentially, with the rest of the community.[154]

151 Regarding the distinction of regulative and constitutive norms and their respective causal and constitutive effect, see generally John Searl, *Speech Acts: An Essay on the Philosophy of Language* (1969); Anthony Giddens, *Central Problems in Social Theory* (1979), p. 66; Nicholas Onuf, *World of Our Making* (1989), p. 52.

152 See Harold Hongju Koh, "Why Do Nations Obey International Law?," 106 (1997) *Yale Law Journal* 2599, 2655 (discussing how institutional habits lead nations to compliance).

153 See Sungjoon Cho, "The Nature of Remedies in International Trade Law," 65 (2004) *University of Pittsburgh Law Review*, 763.

154 But see Joost Pauwelyn, "A Typology of Multilateral Treaty Obligations: Are WTO Obligations Bilateral or Collective in Nature?," 14 (2003) *European Journal of*

B. The fabric of the Basic Law

The Basic Law may denote a sedimented body of social knowledge which countless jurists have long developed, evaluated, and elaborated in the world trade community. It is this epistemic nature of the Basic Law which justifies its unique referential value.[155] Importantly, however, the Basic Law is not a mere mechanical recount of the existing WTO jurisprudence, but rather the Basic Law formulates its teleological reconstruction.[156] Thus, it governs how one WTO member *should* treat another one in trade relations. In this regard, the Basic Law epitomizes the WTO's moral power underpinning the world trade community.[157]

The WTO's moral authority distilled in the Basic Law should not be equated with mere charity: it is a reaffirmation of social ethics embedded in the WTO's community. It is not necessarily a form of altruism: rather, it is a firm realization of the social nature of the WTO's community. In this sense, the Basic Law connotes a set of normative expectations that WTO members may build among themselves and, consequently, it reflects a deep-seated sense of legitimacy within the context of the world trade community.[158] Therefore, this type of moral imagination embedded in the Basic Law speaks to a broad notion of rationality, such as communicative rationality.[159]

The Basic Law may manifest itself in two different – negative and positive – modes: a WTO member *shall not* discriminate against another member; yet, a WTO member *shall* take into consideration another member's situation. First, note that after all these years the trying realities of political economy on the ground still undermine the supreme norm of nondiscrimination in international trade. Therefore, the first tenet of the Basic Law is to reaffirm the backbone of free trade. The Basic Law should proscribe any kind of protectionism so that any WTO member can secure better access to others' markets for agricultural and

International Law, 907 (observing that the nature of WTO obligations remains bilateral).

155 *Cf.* Jeremy Waldron, "Foreign Law and the Modern *Ius Gentium*," 119 (2005) *Harvard Law Review* 129.

156 Even in the United States, the Restatement does not necessarily mean a mere "restating" of the majority opinions of the court. It may reflect what appropriate law is according to an author. Byrne, *supra* note 144, 1030.

157 *Cf.* Michael Barnett and Martha Finnemore, *Rules for the World: International Organization in Global Politics* (2004), pp. 23–4.

158 *Cf.* Charles Taylor, *Modern Social Imaginaries* (2003), p. 23.

159 Mark Johnson, "Imagination in Moral Judgement," 46 (1985) *Philosophy and Phenomenological Research*, 265, 266.

manufactured products. Importantly, the first tenet (nondiscrimination) also paves a firm ground for international economic justice by empowering the poor to make the most of their comparative advantages. In this regard, it is a superior developmental apparatus to any special trade preferences or aid: aid without free trade seldom surpasses free trade without aid.[160]

Developing countries, in particular the least-developed countries (LDCs), tend to rely on ostensibly alluring yet ultimately pernicious special exemptions from multilateral trade norms.[161] Those special exemptions, such as special and differential treatment (SDT) provisions, are exogenous to the Basic Law. Those provisions do not derive from the GATT/WTO jurisprudential practice. Instead, they are largely a product of political bargaining. However, those special exemptions often prove to be against recipients' interest. In return for those exemptions, developing countries are forced to exclude their most promising export products from trade preferences.[162] This is in fact a "reverse" SDT.[163]

Therefore, if developing countries want to fully harness trade for the sake of their development, they must also be subject to, not exempted from, the Basic Law. In other words, developing countries must remain proficient in the WTO language by mainstreaming free trade in their development strategy. The recent prominence of GVCs and their extensive trade potential to developing countries amplify the need for developing countries to stay within the world trade community.[164]

[160] "Mixed Reaction on Trade in Financing for Development Outcome," 6 *Bridges Weekly Trade News Digest* (March 26, 2002), www.ictsd.org/weekly/02-03-26/story3.htm; Ela Soyemi, "Africa Needs Trade, Not Aid," *The Guardian* (April 17, 2010), guardian.co.uk.

[161] See generally Sungjoon Cho, "Reinventing the Development Wheel of the World Trading System" 16 (2013) *Journal of International Economic Law*, 481 (reviewing Sonia E. Rolland, *Development at the World Trade Organization* (2012)).

[162] Michael J. Trebilcock and Robert Howse, *The Regulation of International Trade* (2nd edn, 1999), p. 368.

[163] Ablasse Ouedraogo, "Seminar on Special and Differential Treatment for Developing Countries, Closing Remarks," WTO (March 7, 2000), available at www.wto.org/english/tratop_e/devel_e/sem01_e/sdtrem_e.htm; *cf.* Joseph E. Stiglitz, "Two Principles for the Next Round or, How to Bring Developing Countries in from the Cold," 23 (2000) *World Economics*, 437, 437–8 (criticizing the developed countries' "hypocrisy" when they continuously exhort developing countries towards further market openings, while they still maintain trade barriers in sectors of natural comparative advantage for developing countries).

[164] See Nicolas Imboden, "Bali, the Doha Round, and the Multilateral Legal Framework," 2 *Bridges Africa Review* (November 15, 2013), ictsd.org/i/news/bridges-africa-review/179067/ (observing that "exemptions from rules are not the solution").

For example, the Basic Law invalidates any new trade barriers (such as quotas) to developing countries' major exports (such as textiles) that new regional trading blocs may sneakily erect.[165] Also, the Basic Law may discipline an abuse of temporary trade relief, such as the "transitional safeguard mechanism" under the Agreement on Textiles and Clothing by developed countries against developing countries' lifeline exports, such as textiles and clothing.[166] In sum, a negative form of the Basic Law can be conducive to development by reaffirming classical free trade principles.

However, even when a WTO member pursues legitimate non-discriminatory social policies, these measures may still negatively affect another member's effective market access. For example, higher health or environmental standards in Western countries may effectively block African countries' agricultural exports from accessing Western markets because African producers are often unable to comply with sophisticated Western regulatory standards.[167] These countries may lack both the technical and financial capacities necessary to adopt and implement such high standards. This is why the Basic Law should also manifest itself through a *positive* mode. This positive manifestation of the Basic Law requires a regulating (importing) country to take into full consideration any potential regulatory burdens that an exporting country may incur.

Suppose that a developed country implements an environmental policy that may potentially affect a developing country's exports. In this situation, the developed country shall take into account the developing country's interests by establishing a certain cooperative arrangement, such as a Memorandum of Understanding (MOU), with the latter.[168] Undoubtedly, in a situation involving developed and developing countries, a cooperative arrangement tends to include certain types of technical and financial assistance programs. In fact, such an arrangement can help developed countries achieve their own domestic

[165] See Appellate Body Report, *Turkey – Restrictions on Imports of Textile and Clothing Products*, WT/DS34/AB/R (November 19, 1999).

[166] See Appellate Body Report, *United States – Transitional Safeguard Measure on Combed Cotton Yarn from Pakistan*, WT/DS192/AB/R (October 8, 2001).

[167] See generally John S. Wilson and Victor O. Abiola (eds.), *Standards and Global Trade: A Voice for Africa* (2003).

[168] Appellate Body and Panel Report, *United States – Standards for Reformulated and Conventional Gasoline*, WT/DS2/9 (May 20, 1996) [hereinafter "*Gasoline*"].

regulatory goals by facilitating developing countries' compliance with the former's regulatory standards.

The contemporary trade environment lends credence to this positive mode of the Basic Law. In this highly interdependent world, aggressive regulatory unilateralism is counterproductive.[169] Even recent ambitious developmental aid programs, such as the US "African Growth and Opportunity Act" (AGOA) and the EU's "Everything But Arms" (EBA) initiative, might be of little practical value to those developing countries that could not afford to meet the high regulatory standards of developed (importing) countries.[170] Given this dilemma, the only viable way to achieve both regulatory and developmental goals is to help developing countries build the capacity to meet those standards, as seen in the recent multi-organizational initiative, the "Standards and Trade Development Facility" (STDF), as discussed in Chapter 7. In this regard, the Basic Law, in its positive manifestation, may require developed (importing) countries to consult with developing (exporting) countries lacking technical and financial competencies with a view to a possible cooperative arrangement. In this way, the interests of developing state citizens may be factored into developed state regulatory regimes.

Importantly, the Basic Law mirrors the principle of "good faith," which concerns both negative (non-discrimination) and positive (considerations of a regulation's trade impacts on other members) fabrics of the Basic Law. As the basic duty of a WTO member, a regulating member's refraining from discrimination may translate into treating a fellow WTO member with good faith. At the same time, a regulating state's sincere engagement with an affected exporting state may constitute a good faith effort by the regulating state to factor in any potential harm on other members.

Note that the Basic Law, in the form of the good faith principle, mainly concerns the propriety of a WTO member's behavior, rather than its consequences. The negative mode of the Basic Law does not connote the effect test that purports to capture private damages, such as nullification or impairment under GATT Article XXIII. In other words, even if a

[169] Philippe Cullet, "Differential Treatment in International Law: Towards a New Paradigm of Inter-State Relations," 10 (1999) *European Journal of International Law* 549, 558–9 (emphasizing "solidarity," reflecting the interdependence and integration of the global trading system).

[170] Wilson and Abiola, *supra* note 167, p. v.

discriminatory measure would not actually *ex post* decrease the volume of exports, the regulating country *ex ante* violates the Basic Law as long as its measure remains discriminatory in a systematic sense. In most violation claims, what truly matters is a public, potential harm borne by the WTO system itself, such as the distortion of the equality of competitive relationship in the market.[171]

Likewise, a regulating state's good faith effort to negotiate and conclude a cooperative agreement with an exporting state may suffice to meet the positive mode of the Basic Law: the former need not actually conclude such an agreement.[172] In *US – Shrimp (Article 21.5)*, the Appellate Body emphasized this very point. The Appellate Body held that a regulating state would only have to exert earnest good faith *efforts* to negotiate and complete a cooperative agreement with an exporting state as the former takes any noticeable differences in both countries' regulatory contexts into full consideration.[173]

"Due process" may be another doctrinal manifestation of the Basic Law. In particular, due process has been the central element of the WTO jurisprudence on trade remedies that governs how an investigating authority should treat foreign producers. To some scholars, this can be seen as a WTO version of emerging "global administrative law."[174] In developing the due process line of jurisprudence, the WTO panels and the Appellate Body have relied heavily on procedural obligations scattered in the WTO Antidumping Agreement concerning notification,[175] transparency,[176] reason-giving[177] and right to be heard.[178]

For example, the *Steel Rebar* (2002) panel found that Egypt violated Article 6.8 and Annex II, paragraph 6 of the WTO Antidumping

[171] Section 337, *supra* note 122, ¶ 5.11 (ruling that the "no less favorable treatment" parameter under GATT Article III (National Treatment) "calls for effective equality of opportunities for imported products in respect of the application of laws, regulations and requirements affecting the internal sale, offering for sale, purchase, transportation, distribution or use of products").

[172] Appellate Body Report, *United States – Import Prohibition of Certain Shrimp and Shrimp Products – Recourse to Article 21.5 of the DSU by Malaysia*, DS/58/AB/RW (October 22, 2001).

[173] *Ibid.* at ¶¶ 115, 146.

[174] See generally Richard B. Stewart and Michelle Ratton Sanchez Badin, "The World Trade Organization: Multiple Dimensions of Global Administration Law," 9 (2011) *International Journal of Constitutional Law,* 556.

[175] See, e.g., Agreement on Implementation of Article VI of the General Agreement on Tariffs and Trade, 1868 UNTS 201 (1994), art. 5.5, 6.1, 6.9, 12.1.

[176] See, e.g., *ibid.*, art. 6.7, 12.2. [177] See, e.g., *ibid.*, art. 6.4, 6.9, 12.1.

[178] See, e.g., *ibid.*, art. 6.2, 13.

Agreement because its antidumping authority failed to notify companies under investigation of its decision to reject information the companies had submitted and thus deprived those companies of the opportunity to defend their positions.[179] The *Brazilian Poultry* (2003) panel decided that a tardy notification to exporters made eight months after initiation failed to satisfy the requirement of Article 12.1.[180] The Appellate Body in *Iron Tube* (2003) ruled that the EC violated Article 6.2 when it deprived a Brazilian exporter of the exporter's defense opportunity by failing to disclose its internal note containing the various considerations on which it based its decision.[181]

The WTO tribunal has also focused on the proper exercise of discretion by regulating states. Throughout the course of an antidumping investigation and determination, domestic authorities face numerous moments of decision-making, big and small, regarding how to assess and weigh the facts, as well as how to interpret their own domestic antidumping statutes. Technical complexities, which are a defining nature of antidumping laws and their applications, tend to increase both the depth and width of such discretion. In fact, Article 17.6 of the Antidumping Agreement was designed to safeguard profuse administrative discretion in domestic antidumping investigations and determinations. Undoubtedly, this discretion, if left unchecked, is prone to protectionist abuse. Therefore, the WTO jurisprudence in this field aims to check this administrative discretion and prevent its abuse.

Here, as in domestic judicial review of administrative actions, WTO panels and the Appellate Body have referred to a traditional standard of "reasonableness," which connotes both unbiasedness and objectiveness. For example, the panel in *DRAMS* (1999) highlighted that continuing a preexisting antidumping order requires antidumping authorities to conduct a practical reasoning based on evidence, beyond mere presumption, on the probability of recurrence of dumping if the duty were removed.[182] Likewise, the panel in *HFCS* (2000) rejected

[179] Panel Report, *Egypt – Definitive Anti-Dumping Measures on Steel Rebar from Turkey*, ¶ 7.266, WT/DS211/R (October 1, 2002).

[180] Panel Report, *Argentina – Definitive Anti-Dumping Duties on Poultry from Brazil*, ¶. 7.134, WT/DS241/R (May 10, 2003) [hereinafter "*Poultry from Brazil*"].

[181] Appellate Body Report, *European Communities – Anti-Dumping Duties on Malleable Cast Iron Tube or Pipe Fittings from Brazil*, ¶¶. 119, 149, WT/DS219/AB/R (August 18, 2003).

[182] Panel Report, *United States – Anti-Dumping Duty on Dynamic Random Access Memory Semiconductors (DRAMS) of One Megabit or Above from Korea*, ¶¶ 6.20, 6.43, 6.50, WT/DS99/R (March 19, 1999).

Mexico's argument that the investigating authority enjoyed full discretion to examine the impact of dumping without a clear explanation of omitted factors[183] and ruled that an analysis based on evidence, beyond mere speculation, was required to conclude that a threat of injury existed due to dumped imports.[184] In a similar context, panels and the Appellate Body often condemn specific assessments of facts by domestic authorities on the grounds that an impartial investigating authority could have reached a different outcome.[185] In doing so, they also criticized futile excuses by domestic authorities as *ex post* rationalization.[186]

In sum, the Basic Law, which reflects the object and purpose of the world trade community, can manifest itself in various modes. It may represent a negative obligation, such as non-discrimination, or a positive obligation, such as the duty to cooperate. It can be reified in general principles of law, such as good faith and due process. Considering the communicative role of the Basic Law, these general principles of law embodying the Basic Law offer an effective medium for WTO discourse on account of their unique heuristic value. The procedural trait of the Basic Law, as seen in good faith and due process, is attributable to one of its main hermeneutical functions, that is, reconciling trade and non-trade values. Focusing on procedural principles tends to expand shared grounds that varying stakeholders of the global trading community could co-exist and co-prosper in a synergistic manner.[187]

The ultimate goal of the Basic Law is not to establish an axiomatic norm. Rather, it attempts to schematize a basic normative structure under which the world trade community develops. While its concrete content is subject to change, the notion is still useful in the sense that it

[183] Panel Report, *Mexico – Anti-Dumping Investigation of High Fructose Corn Syrup (HFCS) from United States*, ¶ 7.122, WT/DS132/R (adopted February 24, 2000).

[184] *Ibid.*, ¶ 7.141.

[185] Panel Report, *United States – Antidumping Measures on Stainless Steel Plate in Coils and Stainless Steel Sheet and Strip from Korea*, ¶¶ 6.38, 6.39, WT/DS 179/R (adopted February 1, 2001); Panel Report, *Guatemala – Definitive Antidumping Measures on Grey Portland Cement from Mexico*, ¶ 8.54, WT/DS156/R (adopted November 7, 2001); Panel Report, *Argentina – Definitive Anti-Dumping Measures on Imports of Ceramic Floor Tiles from Italy*, ¶ 6.28, WT/DS189/R (adopted November 7, 2001) [hereinafter "*Ceramic Floor Tiles*"].

[186] *Ceramic Floor Tiles*, *supra* note 185, ¶ 6.27; *Poultry from Brazil*, *supra* note 180, ¶ 7.187.

[187] *Cf.* Stuart Hampshire, *Justice is Conflict* (2000), p. 53.

offers coherent normative guidance on particular cases. Note that the WTO discourse, even with reference to the Basic Law, may not always produce consensus. Instead, a deeper meaning of the Basic Law might be to nurture WTO members' level of discursive tolerance by concretizing unshared grounds and making them ready for future accommodation.[188]

[188] *Cf.* Paul Schiff Berman, *Global Legal Pluralism: A Jurisprudence of Law Beyond Borders* (2012), pp. 327–8; Kwame Anthony Appiah, *Cosmopolitanism: Ethics in a World of Strangers (Issues of Our Time)* (2006), pp. 85, 99.

5

The world trade constitution: external relationships of the world trade community

Because of this distance between us, we can only partially satisfy our need for warmth, but at the same time, we are spared the stab of one another's quills.

– Arthur Schopenhauer[1]

After discussing the internal operation of the world trade community in Chapter 4, I will now address its external relationships with its environment, namely, different legal systems. This book conceptualizes the external social dynamics of the world trade community as the "world trade constitution." This chapter probes the world trade constitution in three different configurations depending on the type of environment that the world trade community embraces: first, a horizontal relationship with non-trade international legal systems (such as multilateral environmental agreements); second, a vertical relationship with domestic legal systems (such as the US legal system); and third, a federalistic relationship with regional trade agreements (such as the North American Free Trade Agreement). Each of these external relationships signifies three main themes: resonance, internalization, and defragmentation, respectively.

I. Defining the world trade constitution

The world trade community is not a self-contained system. It does not exist in a clinical disconnection from other legal systems.[2] Rather, its external relationship with the surrounding environment is as important

[1] Arthur Schopenhauer, *Parerga und Paralipomena: Kleine Philosophische Schriften*, Bande (1851), pp. 1–2, 524.

[2] Appellate Body Report, *United States – Standards for Reformulated and Conventional Gasoline*, 11, WT/DS2/AB/R (May 20, 1996).

as its internal operation discussed in Chapter 4. Fully comprehending the world trade community calls for *inter*-systemic or *inter*-institutional investigations between the WTO and other legal systems concerning such questions as how the WTO responds to non-trade systems (resonance); how its norms penetrate into members' domestic legal systems (internalization);[3] and how it configures itself with regional trade agreements (RTAs) (defragmentation). Thus, while the world trade community is shaped by its own *intra*discourse, its external dynamics reflect the *inter*discourse between the world trade community and other *nomoi*, be they other areas of international law or domestic legal systems.[4]

This chapter embraces the notion of the "world trade constitution" in an effort to conceptualize the world trade community's external relationships.[5] Its main analytical focus is how the world trade community defines, governs, manifests, and eventually constitutes itself in an external legal relationship with other legal systems, such as multilateral environmental treaties, the US legal system, and the North American Free Trade Agreement (NAFTA). The world trade community is constitutive in the sense that it creates a *social* connection with its environment that might not otherwise exist.[6] If the WTO has any meaning, it is because its members construct, and reconstruct, social realities around it as well as identities of its own *and* other institutions.[7]

Modalities of these legal relationships between the WTO and other legal systems may vary. A horizontal relationship may be pluralistic in that the WTO and a multilateral environmental agreement would

[3] Under pure monism, no serious vertical dynamics between international law (WTO norms) and a domestic legal system would arise since international law is immediately and unconditionally incorporated in the domestic legal system. In reality, however, most WTO members are dualist countries, which regard WTO norms as conceptually distinct legal regimes from their own.

[4] Regarding "intradiscourse" and "interdiscourse," see Peter Goodrich, *Legal Discourse: Studies in Linguistics, Rhetoric and Legal Analysis* (1987), pp. 146–51.

[5] Regarding a similar categorization (horizontal and vertical) in explaining the mechanisms of constitutionalism, see Jeffrey L. Dunoff and Joel P. Trachtman, "Economic Analysis of International Law," 24 (1999) *Yale Journal of International Law*, 1, 19; T. Cottier, "Limits to International Trade: The Constitutional Challenge," (2000) *American Society of International Law* 220, 221 (viewing that a horizontal perspective on constitutionalism concerns coherence between different values, while a vertical one involves the balancing of power between different levels of government).

[6] Kenneth W. Abbott, "'Economic' Issues and Political Participation: The Evolving Boundaries of International Federalism," 18 (1996) *Cardozo Law Review*, 971, 974.

[7] W. Richard Scott, "Reflections on a Half-Century of Organizational Sociology," 30 (2004) *Annual Review of Sociology*, 1, 13.

neither assimilate nor exclude each other.[8] Rather, both systems communicate with, and thus influence, each other. In contrast, a vertical relationship may be more orderly, if not entirely hierarchical, than a horizontal relationship in the sense that a domestic legal system should somehow transform the WTO norms into its own law. Also, a federalistic, if not federal, relationship can emerge between the WTO and RTAs because RTAs may complement the WTO's operation while maintaining their organizational autonomy.[9] From a social perspective, this chapter is interested more in actors and processes through which the WTO norms interplay with non-WTO legal systems rather than any universal metric for legal hierarchy between the WTO and other legal systems.[10] The main purpose of the chapter is to envision possibilities for bringing WTO and non-WTO actors together into an extended public sphere.[11]

Admittedly, the very label of "constitution" may invoke, mostly in a misleading way, direct domestic analogy:[12] a reader might associate this c-word with his or her domestic counterpart, a (large C) Constitution, which symbolizes, among other things, democratic representation and universal suffrage.[13] However, the world trade constitution, for the purpose of this book, is an example of a *proto*-constitution, which mainly concerns a supranational coordination of powers exercised by collective actors (states).[14] Therefore, "constitution" as used in this book must be distinguished from a domestic republican constitution presupposing individual persons and establishing a sophisticated government

[8] See notably Paul Schiff Berman, *Global Legal Pluralism: A Jurisprudence of Law Beyond Borders* (2012), p. 12.

[9] See Sungjoon Cho, "Breaking the Barrier between Regionalism and Multilateralism: A New Perspective on Trade Regionalism," 42 (2001) *Harvard International Law Journal*, 419, 453.

[10] See Berman, *supra* note 8, p. 15; see also Gregory Shaffer, "A Structural Theory of WTO Dispute Settlement: Why Institutional Choice Lies at the Center of the GMO Case," 41 (2008) *New York University Journal of International Law and Politics*, 1, 13 (recognizing that the term constitution may accord the WTO a false image of "global hierarchy").

[11] See Berman, *supra* note 8, p. 16.

[12] Regarding the "domestic analogy," see generally Hedley Bull, *The Anarchical Society* (1977).

[13] *Cf.* Mattias Kumm, "The Cosmopolitan Turn in Constitutionalism: On the Relationship between Constitutionalism in and beyond the State," in Jeffrey L. Dunoff and Joel P. Trachtman (eds.), *Ruling the World?: Constitutionalism, International Law, and Global Governance* (2010), p. 263 (contending that a "cosmopolitan" paradigm of constitutionalism should replace the "statist" paradigm of constitutionalism).

[14] *Cf.* Jürgen Habermas, *The Divided West* (Ciaran Cronin trans., 2006), pp. 132–4.

structure.[15] This is not to say that the domestic concept of "Constitution" is entirely foreign to the world trade constitution. One should apply a structural analogy between the domestic constitution and that of an international organization, but with judiciously limited functions.[16] In fact, many scholars have already employed this functional mode of trade constitution,[17] including an apolitical constitution that allocates powers among members based on the rule-based system;[18] an economic constitution that establishes an institutional authority to regulate transactions;[19] a fundamental rights approach to trade constitution that empowers individuals with freedom of trade;[20] and trade constitution as judicial norm-making.[21]

Yet, what makes this book's approach unique is its focus on a *social* paradigm linked to a constitutional analysis. As long as the WTO is deemed a community, distinctive from a mere aggregate of its members, its collective response to different legal systems tends to construct its collective identity and thus constitutes itself.[22]

[15] *Ibid.*

[16] *Ibid.*, p. 134. Regarding a similar view, see John H. Jackson, *Sovereignty, the WTO and Changing Fundamentals of International Law* (2006), p, 267 (arguing that constitution may mean a particular institutional arrangement that "enable[s] the institution to carry out its responsibilities and objectives effectively over a long period of time").

[17] Regarding various definitions, both converging and diverging, see Sungjoon Cho, "Global Constitutional Lawmaking," 31 (2010) *University of Pennsylvania Journal of International Law*, 621; Neil Walker, "Late Sovereignty in the European Union," in Neil Walker (ed.), *Sovereignty in Transition* (2003); Jeffrey L. Dunoff and Joel P. Trachtman, "A Functional Approach to International Constitutionalism," in Jeffrey L. Dunoff and Joel P. Trachtman (eds.), *Ruling the World? Constitutionalism, International Law, and Global Governance* (2009), p. 4 (introducing a "taxonomic" approach to international constitutionalism).

[18] John Jackson, "Reflections on Constitutional Changes to the Global Trading System," 72 (1996) *Chicago-Kent Law Review* 511, 519.

[19] Joel P. Trachtman, "The Constitutions of the WTO," 17 (2006) *European Journal of International Law*, 623.

[20] Ernst-Ulrich Petersmann, "Time for a United Nations 'Global Compact' for Integrating Human Rights Into the Law of Worldwide Organizations: Lessons from European Integration," 13 (2002) *European Journal of International Law*, 621.

[21] Deborah Cass, *The Constitutionalization of the World Trade Organization: Legitimacy, Democracy, and Community in the International Trading System* (2005).

[22] *Cf.* Guy E. Swanson, "An Organizational Analysis of Collectivities," 36 (1971) *American Sociological Review*, 607, 611, 621. Yet some scholars warn that the de-politicizing effects of trade constitution might in fact aggravate underlying conflicts. Jeffrey L. Dunoff, "Constitutional Conceits: The WTO's 'Constitution' and the Discipline of International Law," 17 (2006) *European Journal of International Law*, 647.

II. The horizontal trade constitution: resonance

A. *Conventional narratives: entropic linkage*

No institution is an island; neither is the WTO. The world trade community exists and operates by continuously interacting with its environment, that is to say, with other legal systems that pursue different (non-trade) functions and values from free trade. This interaction is critical to the WTO's evolution *qua* organization because it shapes the contour of the WTO's own identity.[23] More often than not, certain tensions may emerge between the WTO's pursuit of a free trade value and other areas of social regulation that may inhibit such pursuit. The notorious *Tuna–Dolphin* dispute offers a case in point.

In the early 1990s, a GATT panel struck down a US ban on Mexican yellow-finned tuna under the Marine Mammal Protection Act of 1972. The ban targeted a controversial tuna fishing practice that inevitably caused the incidental killing of dolphins on a large scale. Whatever the legal merits of the panel decision, environmentalists led fierce protests against the decision. According to their view, the GATT had arrogantly countermanded a widely popular domestic measure intended to protect innocent dolphins. Some protesters performed a scene in which "GATTzilla," a demonization of GATT as the famed Japanese monster, devoured helpless little dolphins. These protesters depicted the GATT as a cold-blooded monster that cared little about legitimate environmental causes.

In this situation, where trade is inevitably associated with non-trade issues, how should the WTO situate itself? Should the WTO uncompromisingly adhere to its own value (free trade) and ignore other (here environmental) values? Or, should the WTO defer this issue to relevant regulatory organizations, such as multilateral environmental organizations? In this regard, how to manage linkage constitutes the WTO itself *vis-à-vis* other areas of law and institutions. It is in this sense that linkage characterizes the WTO's horizontal constitution. Mismanaging linkage may also pose an ontological threat to the WTO because such a threat, if left unchecked, tends to render the WTO unsustainable.[24] An

[23] Sungjoon Cho, "Toward an Identity Theory of International Organizations," 34(3), (2014), *Northwestern Journal of International Law and Business* (2014), available at papers.ssrn.com/sol3/papers.cfm?abstract_id=968433.

[24] See Philip M. Nichols, "GATT Doctrine," (1996) *Virginia Journal of International Law*, 379, 464 (observing that "[t]o the extent the World Trade Organization translates GATT doctrine into a rigidity that consistently exalts trade above all other societal values, it could seriously undermine the free trade regime's popular acceptance.").

organizational isolation would eventually undermine the legitimacy of the WTO.[25]

Yet in terms of how much and what kind of linkage would be desirable, scholars' views diverge. Some take a rather narrow view on linkage, radically *de*-linking the WTO from non-trade areas. These scholars locate a Madisonian constitution in the WTO system on the ground that the WTO safeguards the free trade principle from special interest groups that seek protection from foreign competition.[26] James Madison warned against parochial factions, which would incessantly promote their special interests at the expense of the public welfare. According to these scholars, a Madisonian constitution could inform the WTO, whose members collectively bound themselves against the Sirens of protectionism to promote free trade. However, while a Madisonian constitution might be a necessary condition for the world trade constitution, it would not establish a sufficient one. This narrow version of trade constitution merely screens anti-discrimination; it does not fully capture regulatory considerations. These scholars basically view the WTO as a de-politicizing mechanism, which reduces interest groups' political influences.[27]

This narrow view on linkage risks turning the world trade community into a self-contained regime. The WTO creators did not intend an insular body; in fact, the Preamble of the WTO Agreement expresses the ideal of an "integrated, more viable and durable multilateral trading system," which certainly extends beyond the narrow anti-protectionist motto that was embedded in the old GATT. In the same context, the Doha Ministerial Declaration recently reaffirmed the Members' commitment to the objective of "sustainable development" under which a dual goal of open markets and adequate social regulation must be "mutually supportive."[28]

At the other extreme, scholars advocate *over*-linking the WTO to non-trade areas. For example, some scholars contend that the WTO tribunal should apply non-WTO norms via *inter se* modifications of WTO

[25] José E. Alvarez, "How Not to Link: Institutional Conundrums of an Expanded Trade Regime," 7 (2001) *Widener Law Symposium Journal*, 1, 15; see also P. J. Kuyper, "The Law of GATT as a Special Field of International Law: Ignorance, Further Refinement or Self-Contained System of International Law?," 25 (1994) *Netherlands Year Book of International Law*, 227, 228.

[26] John O. McGinnis and Mark L. Movsesian, "The World Trade Constitution," 114 (2001) *Harvard Law Review* 511.

[27] *Ibid.*, 514.

[28] World Trade Organization, Ministerial Declaration of 20 November 2001, WT/MIN(01)/DEC/1, available at www.wto.org/english/thewto_e/minist_e/min01_e/mindecl_e.pdf.

obligations between disputants to avoid conflict between WTO norms and non-trade norms.[29] According to this position, non-WTO norms may trump WTO norms in a case where two WTO members dispose of the rule of WTO law by privately suspending certain WTO provisions between themselves. This position originates from an underlying view that the nature of WTO obligation is bilateral.

However, such a view is oblivious to the increasingly collective nature of WTO rights and obligations. In the contemporary era, characterized by global value chains and cross-border M&As, any *inter se* modification is destined to affect third parties one way or another. For example, suppose that the EU and Cambodia sign a bilateral treaty that penalizes high CO_2 emissions through an import ban. If this bilateral treaty is an *inter se* modification, could the EU ban the imports of Cambodian toys when they were allegedly manufactured in a condition where a high level of CO_2 was emitted? What if these toys are actually produced in a Cambodian factory built by US investors? Wouldn't such a modification affect the rights of other WTO members such as the United States?

Furthermore, this porous notion of trade constitution via over-linkage jeopardizes the autonomy of the world trade community, which is essential to its own structural stability, and even its own survival.[30] Non-WTO norms, such as international environmental law or international human rights law, simply cannot supplant WTO norms. As is unequivocally stipulated in Article 3.2 of the Dispute Settlement Understanding ("cannot add to or diminish the rights and obligations provided in the covered agreements"), the WTO tribunal should not locate its legal sources beyond the WTO's domain,[31] unless the WTO itself assimilated non-WTO norms in the agreement.[32] Importantly, the goal of trade constitution is not to eliminate conflict of norms between

[29] Joost Pauwelyn, *Conflict of Norms in Public International Law: How WTO Law Relates to Other Rules of International Law*, (2003), p. 316; Sungjoon Cho, "WTO's Identity Crisis," *Global Law Books* (January 31, 2006), reprinted in 5 (2006) *World Trade Review*, 298.

[30] *Cf.* Richard Nobles and David Schiff, "Introduction," in Fatima Kastner *et al.* (eds.), *Niklas Luhmann, Law as a Social System* (2004), p. 8.

[31] Joel P. Trachtman, "The Domain of WTO Dispute Settlement Resolution," 40 (1999) *Harvard International Law Journal*, 333, 342.

[32] For example, both TBT and SPS stipulate that WTO members should follow certain "international standards" which are non-WTO norms established under international regulatory organizations. Agreement on Technical Barriers to Trade, 1994, 1868 UNTS 120, art. 2.4; Agreement on the Application of Sanitary and Phytosanitary Measures, 1995, 1867 UNTS 493, art. 3.1.

the WTO and other branches of international law by dispensing with the autonomy of the WTO system. Rather, the world trade constitution is to manage such tension and reconcile between these two paramount values from the WTO's *own* perspective.

B. *Resonance: a social framework of the horizontal trade constitution*

As discussed above, trade is pre-ordained to be linked with regulatory matters, such as human health and the environment. Article III (National Treatment) of the GATT itself acknowledges that a domestic regulation may *affect* trade in various ways, such as the "internal sale, offering for sale, purchase, transportation, distribution or use of products, and internal quantitative regulations requiring the mixture, processing or use of products in specified amounts or proportions."[33] However, beneath this ostensible logical connection between trade and non-trade regulatory issues lies a deep, structural dimension that defines the world trade community. The WTO's identity has meaning *only* when it presupposes its environment, such as non-trade systems.[34] If the WTO were the sole institution on earth, its identity would have been a moot point. This rather existential point characterizes the horizontal trade constitution.

Discussing the WTO's horizontal constitution begins with an acknowledgement of the absence of a mega-structure, or a World Constitution. Such a mega-structure would have effectively allocated competencies between the WTO and other international regulatory systems, as seen in a federal state. Admittedly, such a mega-structure might be conceived even without the existence of any formal arrangement, such as a nation state or supranational conference. Crucially, however, any radical ontological claim for a larger social, normative sphere (*nomos*) comprised of the WTO and other areas of international law (e.g., international environmental law) sounds implausible in the absence of any institutionalized form of discourse between these two *nomoi*. For example, international trade law and international environmental law, at least from what each of

[33] General Agreement on Tariffs and Trade, Oct. 30, 1947, 55 UNTS 194, art. 3.

[34] See Sungjoon Cho, "Linkage of Free Trade and Social Regulation: Moving Beyond the Entropic Dilemma," 6 (2005) *Chicago Journal of International Law*, 625; Andrew T. F. Lang, "Reflecting on 'Linkage,' Cognitive and Institutional Change in the International Trading System," 70 (2007) *Modern Law Review*, 523, 541–2 (documenting certain trade law scholars' serious attempt to define and redefine the WTO's *telos* as it is related to non-trade regimes).

these areas of law currently stands for, reveal limited shared grounds in their doctrinal assumptions and operative narratives. The trade reality may not be the same as the environmental reality due to different paradigmatic frameworks and methodologies that each universe adopts in understanding the world around it.[35]

Nonetheless, some commentators postulate the existence of the aforementioned mega-structure overarching the WTO norms and other areas of international law. The recent scholarly narratives of fragmentation characterize such hypothesis.[36] As witnessed in a recent study conducted by the International Law Commission (ILC),[37] many public international lawyers are concerned about a fragmented system of international law, which derives from the uncoordinated existence of specialized legal systems. Here, the ILC unwittingly presupposes a hierarchically postulated unified *nomos*,[38] which is far too remote from the reality, as discussed above. Under this hierarchical framework, the fragmentation narratives naturally highlight negative aspects of linkage, such as tensions, clashes and zero-sum dynamics, between different legal systems.[39]

Yet given the current limited range and depth of discourse between the world trade community and these non-trade *nomoi*, the nature of the WTO's horizontal constitution, as defined in relation to other *nomoi* in the international field, should be to effectively configure pluralistic coexistence with other *nomoi*.[40] Admittedly, there might be potentially

[35] *Cf.* Hans-Georg Moeller, *Luhmann Explained: From Souls to Systems* (2006), p. 24.

[36] See Bruno Simma, "Universality of International Law from the Perspective of a Practitioner," 20 (2009) *European Journal of International Law* 265, 272 (drawing on the 2006 International Law Commission Report on Fragmentation, arguing for a "normative hierarchy" in international law based on legal concepts such as *jus cogens* and obligations *erga omnes*).

[37] International Law Commission (58th Session), "Fragmentation of International Law: Difficulties Arising from the Diversification and Expansion of International Law," A/CN.4/L.682 (April 13, 2006).

[38] Dunoff and Trachtman, *supra* note 5, 8. Dunoff and Trachtman observed some scholars, such as Martti Koskenniemi, characterized the pursuit of de-fragmented international law via constitutionalization as a "hegemonic project." *Ibid.*, 8–9 (citing Martti Koskenniemi, *Global Legal Pluralism: Multiple Regimes and Multiple Models of Thought* (2005), p. 5 (unpublished manuscript) (on file with authors)).

[39] Cho, *supra* note 34, 645–6 (observing an "entropic dilemma" in the contemporary linkage debates which focus on mutually canceling dynamics between trade and non-trade values, such as the environmental protection).

[40] *Cf.* Daniel Halberstam, "Constitutional Heterarchy: The Centrality of Conflict in the European Union and the United States," in Jeffrey L. Dunoff and Joel P. Trachtman (eds.), *Ruling the World?: Constitutionalism, International Law, and Global Governance* (2010), pp. 263, 328 (defining such a nonhierarchical order as "heterarchy").

diverging conclusions between the WTO and another international regulatory regime over any overlapping subject matter.[41] Also, there might be some uncoordinated inter-institutional dynamics, such as forum-shopping and "regime shifting."[42] Yet these ostensibly suboptimal phenomena are not necessarily defects in and of themselves; rather, they simply reflect the de-centralized status quo of the international sphere, at least as of today.

In this regard, a cardinal operational paradigm for linkage should be "resonance"[43] between the WTO and non-trade systems, rather than a hierarchy. While both the WTO and non-trade systems maintain their systematic autonomy, they can still mutually constitute each other in the sense that the WTO creates its own reality by relating to non-trade systems,[44] just as an adolescent forms his or her identity by relating himself or herself to peers or generalized others. This "other-reference"[45] is a critical aspect of interdiscourse because the WTO can make sense of itself only by making sense of other (non-trade) systems.[46] In fact, the main institutional goal of the WTO, i.e., sustainable development, could not be fully constructed without reference to multilateral environmental systems, such as the Rio Declaration on Environment and Development or the Convention on International Trade in Endangered Species of Wild Fauna and Flora (CITES).[47]

From a practical standpoint, this other-reference may result in reconciliation between trade and non-trade values. Suppose that a US tobacco company believes that it may freely export its cigarettes to the Thai market because both the United States and Thailand are WTO members. If Thailand bans the import of the US cigarettes in order to protect the former's domestic tobacco industries, such a ban may be illegal under the WTO norms: the ban would violate GATT Article III: 4, XI: 1, and/or possibly the TBT agreement, depending on factual circumstances. However, what if Thailand bans the US cigarettes not because the former

[41] See K. Alter and S. Meunier, "Banana Splits: Nested and Competing Regimes in the Transatlantic Banana Trade Dispute," 13 (2006) *Journal of European Public Policy* 362–82.

[42] Laurence R. Helfer, "Regime Shifting: The TRIPs Agreement and New Dynamics of International Intellectual Property Lawmaking," (2004) *Yale Journal of International Law*, 1.

[43] *Cf.* Niklas Luhmann, *Ecological Communication* (John Bednarz, Jr. trans., 1989), p. 21.

[44] *Cf.* Moeller, *supra* note 35, p. 66. [45] *Ibid.*, p. 36. [46] *Ibid.*, p. 37.

[47] United Nations Conference on Environment and Development, Rio de Janeiro, Brazil, June 3–14, 1992, Rio Declaration on Environment and Development, UN Doc. A/CONF.151/26/Rev.1 (Vol. I), Annex I (Aug. 12, 1992); Convention on International Trade in Endangered Species of Wild Fauna and Flora, March 3, 1973, 993 UNTS 243.

wants to protect its domestic industry but because it wants to protect the health of its people?

Also suppose that the US cigarettes contain certain toxic chemicals administered to enhance their flavor. Thailand would then have every legitimate regulatory reason to ban the import of the US cigarettes even though such a ban would negatively affect US tobacco industries. In this example, two different values, trade and human health, are inter-linked. In a provisional sense, a tension exists between these two values because any blind faith in free trade could undermine protection of people's health, and vice versa. If left unattended, such tension may lead to a real conflict. Conflicts tend to increase entropy, which each system resists for the sake of its own survival.[48]

Therefore, each system provides some kind of mechanism, such as GATT Article XX (General Exceptions) and WTO side agreements (SPS/TBT), to help the system reconcile with its environment (other systems). While scales and modalities of such reconciliation vary within each particular context, it is this process of reconciliation, or interaction, with the surrounding environment that constitutes the very identity of each system.

The old GATT largely failed in the aforementioned interdiscourse in the form of other-reference. For example, in *Thai Cigarette*, a GATT panel ignored an expert opinion provided by the World Health Organization that a ban on harmful reconstituted tobaccos from multinational tobacco companies could be an effective policy tool to protect the health of people in developing countries. This pro-trade bias was harshly criticized and cost the GATT's reputation dearly.[49] The new WTO system, in particular two critical side agreements, the Agreement on Technical Barriers to Trade (TBT) and the Agreement on the Application of Sanitary and Phytosanitary Measures (SPS), addressed this structural deficit by incorporating other-reference, such as relevant international standards, into the main body of WTO norms.

Importantly, however, linking the WTO to non-trade systems does not translate to the WTO's transfiguration into a different organization: linkage does not change the WTO's status as a *trade* system. Although

48 See generally Talcott Parsons, *The System of Modern Societies* (1971).

49 See Robert Howse, "Managing the Interface between International Trade Law and the Regulatory State: What Lessons Should (and Should Not) Be Drawn from the Jurisprudence of the United States Dormant Commerce Clause," in Thomas Cottier and Petros C. Mavroidis (eds.), *Regulatory Barriers and the Principle of Non-Discrimination in World Trade Law* (2000), p. 142.

the WTO is not disconnected from its environment, it is still operationally closed in the sense that it can still differentiate internal needs from external problems and maintain its own institutional homeostasis.[50]

Suppose that a WTO panel faces an internal need to determine whether a defending party's alleged environment regulation relates to the conservation of exhaustible resources under GATT Article XX (g). Would endangered species, such as sea turtles, fall within the rubric of these "exhaustible resources"? One might argue that exhaustible resources mean typical natural resources such as coal and natural gas. In fact, this is exactly what the framers of GATT envisioned in the 1940s. From the WTO's internal perspective, the WTO panel would render whatever best interpretation it could think of. However, a trade organization (WTO)'s self-reference on a non-trade issue (such as exhaustible resources) tends to invite perturbations from its surroundings, such as multilateral environmental organizations, NGOs and civil society. This external irritation, if left unchecked, threatens the WTO's legitimacy and institutional sustainability.

In this situation, could the WTO panel refuse to adjudicate such a dispute, and declare that it is incapable of ruling on a non-trade issue?[51] The problem here, however, is that this hypothetical dispute would not entirely concern a non-trade (environmental) issue. It is still a trade dispute in that a defending country's *ban* on such endangered species is at stake. In this coupled situation involving both trade and non-trade issues, the WTO cannot simply replace its own operation with that of a capable organization, such as the CITES.[52] In other words, the WTO simply cannot suspend, or disapply, its own provisions and instead apply relevant provisions of the CITES in its own dispute resolution. If so, the WTO would lose the operational closure that distinguishes itself from its environment: it would have been absorbed into an environmental organization.

Without losing its organizational autonomy, namely, without succumbing to its environment in a hierarchical sense, the WTO can still resonate with its environment. For example, the WTO panel can

[50] *Cf.* Niklas Luhmann, "Operational Closure and Structural Coupling: The Differentiation of the Legal System," 13 (1992) *Cardozo Law Review*, 1419, 1420.

[51] It would be the so-called "*non liquet*" situation under the Roman Law. See Alfredo Mordechai Rabello, "Non Liquet: From Modern Law to Roman Law," 10 (2004) *Annual Survey of International and Comparative Law*, 1.

[52] Convention on International Trade in Endangered Species of Wild Fauna and Flora, March 3, 1973, 993 UNTS 243.

reference a multilateral environmental agreement (MEA) as to the meaning of exhaustible resources and take the latter's professional interpretation into account when it renders its own ruling. At the same time, however, such referencing itself is part of the WTO's own operation. The WTO does not allow the external environment to dictate terms and conditions of such resonance. The WTO is not bound by such referential information in a technical sense; rather, it retains the authority to decide whether to follow that information. The WTO communicates with its environment based on its own internal needs and through its own internal procedures. This way, the WTO maintains its operational closure as it is still open to its environment.[53]

C. *Resonance as discursive coupling*

Both the narrow and broad view, as discussed above, betray the fundamental problem of purely legalistic conceptualization of linkage. Linkage is not necessarily an on–off phenomenon captured by a binary code of legal and illegal. Such rather simplistic postulation loses sight of a rich interactive process represented by discourse between the world trade community and other areas of international law. This interdiscourse between different legal systems maps itself onto the horizontal trade constitution. Normative gravity existing between the WTO's *nomos* and that of another area of international law need not necessarily be conflicting or tension-generating. Institutionalizing operable communicative paths between the WTO and other international regulatory regimes greatly contributes to the prevention of any entropic normative consequences, and thus helps achieve greater coherence between regimes.[54]

The interdiscourse, as the *modus operandi* of the WTO's horizontal constitution, is an extension of intradiscourse discussed in Chapter 4. Those institutionalized forms of WTO discourse, such as adjudication, peer review, and consultation, also serve as valuable avenues for inter-institutional communication between the WTO and other international

[53] In fact, this operational closure with openness to the environment is common among legal systems. See Bernhard Schlink, "Open Justice in a Closed Legal System," 13 (1992) *Cardozo Law Review*, 1713, 1715–16 (observing that the German Supreme Court may embrace non-legal, such as economic and political, arguments in interpreting the "principle of proportionality").

[54] Cho, *supra* note 34, 648; Pierre Sauvé and Americo Beviglia Zampetti, "Subsidiarity Perspectives on the New Trade Agenda," 3 (2000) *Journal of International Economic Law*, 83, 104.

regulatory regimes. Out of these forms, adjudication tends to exhibit the most salient case for the WTO's horizontal constitution.

In adjudicating individual cases, the WTO tribunal can reconcile trade and non-trade (social) values in a non-conflicting way. Under the old GATT, the embedded pro-trade bias in the textual dichotomy between free trade obligations (such as National Treatment) and social exceptions (such as protection of human health) hindered GATT panels from adopting interpretations accommodating those social concerns. However, the launch of the new WTO system with a more mature integrationist teleology transformed the tribunal's hermeneutical attitude. As was seen in early WTO cases such as *Gasoline* and *Turtle*, the Appellate Body took seriously the legitimacy of social regulations protecting human health or the environment. While the WTO tribunal does not *apply per se* non-WTO norms (treaties), it may still reference or take into account those non-WTO norms in a way that narrows cognitive distances between WTO norms and non-WTO norms.[55] For example, although the Appellate Body did not apply the United Nations Convention on the Law of the Sea (UNCLOS) and the Convention on International Trade in Endangered Species of Wild Fauna and Flora (CITES) in *Turtle*, the Appellate Body did *reference* these non-trade norms to substantiate its evolutionary interpretation of exhaustible natural resources.[56] Thus, the WTO Appellate Body is open to non-trade norms to the extent that it still holds primary competence in various linkage situations.[57]

[55] See e.g., Trachtman, *supra* note 31, 333 (arguing that the WTO tribunal may use non-WTO norms as interpretive guidance instead of directly applying them); William J. Davey and André Sapir, "The *Soft Drinks* Case: The WTO and Regional Agreements," 8 (2009) *World Trade Review*, 1, 18 (viewing that the WTO tribunal can "refer to and analyze [non-WTO] agreements to the extent it is necessary to determine rights and obligations under the WTO agreements."). *Cf.* Geraldo Vidigal, "From Bilateral to Multilateral Law-making: Legislation, Practice, Evolution and the Future of Inter Se Agreements in the WTO," 24 (2013) *European Journal of International Law*, 1027, 1050 (emphasizing that "taking due account" of non-WTO norms does not accord these norms an exception status *vis-à-vis* WTO norms).

[56] Appellate Body Report, *United States – Import Prohibition of Certain Shrimp and Shrimp Products*, ¶ 168, WT/DS58/AB/R (98–0000)(October 12, 1998).

[57] Laurence Boisson de Chazournes and Makane Moïse Mbengue, "Trade, Environment and Biotechnology: On Coexistence and Coherence," in Daniel Wüger and Thomas Cottier (eds.), *Genetic Engineering and the World Trade System* (2008), p. 228. The 2004 WTO Consultative Body Report (the "Sutherland Report") also highlighted that the WTO should maintain its "*sui generis*" status *vis-à-vis* other international organizations. Report by the Consultative Board to the former Director-General, Supachai Panitchpakdi, "The Future of the WTO: Addressing Institutional Challenges in the New Millennium," (2004), ¶ 159–60, available at www.wto.org/english/res_e/publications_e/future_wto_e.htm ("The guiding

This discursive coupling may occur in a situation of parallel litigation in the WTO tribunal and a non-WTO tribunal. The *Swordfish* dispute is a case in point. In 2000, Chile denied Spanish ships access to its port on account of the latter's alleged overfishing of swordfish. The EU, representing Spain, filed a WTO complaint against Chile for the latter's violation of free transit under GATT Article V.[58] In response, Chile filed a complaint against the EU in the International Tribunal on the Law of the Sea (ITLOS) for Spain's violation under the United Nations Convention on the Law of the Sea (UNCLOS).[59] Although disputants ultimately suspended both proceedings after a settlement, how should the WTO panel have decided had the ITLOS issued its decision before the WTO panel? The WTO panel probably could have located some discursive room for interdiscourse. The WTO panel could have achieved this if it had applied GATT Article XX exceptions to the Chilean Fishery Law that had led to the denial of transit to Spanish ships.[60] Here, the ITLOS ruling would have provided the WTO with useful facts and information concerning the validity of Chile's allegation of Spanish overfishing of swordfish under the UNCLOS.

Admittedly, not all disputes might be susceptible to interdiscourse. Recently, emerging trade–regulatory disputes in areas such as climate change and renewable energy provide cases in point. In these disputes, WTO members diverge to a great degree over the subtle balance between free market access and due regulatory intervention. The stark differences in the level of economic development, culture, and the sense of fairness among WTO members complicate the formation of shared grounds. Under these constraints, a judgmental mode of WTO discourse (adjudication) would bear few fruits.[61]

Instead, a more flexible mode of discourse, such as peer review, would better serve the world trade community in building up acceptable

line for granting observer status to international organizations, as for cooperative agreements, is the contribution 'horizontal coordination' can offer to the activities of the WTO.").

58 Request for Consultations, *Chile – Measures Affecting the Transit and Importation of Swordfish*, WT/DS/193/3 (April 6, 2001).

59 *Case Concerning the Conservation and Sustainable Exploitation of Swordfish Stocks in the South-Eastern Pacific Ocean* (*Chile* v. *European Community*), Case No. 7, Order of December 20, 2007, ITLOS Rep.

60 See Pascal Lamy, "The Place and Role of the WTO (WTO Law) in the International Legal Order," Address before the European Society of International Law (May 19, 2006).

61 Paul Blustein, "Why 2010 Could Mark the Death of the Global Trade System as We Know It," *Foreign Policy* (January/February 2010), available at www.foreignpolicy.com/articles/2010/01/04/rip_wto (warning that litigating on "green tariffs" in the WTO might lead to a deadlock).

programs that may subsequently be concretized as norms. In this regard, various WTO committees, such as the Committee on Technical Barriers to Trade and the Committee on Subsidies and Countervailing Duties, offer sector-specific discursive venues where WTO members can expand their shared understanding of relevant facts and norms by learning from each other. Along the same line, the Doha Declaration called for the establishment of certain avenues for regular information exchange between the WTO and MEAs. These avenues may include those MEAs' observership in the WTO Committee on Trade and Environment.[62]

Likewise, both the TBT and SPS Agreements expressly require WTO members to participate actively in regulatory discourse under the auspices of representative non-trade organizations, such as the "International Organization for Standardization (ISO),"[63] the "International Electrotechnical Commission (IEC),"[64] and the "Codex Alimentarius Commission."[65] For example, SPS Article 3.5 requires the SPS Committee to "develop a procedure to monitor the process of international harmonization and coordinate efforts in this regard with the relevant international organizations." Article 12.3 also mandates the SPS Committee to "maintain close contact with the relevant international organizations," such as the Codex Alimentarius Commission, in order to "secur[e] the best available scientific and technical advice." These cross-institutional discursive platforms build a more extensive international dialogue based on shared norms and values. Furthermore, both the TBT and SPS Agreements mandate that WTO members subscribe to relevant international standards which these international organizations establish under their professional capacities.

Importantly, given that many countries still lack adequate regulation, regulatory dialogue, particularly in the form of capacity-building assistance, is key to achieving a synergistic, positive-sum outcome between trade and certain regulatory goals, such as human health. In this regard, the recent APEC initiative on wine safety ("APEC Wine Regulatory

[62] World Trade Organization, Ministerial Declaration of 20 November 2001, WT/MIN(01)/DEC/1, available at www.wto.org/english/thewto_e/minist_e/min01_e/mindecl_e.pdf.

[63] International Organization for Standardization, "About ISO," available at www.iso.org/iso/home/about.htm (last visited October 28, 2013).

[64] International Electrotechnical Commission, "About the IEC," available at www.iec.ch/about/ (last visited October 28, 2013).

[65] World Health Organization, "The Codex Alimentarius Commission," available at www.codexalimentarius.net/default.htm (last visited October 28, 2013).

Forum") offers a propitious example.[66] Despite the skyrocketing demand of wine products in the Asia Pacific region, a number of non-tariff barriers, such as duplicate export certificates, have hampered wine trade in the region due to the high cost incurred by wine businesses. In an effort to consolidate certificate requirements across APEC countries and thus to reduce unnecessary compliance costs, the Forum locates the potential need for capacity building by surveying members' wine testing capabilities. The Forum responds to such a need by information sharing and technical exchanges on wine risk assessment. This regulatory dialogue eventually leads to standardization in wine regulation, contributing to a dual goal of increased wine trade and better regulation of wine products.

In sum, the WTO's horizontal constitution stands for "trade and environment," not "environment and trade." The aforementioned linkage in terms of cognitive openness should not destabilize or undermine the WTO's normative integrity. After all, the WTO's community maintains its normative autonomy through its self-referential communication (intradiscourse).[67] At the same time, however, the WTO also engages in structural coupling with its environment, that is, its operational interaction with other areas of international law (interdiscourse). The true purpose of the WTO's horizontal constitution is to build trust with non-trade legal systems,[68] while it also effectively screens out disguised protectionism in the name of those non-trade legal systems.

III. The vertical trade constitution: internalization

A. *Conventional narratives: compliance and enforcement*

Another external dimension of the WTO's constitution concerns how the WTO norms may permeate into members' domestic legal systems. Conventional international relations (IR) and international law scholars

[66] See APEC, "Streamlining Regulations Boosts Wine Trade" (January 24, 2014), available at www.apec.org/Press/Features/2014/0124_wine.aspx.

[67] *Cf.* Robert van Krieken, "Legal Reasoning As a Field of Knowledge Production: Luhmann, Bourdieu, and Law's Autonomy," Paper Presented at the Annual Meeting of the Law and Society Association, Chicago, Illinois (May 27, 2004); *cf.* Goodrich, *supra* note 4, p. 146 (highlighting a pivotal nature of "intradiscourse" which is self-defining, self-articulating and self-authorizing).

[68] See Franz Xaver Perrez, "Risk Regulation, Precaution and Trade," in Daniel Wüger and Thomas Cottier (eds.), *Genetic Engineering* (2008), pp. 246, 274.

tend to label this issue as compliance. While their views vary in line with their theoretical backgrounds, conventional IR theorists highlight certain exogenous factors, such as power, interest, and utility, in explaining compliance as a particular type of state behavior. In other words, under this rationalist framework, states would behave if, *only* if, behaving (compliance) is in their interest or violating (non-compliance) would entail certain disutilities, such as a sanction.[69]

Both neorealists and public choice theorists believe that WTO members comply with WTO norms only when those norms serve interests of powerful domestic lobbies.[70] Neoliberals may find such compliance congruent to domestic preferences in cases where both WTO norms and domestic values coincide.[71] In these rationalist views, legalization may restrict egocentric interpretation and raises the cost of misbehaving.[72] A more sophisticated rationalist thesis of compliance may be found in the reputational effect. Some scholars argue that members of the International Monetary Fund (IMF) would comply with IMF rules for fear of any negative signal that non-compliance might bring to market participants, such as other governments and private actors (potential investors).[73] Yet, if the market, as a "surrogate for power," is biased toward interests of the powerful,[74] any normative signal from the market that is associated with reputation may be in sync with the national interest of those powerful states.

This exogenous approach leads naturally to a remedial accent on compliance, which tends to overemphasize a judgmental, and thus a binary, aspect of underlying obligations imposed on WTO members in the shadow of enforcement. Undeniably, the sophisticated enforcement mechanism stipulated in Articles 21 and 22 of the WTO DSU has been regarded as one of the most notable innovations of the new WTO system. With highly elaborated procedural provisions and no veto power, the "GATT with teeth" certainly appears better positioned to

[69] Claire R. Kelly, "Realist Theory and Real Constraints," 44 (2004) *Virginia Journal of International Law*, 545, 586; Kenneth W. Abbott and Duncan Snidal, "Hard and Soft Law in International Governance," 54 (2000) *International Organization*, 421, 430.

[70] See Audie Klotz, *Norms in International Relations: The Struggle against Apartheid* (1995), p. 25 (observing that realists view norms as coercion and constraints).

[71] Kelly, *supra* note 69, 586. [72] Abbott and Snidal, *supra* note 69, 427.

[73] Beth A. Simmons, "Money and the Law: Why Comply with the Public International Law of Money?" 25 (2000) *Yale Journal of International Law* 323, 355–7; see also Andrew T. Guzman, *How International Law Works: A Rational Choice Theory* (2008).

[74] Kelly, *supra* note 69, 592.

bring compliance than the old GATT.[75] This enforcement mechanism under the WTO DSU is indeed a brainchild of rationalism. To force such compliance, the WTO imposes negative material conditions, for example, *dis*-incentives such as retaliatory tariffs, on violating members.

Notably, the conventional focus on compliance betrays a state-centered premise nurtured by dualism. Under dualism, the WTO system is a separate legal universe from the domestic system. Whether and how to transform the WTO norms into domestic norms is basically at each member's discretion. Thus, compliance carries an innate ambiguity around it. Likewise, most WTO members do not allow private parties to directly rely on WTO norms either offensively, such as in a cause of action, or defensively, such as in an affirmative defense.[76] This denial of self-executing or direct effect is a hallmark of dualism.

Yet some would oppose this strict dualism and attempt to explore a monist configuration between the WTO and domestic legal systems. In a broad brush, this position echoes Georges Scelle's "role-splitting" (*dédoublement fonctionnel*).[77] Under this view, a WTO member should play an active agency role in administering and enforcing WTO norms within its domestic legal system. Similarly, some scholars argue that certain fundamental WTO obligations, such as the non-discrimination principle, must be constitutionalized so that even private parties may invoke them in domestic courts.[78] While these monistic views might not be readily applicable to the reality, they tend to divulge the dualist dilemma, in particular its failure to allow international norms to pierce the statist veil and reach out to private parties in the domestic legal system.

However, the rationalist preoccupation with law as coercion (enforcement) tends to dismiss important non-material dimensions of WTO norms, such as their rhetorical power,[79] as discussed in Chapter 4. At the same time, as long as the national interest structures state behavior, such as compliance, there is little conceptual space for individual economic

[75] Miquel Montaia i Mora, "A GATT with Teeth: Law Wins Over Politics in the Resolution of International Trade Disputes," 31 (1993) *Columbia Journal of Transnational Law*, 103, 103–80.

[76] Uruguay Round Agreements Act, Pub. L. No. 103–465, 108 Stat. 4809, 4818 (1994).

[77] Antonio Cassese, "Remarks on Scelle's Theory of 'Role Splitting' (dédoublement fonctionnel) in International Law," 1 (1990) *European Journal of International Law*, 210.

[78] Ernst-Ulrich Petersmann, "Theories of Justice, Human Rights, and the Constitution of International Markets," 37 (2003) *Loyola of Los Angeles Law Review*, 407, 427.

[79] *Cf.* Berman, *supra* note 8, p. 21.

players, such as importers and consumers. These individual parties remain largely invisible in this sovereign black box. This blind spot appears particularly troubling amid the recent phenomenon of "postnational constellation,"[80] where the role of non-state actors has become increasingly important.

B. *Internalization: a social framework of the vertical trade constitution*

While the conventional, rationalist views may offer a simple yet powerful heuristic on compliance, they still fail to present a complete picture of compliance, as discussed above. Moreover, the emphasis on enforcement appears inherently problematic in the current anarchical state of the international sphere, which lacks any centralized supreme authority. For example, power disparity among WTO members inevitably engenders inequality at the enforcement stage. The recent online gambling saga between the United States and Antigua is a case in point. Antigua prevailed over the United States in a WTO case where the WTO Appellate Body ruled that the US ban on online gambling violated the General Agreement on Trade in Services. Although some celebrate Antigua's legal victory in the WTO as David's defeat of Goliath, it might be in fact a Pyrrhic victory for Antigua from a long-term perspective.[81] Antigua, a small country, would not want its relationship with the United States, the superpower, to deteriorate.

Moreover, the end result of enforcement (retaliation) might contradict the very purpose of free trade: it would hurt individual economic players of the retaliating country, such as retailers and consumers. Past experience under the old GATT also tends to question the wisdom of the WTO-style enforcement mechanism: even without such formal enforcement mechanism, the old GATT demonstrated an excellent record for compliance.[82] In fact, enforcement might even undermine the culture of dialogue and poison the domestic political atmosphere for future compliance.

Focusing mainly on a static dyad of compliance and violation, the conventional views largely ignore the jurisgenerative process under which

[80] Habermas, *supra* note 14, p. 161.

[81] Sungjoon Cho and Simon Lester, "The WTO and Copyright Piracy," *The Huffington Post* (February 12, 2013).

[82] See Robert E. Hudec, *Enforcing International Trade Law: The Evolution of the Modern GATT Legal System* (1993).

the WTO discourse cascades into domestic legal systems.[83] What truly matters in the long term is a habituated change of state behavior, not an episodic event of compliance.[84] Conventional IR/international law scholars seldom probe norm internalization through habituation and socialization with WTO norms.[85] In this regard, constructivism can help overcome such theoretical blind spots by highlighting the rich process in which WTO members internalize the WTO discourse in an endogenous fashion. Constructivist scholars such as Harold Koh, Martha Finnemore and Kathryn Sikkink focus on the vertical dynamics by which one can investigate how domestic actors learn, familiarize and assimilate international law in the domestic legal system. This is a different research project from mainstream IR theories that are basically interested in direct causal relationships between state behaviors and certain (material) exogenous factors, such as power and interest.[86]

Once fully internalized, WTO norms are capable of imbuing a sense of collective identity into a WTO member's conventional egoistic identity. Here, the WTO member tends to behave in a cultural dimension beyond an instrumental one. In other words, the WTO member complies with WTO norms not necessarily because such compliance would bring to it certain material benefits but because the member deems such compliance appropriate. As a corollary, if the WTO member has failed to fully internalize certain WTO norms, it tends to comply only to the extent that such compliance satisfies its own instrumental goals.[87] In the latter situation, if any further compliance stops serving its

[83] See Benedict Kingsbury, "The Concept of Compliance as a Function of Competing Conceptions of International Law," 19 (1998) *Michigan Journal of International Law*, 345, 368 (trenchantly observing that different "theories" of international law tend to beget different views on compliance since these diverging theories have different accounts on the relationship of international law to state behaviors).

[84] See Harold Hongju Koh, "Why Do Nations Obey International Law?," 106 (1997) *Yale Law Journal*, 2599, 2655 (discussing how institutional habits lead nations to compliance).

[85] Regarding a notable exception, see Robert Wolfe, "See you in Geneva! Legal (Mis)representations of the Trading System," 11 (2005) *European Journal of International Relations*, 339 (observing that dense interactions within the SPS Committee tend to function better in enhancing WTO members' understanding of, and thus compliance with, the SPS Agreement than adjudicated decisions which are often confusing and incomprehensible).

[86] Kingsbury, *supra* note 83, 368. Of course, constructivist theories on compliance may also be prone to the "rationalist criticism" in that these theories fail to explain certain conditions under which international law really becomes "effective." *Ibid.*, 359.

[87] See Russell Hardin, "Self-Interest and Group Identity," in A. Breton *et al.* (eds.), *Nationalism and Rationality* (1995), p. 14; Russell Hardin, *One for All: The Logic of Group Conflict* (1995).

selfish goals, the member tends to violate those rules, as seen in the case of efficient breach.[88] Here, although WTO norms are shared by this violating member as a *common* knowledge, they still fail to penetrate into its belief system and thereby constitute a *collective* knowledge. Such failure is a serious impediment to the stabilization of WTO members' collective expectations. Under these circumstances, compliance would not feature "social proof" that signals the belongingness to the world trade community.[89]

Note that WTO norms are an objectified social reality under the vertical WTO constitution with or without internalization by an individual WTO member. A WTO member cannot simply wish away these norms' existence. Furthermore, any subjective (domestic) interpretation inconsistent with the WTO's social reality will be given an "inferior ontological status," such as a violation, and will be kept away from the WTO's symbolic universe.[90] Thus, the vertical WTO constitution maintains its institutional order by distinguishing what is meaningful from what is meaningless within its symbolic universe, and therefore by preventing anomic chaos threatened by precarious subjective (domestic) reality.[91]

From the social perspective, even enforcement may signify a different meaning from the conventional view. It might not necessarily be seen as a retaliatory system. Rather, it might be interpreted as a form of social ritual whose purpose is to reinforce the collective identity of members belonging to the world trade community. It is yet another post-adjudicative forum for discourse that offers a violating member a *second* chance to conform to what has been regarded as appropriate for the world trade community.

From this perspective, any material deterrent force in the form of disutilities, such as suspension of concessions, might not be of cardinal significance. After all, actual materialization of retaliation under Article 22.6 of DSU is rare because it depends on a number of factors, such as a

[88] Alan O. Sykes, "The Remedy for Breach of Obligations under the WTO Dispute Settlement Understanding: Damages or Specific Performance?," in Marco Bronckers and Reinhard Quick (eds.), *New Directions in International Economic Law: Essays in Honor of John H. Jackson* (2000), pp. 347, 356.

[89] *Cf.* Robert Axelrod, "An Evolutionary Approach to Norms," 80 (1986) *The American Political Science Review*, 1095, 1105.

[90] *Cf.* Peter L. Berger and Thomas Luckmann, *The Social Construction of Reality: A Treatise in the Sociology of Knowledge* (1966), p. 115.

[91] *Cf. ibid.*, p. 103.

political situation. Yet Article 21.5 (surveillance) procedure provides both disputants with additional opportunities to continue their discursive engagement in the form of argumentation, persuasion, learning, and perspective-taking. Admittedly, this additional legal discourse may not always guarantee mutual understanding between disputants: it may leave an original conflict unresolved. Nonetheless, such an additional discursive forum tends to help the world trade community on the whole to reaffirm and further disseminate WTO norms.

In sum, the concept of vertical trade constitution connotes a dynamic, and often repeated, interrelationship between the world trade community and domestic legal systems. Repeated discursive interactions between the world trade community and a domestic legal system are conducive to internalization of WTO norms. As discussed below, the *Charming Betsy* doctrine encourages the US court to adjust its statutory interpretation to international law, including WTO norms. Likewise, the US Court of International Trade's occasional reference to WTO tribunal decisions on related issues, such as appropriate trade remedies, enhances the susceptibility of corresponding WTO norms in the US legal system.[92]

Finally, internalization is inextricably linked to the legitimacy of the world trade community. Internalization is to integrate the world trade community's institutional order into a domestic legal system to make such order subjectively (domestically) meaningful.[93] Via internalization, a WTO member may configure its social location within the WTO's symbolic universe.[94]

C. *Internalization as a discursive pathway*

Internalization as a social phenomenon denotes a *process* driven by discourse, rather than an on-off event of compliance-cum-enforcement, as discussed above. Scholars who share this sociological view describe this discursive pathway in various ways. Some political scientists explain internalization as a final stage of a broader normative lifecycle. Under this analysis, social agents as norm sponsors first attempt to persuade norm leaders to embrace new norms; second, after a certain tipping point, the norms cascade to many other states in a socialization process; and finally, the norms become natural to the extent that

[92] See Sungjoon Cho, "Transnationalizing the Judicial Sphere" (October 27, 2013) (unpublished manuscript) (on file with the author).

[93] *Cf.* Berger and Luckmann, *supra* note 90, p. 92.

[94] *Ibid.*, p. 96.

they generate no further serious debates.[95] Other sociologists focus on the interrelationship between global norms and domestic implementation. They argue that external actors (such as international organizations and sovereign states) and internal actors (such as corporations and professionals) interact with each other in a recursive cycle of global norm-making and domestic law-making (and implementation).[96]

Among these legal scholars, Professor Harold Koh illustrates this discursive pathway in his notion of "transnational legal process," a chain process of "interaction, interpretation and internalization." According to Professor Koh, various actors, public (bureaucrats) and private (NGOs and businesses), network with each other and coalesce to augment the adhesiveness of certain global norms to the domestic legal system. It is this stickiness that can transform potential violations to compliance in the form of habituated behavior.[97]

In this discursive pathway, WTO norms are subject to an evolutionary dynamic.[98] First, norm entrepreneurs, including trade diplomats (such as United States Trade Representative officials), trade lawyers, and pro-trade organizations (such as the Cato Institute and the Consuming Industries Trade Action Coalition) may introduce and market certain WTO norms, such as a new WTO Appellate Body Report. They may also frame various trade-related business behaviors and government policies on such norms.

For example, the WTO zeroing ruling prompted US domestic consumer groups to double their efforts to repeal this competition-inhibiting practice in the name of US consumers and consuming industries.[99] The outcome is

[95] Martha Finnemore and Kathryn Sikkink, "International Norm Dynamics and Political Change," 52 (1998) *International Organization* 887, 895–6.

[96] Terrence C. Halliday and Bruce G. Carruthers, "The Recursivity of Law: Global Norm Making and National Lawmaking in the Globalization of Corporate Insolvency Regimes," 112 (2007) *American Journal of Sociology*, 1147.

[97] Harold Hongju Koh, "How Is International Human Rights Law Enforced?" 74 (1999) *Indiana Law Journal*, 1397, 1412.

[98] *Cf.* Finnemore and Sikkink, *supra* note 95, 894–909.

[99] See Consuming Industries Trade Action Coalition (CITAC), *Rebuttal Comments on the Commerce Department's "Zeroing" Proposal*, 71 Fed. Reg. 11189 (March 6, 2006), available at www.citac.info/about/issues/zeroing/CITAC_On_Zeroing_2300285_1.pdf (urging the Department of Commerce to "eliminate zeroing from *all* antidumping calculation methodologies") (emphasis added); Robin Lanier, *A Letter to Secretary of Commerce (Re: "Zeroing" of Duties)* (January 6, 2005) (proposing to "eliminate the practice of zeroing in all dumping cases"). Harold Koh defines this phenomenon as "legislative internalization" which "occurs when domestic lobbying embeds international law norms into binding domestic legislation or even constitutional law that officials of a noncomplying government must then obey as part of the domestic legal

an enhanced level of political tolerance toward market openness as well as a selective "*de facto* delegation" of trade authority from domestic political branches to the world trade community.[100] Once WTO norms emerge with the help of those norm entrepreneurs, they diffuse to other economic players and policymakers. In this normative life cycle, communicative elements, such as peer pressure, persuasion, networking and social marketing, play a critical role.[101] These rich sets of communications construct, or reconstruct, a collective social reality among WTO members.

Here, one needs to be mindful of oft-underestimated "disaggregated" roles of public actors in the sector-specific departments and agencies of the executive branch.[102] Indeed, these working-level government officials are the ones who actually shape the depth and the modalities of internalization of WTO norms on a quotidian basis. For example, some of the WTO's basic disciplines in the area of human health regulation, such as risk assessment, have been entrenched in EU administrative processes in a way that gives the EU regulatory leverage by inviting various inputs (notice and comments) from interested parties.[103] Importantly, this due process requirement generates a set of administrative documents that can facilitate subsequent litigation.[104]

Concededly, however, a particular domestic governance structure may complicate the internalization process. For example, in its recent jurisprudence on the precautionary principle as applied to genetically modified organisms (GMOs), the European Court of Justice (ECJ) appears to have internalized the WTO jurisprudence that followed a moderated version of the principle under the SPS Article 5.7.[105] Nonetheless, some EU member states are still defiant to this weak version of the precautionary principle and adhere to a strong version of the precautionary

fabric." Harold H. Koh, "Why Do Nations Obey International Law?" 106 (1997) *Yale Law Journal*, 2657.

100 See Judith L. Goldstein and Richard H. Steinberg, "Negotiate or Litigate?: Effects of WTO Judicial Delegation on U.S. Trade Politics," 71 (2008) *Law and Contemporary Problems*, 257 (discussing how the Appellate Body may successfully push for trade openness in the US and the EU).

101 Admittedly, such constructivist thesis does not monopolize the analysis of the norm life-cycle. Rationalism, such as "strategic social construction," may also explain the cycle. Finnemore and Sikkink, *supra* note 95, 909–15.

102 See notably Anne-Marie Slaughter, *A New World Order* (2004), p. 12 (discussing the recent trend of "disaggregation" of a state into functional units, such as departments or courts, in terms of global regulatory cooperation through government networks).

103 Shaffer, *supra* note 10, 66. 104 *Ibid.*

105 Joanne Scott, "European Regulation of GMOs and the WTO," 9 (2003) *Columbia Journal of European Law*, 213, 228.

principle through their own national statutes.[106] Although the *EC–Biotech* panel struck down these national safeguard measures reflecting the strong version of the precautionary principle, internal tensions as to the internalization of the WTO jurisprudence on the precautionary principle still remain within the EU.[107]

In order to facilitate these internalizing efforts, WTO organs may send a subtle yet prudent signal to domestic bureaucrats. For example, a WTO tribunal's well-crafted hermeneutics can greatly assist domestic norm sponsors in their internalizing efforts. In general, any internalization process tends to become complicated if the legislative branch is involved. Any WTO-mandated modification or repeal of a domestic statute may antagonize domestic lawmakers. Yet, the WTO tribunal may avoid this tricky internalization path by adjusting its interpretive focus not on the substance but on the *manner* in which a domestic measure in question was applied: whether it was applied in an unfair and arbitrary manner or whether its application was in accordance with due process.[108] This subtle hermeneutics is indeed typical for constitutional adjudication, which tends to avert a downright doctrinal conclusion in those disputes involving two conflicting values such as free trade and regulatory protection.[109]

[106] Antonia Eliason, "Science Versus Law in WTO Jurisprudence: The (Mis)Interpretation of the Scientific Process and the (In)Sufficiency of Scientific Evidence in EC-Biotech," 41 (2009) *New York University Journal of International Law and Policy*, 341, 367. Miguel Poiares Maduro observed that occasional resistance to the supremacy of EU rules by some member states tends to render EU norms as a "contested or negotiated normative authority." Miguel Poiares Maduro, "Courts and Pluralism: Essay on a Theory of Judicial Adjudication in the Context of Legal and Constitutional Pluralism," in Jeffrey L. Dunoff and Joel P. Trachtman (eds.), *Ruling the World?: Constitutionalism, International Law, and Global Governance* (2010), p. 357.

[107] For example, France nailed down the precautionary principle in its Constitution in 2005. The French Supreme Administrative Court (Conseil d'État) held in a 1998 case (*Sarran*) that its Constitution would prevail over any conflicting international agreements. Eliason, *supra* note 106, 369; *Sarran et Levacher* Conseil d'État [CE] [Court of the State], Oct. 30, 1998, D.P. Ill 1998.

[108] "Public law litigation is . . . less intrusive . . . because it is ordinarily limited to adjusting the *manner* in which state and federal policy . . . is carried forward. Its target is generally administrative rather than legislative action, action that is thus derivative rather than a direct expression of the legislative mandate." Abram Chayes, "The Role of the Judge in Public Law Litigation," 89 (1976) *Harvard Law Review*, 1281, 1315 (emphasis added).

[109] Daniel A. Farber and Robert E. Hudec, "GATT Legal Restraints on Domestic Environmental Regulations," in Jagdish N. Bhagwati and Robert E. Hudec (eds.), *Fair Trade and Harmonization: Prerequisites for Free Trade?, Vol. 2: Legal Analysis* (1996), pp. 59, 85.

For example, in *Shrimp–Turtle*, the WTO Appellate Body reviewed the propriety of the US environmental statute (Section 609) in its actual application, rather than second-guessing the substantive merits of the statute itself.[110] Although the United States lost the case, the Appellate Body's nuanced interpretation did not overburden the United States in its compliance with the Appellate Body decision. The United States did not need to repeal its law (Section 609); it only had to change its application of the statute.[111] Naturally, this interpretation is facilitative of internalization since the executive actors, such as the Department of State, the Department of Commerce, and the Environmental Protection Agency, are in a much more flexible position in the internalizing process when no formal legislative action is needed.

This interpretive focus on the process/application, rather than on the substantive merits, enables the WTO tribunal to identify various procedural flaws in the domestic administrative action. In remedying these procedural flaws, executive agencies can empower themselves to effectively internalize WTO norms into the domestic arena.[112] Indeed, the Appellate Body's recent emphasis on the consistency of a measure corroborates such proceduralist interpretive focus. In a series of high profile disputes involving the TBT Agreement, the Appellate Body has recently held that any negative trade impacts caused by a technical regulation on imported products may be tolerated as long as the regulation is applied in an *evenhanded* manner.[113]

Domestic courts can also serve as a crucial conduit for internalizing WTO norms. For example, a domestic litigant may be tempted to sue his or her own government or other individuals in the domestic court for

[110] Appellate Body and Panel Report, *United States – Import Prohibition of Certain Shrimp and Shrimp Products*, ¶ 180, WT/DS58 (November 6, 1998); *cf.* Andrew T. Guzman, "Food Fears: Health and Safety at the WTO," 45 (2004) *Virginia Journal of International Law*, 1, 4 (justifying this proceduralism *vis-à-vis* substantivism in terms of costs from the standpoint of law and economics).

[111] In a reaction to the Appellate Body decision in *Shrimp – Turtle*, the USTR underscored that the US law (Section 609) had been left intact by the decision. USTR, "Press Release: WTO Appellate Body Found US Sea Turtle Law Meets WTO Criteria But Faults US Implementation," (October 12, 1998).

[112] Shaffer, *supra* note 10, 65.

[113] Report of the Appellate Body, *United States – Certain Country of Origin Labelling Requirements*, WT/DS386/AB/R, (circulated on June 29, 2012); Report of the Appellate Body, *United States – Measures Concerning the Importation, Marketing, and Sale of Tuna and Tuna Products*, WT/DS381/AB/R, (circulated on May 16, 2012); Report of the Appellate Body, *United States – Measures Affecting the Production and Sale of Clove Cigarettes*, WT/DS406/AB/R, (circulated on April 4, 2012).

violating WTO norms. Yet the WTO Agreement does not require this self-execution or direct effect; instead, that decision is left to each domestic legal system. Both the United States and the EU deny such self-execution or direct effect, respectively,[114] while other WTO members, such as Korea, recognize the possibility of such direct applicability in the national court.[115] Importantly, however, domestic courts can still communicate with the WTO's community (norms) even in the absence of this direct internalization channel. A more subtle, nuanced discursive engagement than self-execution or direct effect is conceivable between the world trade community and domestic judicial systems. Domestic courts, through various means and patterns, can cite, quote and incorporate WTO norms in their own rulings. In doing so, domestic courts can synchronize their hermeneutical circle with WTO norms and thus engender a domestic judicial discourse (jurisprudence) that coheres with WTO norms.

The point is that domestic judges are willing, not required, to receive and use WTO norms in interpreting their own laws and regulations. For example, the US Court of International Trade and the US Court of Appeals for the Federal Circuit often reference WTO panel or Appellate Body decisions in addressing similar cases. Although these domestic courts do not *apply* WTO decisions, they still discursively engage with the WTO court. Note that both the US trade court and the WTO court share the same epistemic grounds in the area of international

[114] Uruguay Round Agreements Act, Pub. L. No. 103–465, 108 Stat. 4809 (1994); Meinhard Hilf, "The Role of National Courts in International Trade Relations," 18 (1997) *Michigan Journal of International Law*, 321, 338–9 (summarizing the European Court of Justice (ECJ)'s jurisprudence which denied direct applicability of GATT law); but see Carlos Manuel Vazquez, "Treaties as Law of the Land: The Supremacy Clause and the Judicial Enforcement of Treaties," 122 (2008) *Harvard Law Review*, 599 (arguing that the Supremacy Clause sets a "default rule" of self-execution of all treaties, which may be reversed only by an explicit declaration of non-self-execution).

[115] Under Article 6, Section 1 of the Korean Constitution, international agreements concluded and decreed in due course as well as generally recognized international law rules shall have the same effect as domestic statutes. Constitution of the Republic of Korea, July 17, 1948, art. 6:1 (Korea); see also Supreme Court [S. Ct.], 2004Chu10, September 9, 2005 (S. Kor.) ("Since General Agreement on Tariffs and Trade 1994 is an integral part of WTO Agreement which the National Assembly had given ratification and now in operation . . . according to Article VI:1 of the Korean Constitution, the effect of the treaty is equivalent to national law. Therefore, if an act by a local assembly violates GATT, it is invalid.") (translated and cited in Ji Hyun Sohn, "The Relationship between WTO Law and National Law: Critical Analysis on Jurisprudence of Korean National Courts," 2 (2007) *Korean University Law Review*, 138, 138–9).

trade over such issues as tariffs and trade remedies. Therefore, the WTO court's rulings on the same legal issues adjudicated by the domestic court can aid the latter's own interpretive process as persuasive, not binding, authority.[116] In this context, the celebrated *Charming Betsy* doctrine, under which courts should interpret domestic statutes in a way that will be consistent with international law,[117] tends to offer a useful rationale for the domestic court's discursive engagement with the WTO court.

Discursive engagement is a nuanced path to internalization since it tends to complement domestic judicial review by revealing creative claims and interpretations not readily available at home.[118] Even though domestic judges do not necessarily follow the WTO decisions in the end, they still read and consider those decisions in the course of their interpretation.[119] Given that domestic judges are repeat players, this voluntary discursive engagement could generate certain empathy toward the WTO jurisprudence in the future. After all, decisions by the WTO court and domestic courts might converge in part and diverge in part depending on the subject matter and circumstances.[120]

In some particular issue areas, domestic courts are wittingly or unwittingly within the premise of strong normative convergence when they adjudicate disputes whose main legal issues overlap with those of the WTO. A number of WTO norms, in particular those governing trade remedies, for example antidumping measures, feature certain procedural disciplines, such as transparency and due process. Because most domestic administrative statutes, including customs regulations governing antidumping measures, are also subject to the same disciplines, a

[116] Cho, *supra* note 92.

[117] *Murray* v. *Schooner Charming Betsy*, 6 US 2 Cranch 64 (1804); see Ralph G. Steinhardt, "The Role of International Law as a Canon of Domestic Statutory Construction," 43 (1990) *Vanderbilt Law Review*, 1103, 1197.

[118] Laurence R. Helfer, "Constitutional Analogies in the International Legal System," (2003) *Loyola Los Angeles Law Review*, 193, 193; see also Vicki C. Jackson, "Constitutional Comparisons: Convergence, Resistance, and Engagement," 119 (2005) *Harvard Law Review*, 109, 112 ("Constitution can best be viewed as a site of engagement with the transnational, informed but not controlled by consideration of other nations' legal norms and the questions they put to interpreters of our specifically national constitution.").

[119] I thank Greg Shaffer for this insight.

[120] *Cf.* Robert B. Ahdieh, "Between Dialogue and Decree: International Review of National Courts," 79 (2004) *New York University Law Review*, 2029; Paul Schiff Berman, "Global Legal Pluralism," 80 (2007) *Southern California Law Review*, 1155, 1198; *cf.* Maduro, *supra* note 106, p. 357 (characterizing the relationship between the EU law and member states' domestic legal systems as a "contested or negotiated normative authority").

domestic court's decision could echo, if not directly follow, the WTO's jurisprudence. In many cases, such normative convergence functions as a judicial bulwark against protectionism, which serves both a national *and* a global interest.

Another judicial avenue that both litigants and domestic courts can utilize when internalizing certain WTO norms is recourse to fundamental constitutional principles mirroring WTO norms. Certain WTO norms, such as the nondiscrimination principle, may share their core normative content with their domestic counterparts. Suppose that the US federal court reviews a parochial measure enacted by Massachusetts to discriminate against out-of-state businesses, including foreign producers. On its face, this protectionist state measure is inconsistent with the National Treatment obligation under the WTO. At the same time, it also violates the Commerce Clause under the US Constitution. For example, in *Goya De Puerto Rico Inc.* v. *Neftali Santiago* (1999), a US court struck down a Puerto Rican inspection regulation that had incurred significant costs to importers of pigeon pea, but not to local producers of pigeon pea.[121] In this case, the US court held that this "facially discriminatory" regulation violated the Commerce Clause of the US Constitution.[122] The WTO court would have ruled that the Puerto Rican inspection regulation violated the National Treatment principle under the WTO had the exporting country sued the United States.

Here, the US court indirectly upheld the WTO's non-discrimination principle by rendering a similar conclusion through its normative counterpart under the US Constitution. One might argue that the Commerce Clause offers a powerful agency by which the US court can channel, in an osmotic way, WTO norms into the domestic legal system.[123] This agency tends to remedy negative political externalities created by certain rent-seekers as they pursue their parochial goals at the expense of collective (public) welfare.[124]

[121] *Goya De Puerto Rico Inc.* v. *Neftali Santiago*, 59 F. Supp. 2d 277 (1999). [122] *Ibid.*

[123] Seyla Benhabib, *Another Cosmopolitanism* (2006), p. 74; Berman, *supra* note 120, 1185. Admittedly, the intensity of such judicial osmosis depends mostly on the maturity of a given constitutional regime. For example, the EU rules (in particular the "CILFIT doctrine") "require national courts to decide as European courts and to internalize in their decisions the consequences to the European legal order as a whole." Maduro, *supra* note 106, p. 375.

[124] See John O. McGinnis, "The Appropriate Hierarchy of Global Multilateralism and Customary International Law: The Example of the WTO," 44 (2003) *Virginia Journal of International Law*, 229, 230 (observing that international fields are prone to these political externalities due to the lack of civic supervision).

As discussed above, the concept of internalization within the meaning of a vertical constitution proposed here should not be equated with any top-down imposition of narrowly-defined obligations. Rather, internalization may connote more than sovereign acts of transformation (implementation). Internalization may involve a variety of interventions by non-state actors. Note that the world trade community is also comprised of *private* actors,[125] who hold enormous stakes in global trade.[126] In fact, an important characteristic of the new paradigm proposed in this book is that it goes beyond the old state-centered, territory-based framework that characterized international law for so many years. As active participants of the world trade community, private businesses are not merely passive respondents of WTO norms filtered by their governments. Instead, operating in tune with the WTO language, these businesses can collaborate with public actors in a way that directly contributes to achieving WTO goals, such as market access-cum-development.

For example, West African countries' use of aflatoxins in harvested grains has majorly impeded these countries' ability to access European markets. Under the SPS Agreement, importing countries may ban agricultural products containing aflatoxins on sanitary grounds. Obviously, most West African countries lack the necessary capacity to duly monitor and lower the level of aflatoxins. This capacity gap also deprives food-processing companies, such as Nestlé, of potential market access for their own products that use West African grains. Facing a perfect occasion for a win–win situation, Nestlé, in partnership with the International Institute of Tropical Agriculture (IITA), developed aflatoxin control technologies that could help West African farmers manage their crop production in a sustainable manner. This private initiative of capacity building brought 3,000 farmers US $900,000, producing about US $126 million in direct socio-economic benefits for the West African region.[127]

This emerging phenomenon of "public–private partnership" (PPP) is more than a mere noticeable anecdote: it has become an undeniable trend.

[125] See notably Panel Report, *United States – Sections 301–310 of the Trade Act of 1974*, ¶¶ 7.76, WT/DS152/R (January 27, 2000) ("The multilateral trading system is, per force, composed not only of States but also, indeed mostly, of individual economic operators. The lack of security and predictability affects mostly these individual operators.").

[126] See generally G. Richard Shell, "Trade Legalism and International Relations Theory: An Analysis of the World Trade Organization," 44 (1995) *Duke Law Journal*, 829, 906, n. 349.

[127] Horacio Rodriguez Vazquez, "Standard and Trade Development Facility, Public-Private Partnership to Enhance SPS Capacity: What Can We Learn from this Collaborative Approach?," (2012) *Standards and Trade Development Facility*, 3.

In particular, development-related PPP projects are now legion, including such agencies as the German Federal Ministry for Economic Cooperation and Development (BMZ), the Danish International Development Agency (Danida), the Ministry of Foreign Affairs in the Netherlands, and the United States Agency for International Development (USAID). Even the WTO's "Aid for Trade" program recognizes the essential value of PPP for the success of trade-promoting development aid.

Depending on its target and style, the PPP can assume various forms, including "SPS dialogue" (convening public and private representative to discuss particular SPS (food safety) issues), "SPS infrastructure" (addressing infrastructure such as cold storage or diagnostic laboratories), "value chain development" (engaging public and private stakeholders to increase regulatory compliance in a particular production chain), "trade facilitation" (streamlining customs procedures), and "co-regulation" (mixing primary regulation and corresponding self-regulation).[128]

PPP occupies a unique place in the world trade community. All private actors, including food processors and exporters, are within the normative gravitational field of the WTO. To the extent that the SPS Agreement permits an importing country to ban certain agricultural products for sanitary reasons, food processors and exporters lose market access to that country. Here, those food processors and exporters are given two choices. First, they may lobby their own government to file a complaint in the WTO against the importing country, claiming that the ban is illegal. Then, depending on the WTO tribunal's decision, the importing country may repeal its ban, restoring the market access for those food processors and exporters. Second, those food processors and exporters may comply with the importing country's standard, as Nestlé elected to do. Given the ample regulatory autonomy bestowed by the SPS Agreement, the second option appears more promising than the first one. What is common between these two options is that not only WTO members but also private actors base their decision-making on the WTO norms. In other words, both public and private actors *speak* the WTO language.

In sum, vertical trade constitution as internalization symbolizes the transformation of the collective meaning-contexts of the world trade community into each WTO member's own socio-cultural structure.[129] Thus, internalization is "vernacularization" in the sense that the esoteric world trade

[128] *Ibid.*

[129] *Cf.* Alfred Schutz and Thomas Luckmann, *The Structures of the Life-World* (Richard M. Zaner & H. Tristram Engelhardt, Jr. trans., 1973), p. 83.

constitution transposes itself as exoteric local norms. International norms become truly effective only when they are translated into local meaning contexts.[130] In this regard, as discussed in Chapter 4, the three modes of WTO discourse may influence such transposition into domestic meaning contexts. In a less formal and less organized legal discourse, such as peer review, the policy signal content is embedded in the discursive situation itself, rather than explicitly announced.[131] For example, when an exporting country raises an issue with an importing country's newly enacted sanitary measure as a specific trade concern at the SPS Committee and both countries engage in a series of dialogues, they define and refine what might or might not be a legitimate policy or a violation between themselves. This deliberative process often results in meaningful behavioral changes on the part of importing countries, as shown in a quite positive record of resolving these specific trade concerns in the SPS Committee.[132]

In contrast, in a more regularized and formalized mode of discourse, such as adjudication, normative content is delivered under an aura of authority. Repeated and habituated, an "authority signal"[133] flown from the WTO court in the form of its case law (jurisprudence) tends to be more visible, and thus more taken-for-granted, than the aforementioned communication flow of policy content.[134] What has happened in the zeroing saga tends to offer a plausible hypothesis that even a superpower, such as the United States, cannot simply dismiss the social reality that WTO adjudication has densely institutionalized over the past six decades. The potential cost incurred to the United States by denying the normative force of the WTO adjudication, which the rest of the WTO members have more or less taken for granted, is self-alienation from the world trade community. Such a cost would be high, perhaps prohibitively so, considering the ever-increasing interdependency among trading nations in the contemporary world.

Finally, a discursive flow is not made solely of content and authority. In such a legal discourse as negotiation–consultation, "control intention" also

[130] Sally Engle Merry, *Human Rights and Gender Violence: Translating International Law into Local Justice* (2006), p. 1; Berman, *supra* note 120, 1185.

[131] W. Michael Reisman, "International Lawmaking: A Process of Communication," 75 (1981) *American Society of International Law Proceedings*, 101, 108–9.

[132] See Sungjoon Cho, "From Control to Communication: Science, Philosophy and World Trade Law," 44 (2011) *Cornell International Law Journal*, 249.

[133] Reisman, *supra* note 131, 110.

[134] *Cf.* Lynne G. Zucker, "The Role of Institutionalization in Cultural Persistence," 42 (1977) *American Sociological Review*, 726, 730 ("For acts low on institutionalization, direct social control . . . is necessary, while for acts high on institutionalization, all that is required is transmission.").

matters.[135] A WTO negotiation is still a legal discourse in the sense that it is conducted under the shadow of preexisting WTO norms. Even bargains between WTO members cannot depart from certain minimum legal parameters: negotiation results should not be inconsistent with WTO rules.[136] At the same time, however, the negotiation itself originally produces legal texts and determines legal pathways. Therefore, the notion of power cannot be entirely dismissed in the negotiation setting.

Note that internalization is not necessarily a one-way process. This localization, once reconstructing domestic preferences,[137] may even feed back into the WTO's norm-building process.[138] For example, a complying WTO member may also encourage or push other members to follow the decision. When the WTO Appellate Body struck down one of the European Union's protectionist antidumping practices (zeroing) in 2001, the EU not only implemented the ruling internally, but it also chased after another big user of the same practice, the United States. The EU challenged the United States' zeroing practice in the WTO and prevailed: the WTO Appellate Body also invalidated the US zeroing practice in a sweeping fashion. Therefore, the EU's action greatly contributed to the firm establishment of anti-zeroing jurisprudence in the WTO.[139]

D. *Externalization: the obverse side of the vertical trade constitution*

Given that discourse is a two-way action, internalization might confront a counter flow of communication in the form of contestation from the domestic side. If internalization is a default pattern under constructivism,

[135] Reisman, *supra* note 131, 111–12.

[136] All settlements must be consistent with the WTO norms. Understanding on Rules and Procedures Governing the Settlement of Disputes, art. 3.5, April 15, 1994, Marrakesh Agreement Establishing the World Trade Organization, Annex 2, 1869 UNTS 401 [hereinafter "DSU"]. ("All solutions to matters formally raised under the consultation and dispute settlement provisions of the covered agreements, including arbitration awards, shall be consistent with those agreements."). These settlements must be notified to third parties that may raise any objections. *Ibid.*, art. 3.6 ("Mutually agreed solutions to matters formally raised under the consultation and dispute settlement provisions of the covered agreements shall be notified to the DSB and the relevant Councils and Committees, where any Member may raise any point relating thereto.").

[137] Claire R. Kelly, "The Value Vacuum: Self-Enforcing Regimes and the Dilution of the Normative Feedback Loop," 22 (2001) *Michigan Journal of International Law*, 673, 693.

[138] *Ibid.*, 690–1.

[139] See generally Sungjoon Cho, "Global Constitutional Lawmaking," 31 (2010) *University of Pennsylvania Journal of International Law*, 621.

this externalization is a default pattern of neorealism, which Kenneth Waltz described as the "second image."[140] Yet a more sophisticated thesis of the second image might be located among liberal constructivists, such as Gerard Ruggie.

In his pioneering work in the early 1980s, Gerard Ruggie characterized the post-war international economic order as a subtle compromise of "embedded liberalism" in which the classical nineteenth century liberal international economic order was conditioned by domestic political authority and social purposes.[141] Ruggie's notion of embedded liberalism originated from Karl Polanyi's concept of embeddedness.[142] Polanyi had originally observed that every market economy is socially embedded in the sense that society is destined to tame an ever-expanding market force.[143] Ruggie employed Polanyi's observation in explaining the GATT's mission, which he viewed as a pursuit of trade liberalization constrained by domestic social stability.[144]

The GATT was structured, Ruggie argued, so that free trade principles, such as National Treatment and Most-Favored Nation, are qualified by domestic interventions, such as safeguards and various exceptions.[145] The grand bargain of embedded liberalism, which he read into the original GATT, retains a strong domestic foundation, such as the New Deal in the United States or social market economy in Europe. According to Ruggie, domestic politics are what underpins the compromise.[146] In this sense, perhaps the GATT might be understood as an international extension of the New Deal.[147]

[140] Kenneth Waltz, *Man, the State and War: A Theoretical Analysis* (1959), p. 8.

[141] John Gerard Ruggie, "International Regimes, Transactions, and Change: Embedded Liberalism in the Postwar Economic Order," 36 (1982) *International Organization*, 379, 382.

[142] *Ibid.*; John Gerard Ruggie, "Introduction," in John Gerard Ruggie (ed.), *Embedding Global Markets: An Enduring Challenge* (2008), p. 2.

[143] Karl Polanyi, *The Great Transformation* (1944), p. 131.

[144] Ruggie, *supra* note 142, p. 2. [145] Ruggie, *supra* note 141, 393, 396–7.

[146] Ruggie, *supra* note 142, p. 4.

[147] See Anne-Marie Burley, "Regulating the World: Multilateralism, International Law, and the Projection of the New Deal Regulatory State," in John Gerard Ruggie (ed.), *Multilateralism Matters: The Theory and Praxis of an Institutional Form* (1993), p. 125. However, this domestic embeddedness, as a stylized theme of externalization, remains rather a contentious point. Ironically, embedded liberalism, while attempting to legitimate the WTO by legitimating the domestic trade politics, might undermine the WTO's normative gravitational force; *cf.* Kelly, *supra* note 137, at 694 (acknowledging the risk of undue hegemonic influences which affect the identity formation).

Ruggie observed that the source of the continuity of the trade regime, which survived the hegemonic decline and thus contested the hegemonic stability thesis, is the state, not the trade regime itself. Thus, his shared social purpose concept basically reflects a collective accentuation of *domestic* interventionism for the sake of domestic stability. It is not necessarily the social purpose that the trade constitution would pursue on its own terms in the international arena via free trade.[148]

At the same time, however, Ruggie acknowledged the dilemma of embedded liberalism, essentially that the theory eventually invites domestic power play into the international arena. He admitted that domestic interventionism under the embedded liberalism compromise shifted adjustment burdens disproportionately from "regime-makers" to "regime-takers."[149] This development failure testifies to the nature of GATT negotiations, which were conducted in a way that could minimize political cost of adjustment, not in a way that could maximize the GATT's collective potential. In other words, GATT negotiators preferred intra-industry trade liberalization, which accompanied few adjustment problems, to inter-industry trade liberalization, which was closer to a classical Ricardian model yet would trigger political upheavals among those negatively affected by trade liberalization.[150]

Likewise, some business circles have recently criticized the WTO's inattention to the so-called new areas, such as intellectual property rights and investment. They have pushed these agendas through regional trading agreements, such as the Trans-Pacific Partnership. Understandably, those businesses and their governments (developed countries) have every incentive to transplant their advanced regulatory regimes to other trading partners.[151] Although this forced harmonization backed by parochial interests may be commonsensical in domestic political terms, it jeopardizes the very purpose of the global trading system: it tends to raise the cost of doing business in the global value chains and in particular it may prevent developing countries from benefiting from extended market access.[152]

148 See Andrew T. F. Lang, "Reconstructing Embedded Liberalism: John Gerard Ruggie and Constructivist Approaches to the Study of the International Trade Regime," 9 (2006) *Journal of International Economic Law*, 81, 99; A. Blackett, "Toward Social Regionalism in the Americas" 23 (2002) *Comparative Labor Law and Policy Journal*, 901, 911 (criticizing the embedded liberalism's "single-nation optic").

149 Ruggie, *supra* note 141, 413. 150 *Ibid.*, 402–3.

151 Simon Lester, "How Much Global Governance Should There Be?," *Vox* (January 20, 2013), available at www.voxeu.org/article/how-much-global-trade-governance-should-there-be.

152 See Sungjoon Cho, "Defragmenting World Trade," 27 (2006) *Northwestern Journal of International Law and Business*, 39.

Nonetheless, the world trade community may still hold space for externalization. Given the intersubjective nature of constructivist dynamics, it is not entirely inconceivable that certain, but not all, domestic norms channel into other WTO members in the course of discourse, as liberal constructivists might envision.[153] Thus, while the domestic politics may be embedded in the world trade community, the latter may also be enmeshed in the former.[154] Where in the spectrum of internalization–externalization the trade constitution strikes a balance in the end remains largely an empirical question, depending on the particular state and situation involved. It is also conceivable that a certain subjective experience of an individual WTO member, which concerns its uniquely sensitive socio-cultural matter, defies objectification around the WTO language.[155] This type of issue often stays outside of the world trade community. For example, soon after the EU challenged a US statute (the Helms–Burton Act), which expanded its trade embargo against Cuba to those transacting with Cuba, before the WTO, that political hot potato gradually disappeared from the WTO scene.

IV. The federalistic trade constitution: defragmentation

A. Conventional narratives: globalism v. regionalism

Compared with the aforementioned horizontal and vertical trade constitution, trade regionalism casts a unique question in terms of the world trade constitution. Regional trade agreements (RTAs), such as the North American Free Trade Agreement (NAFTA) and the European Union (EU), constitute the WTO's environment, namely, *other* legal systems. While RTAs pursue a higher level of free trade than the WTO, their members share fruits of further trade liberalization exclusively among themselves, not with the rest of WTO members.

This intrinsic discriminatory nature embedded in RTAs may wreak havoc on the world trading system, as in the notorious history of inter-war economic balkanization. In a desperate attempt to escape from the

[153] *Cf.* Thomas Risse-Kappen, "Collective Identity in a Democratic Community," in Peter J. Katzenstein (ed.), *The Culture of National Security: Norms and Identity in World Politics* (1996), pp. 268–71.

[154] *Cf.* Robert O. Keohane, "Compliance with International Commitments: Politics within a Framework of Law," 86 (1992) *American Society of International Law Proceedings*, 167, 179–80 (defining "enmeshment" as a situation in which certain institutional arrangements may affect the domestic decision-making process for making international commitments).

[155] *Cf.* Schutz and Luckmann, *supra* note 129, p. 264.

quagmire of the Great Depression, major economies competitively relied on exclusive economic blocs to the detriment of non-members. This competitive trade regionalism contributed to the rise of the Axis, which in turn precipitated the outbreak of the Second World War.[156]

This historical background has ever since set a critical tone in the conventional debates on the dyad of globalism and regionalism. In the post-war architecture of the world trading system, namely the GATT, RTAs remained contested. While the globalist United States preferred the dismantling of trade regionalism in the GATT, other major economies that harbored the Commonwealth and colonial relationships, such as the United Kingdom and France, desired to keep those blocs legal under the GATT.[157] Even the United States had some strategic need for European regionalism to check Soviet expansion. Therefore, the current form of Article XXIV emerged as a compromise between free trade and political considerations. Echoing Jacob Viner's trade creation-diversion formula,[158] Article XXIV permits the establishment of an RTA only when it substantially liberalizes trade among RTA members (paragraph 8) and it does not increase a net incidence of trade restriction *vis-à-vis* non-members (paragraph 5). In sum, RTAs are supposed to complement, not replace, the multilateral trading system.[159]

This institutional equilibrium envisioned under GATT Article XXIV had largely been maintained until neo-regionalism emerged in the late 1980s and early 1990s. The disappointingly timid pace of the Uruguay Round negotiations as well as the intensification of European integration propelled new regionalist fervor among major economies.[160] This proliferation of RTAs has since continued, increasing the number of RTAs to

[156] See Patricia Clavin, "The Triumph of Regionalism over Globalism: Patterns of Trade in the Interwar Period," in Till Geiger and Dennis Kennedy (eds.), *Regional Trade Blocs, Multilateralism, and the GATT: Complementary Paths to Free Trade* (1996), pp. 31–3.

[157] See John H. Jackson, *World Trade and the Law of GATT* (1969), pp. 576–7.

[158] Jacob Viner, *The Customs Union Issue* (1950), pp. 44–5 ("Where the trade-creating force is dominant, one of the members at least must benefit, both may benefit, the two combined must have a net benefit, and the world at large benefits; but the outside world loses, in the short-run at least, and can gain in the long-run only as the result of the general diffusion of the increased prosperity of the customs union area. Where the trade-diverting effect is predominant, one at least of the member countries is bound to be injured, both may be injured, the two combined will suffer a net injury, and there will be injury to the outside world and to the world at large. The question as to what presumptions can reasonably be held to prevail with respect to the relative importance in practice of the two types of effects will be examined subsequently.").

[159] Ken Heydon, "Regionalism: A Complement, Not a Substitute," in *Regionalism and the Multilateral Trading System* (OECD Trade Policy Working Paper 2003), p. 3.

[160] Cho, *supra* note 152, 52–3.

379 (in force) and 575 (notified) as of July 2013, more than a half of which were created after the launch of the WTO in 1995.[161] The legal vacuum around GATT Article XXIV was also responsible for such proliferation.[162] Article XXIV has in fact never disqualified a single RTA based on paragraph 5 and/or 8. Neither the GATT panel nor the special committee provided any necessary disciplines on the formation of RTAs. Many scholars fear that the recent proliferation of RTAs undermines the multilateral trading system as such proliferation reveals a tripartite failure of trade, regulation, and development.[163] The Sutherland Report eloquently describes this structural peril brought by RTAs:

> [N]early five decades after the founding of the GATT, the MFN is no longer the rule: it is almost the exception. . . . [W]hat has been termed the "spaghetti bowl" of customs unions, common markets, regional and bilateral free trade areas, preferences and an endless assortment of miscellaneous trade deals has almost reached the point where MFN treatment is exceptional treatment. Certainly, the term might now be better defined as LFN, Least Favored-Nation treatment.[164]

Nonetheless, RTAs still remain a politically attractive option mainly because they are easier to complete than a multilateral deal under the WTO, as seen in the recent surge of regionalism after the Doha failure.[165] In regional deals, parties may conveniently exempt sensitive areas from liberalization commitments.[166] Also, powerful parties may exert their political influence over less powerful counterparts more easily than in the WTO negotiations. In fact, ever since the collapse of the Cancún meeting in 2003, the United States has shifted its gears to regional trade deals and completed several agreements with Australia, Central American countries, Morocco, Bahrain,

[161] WTO, "Regional Trade Agreements," available at www.wto.org/english/tratop_e/region_e/region_e.htm (last visited October 23, 2013).

[162] Cho, *supra* note 9, 421.

[163] Cho, *supra* note 152, 62–75; see also WTO News: Speeches, "Lamy Says Trade Pacts Pose New Challenge to the Multilateral Trading System" (July 20, 2011), available at www.wto.org/english/news_e/sppl_e/sppl202_e.htm; Jennifer Hillman, "Conflicts Between Dispute Settlement Mechanisms in Regional Trade Agreements and the WTO – What Should the WTO Do?," 42 (2009) *Cornell International Law Journal*, 193, 205 (observing that the recent proliferation of RTAs increases the tension as to WTO members' rights between the WTO and those RTAs and arguing that the current Doha round negotiations should address these problems).

[164] Sutherland Report, *supra* note 57, p. 19.

[165] See Bernard K. Gordon, "Trading Up in Asia: Why the United States Needs the Trans-Pacific Partnership," 91 (2012) *Foreign Affairs*, 17.

[166] Cho, *supra* note 152, 64.

Panama, Colombia, and Korea. Such politically motivated regional deals beget equally political regional responses. A sudden shift to trade regionalism by the United States generated a domino effect,[167] as seen in the so-called "reactionary regionalism" in East Asia.[168] Yet, these politically motivated RTAs, once established, may not live up to their original fanfare. Given the low utilization ratio, some of them might not be commercially viable, although they are politically palatable.[169]

B. *Defragmentation: a social framework of the federalistic trade constitution*

A social framework may justify the longstanding apprehension to ever-propagating RTAs. In particular, structural functionalism posits that parts contribute to the solidarity of a whole system.[170] From this theoretical stance, RTAs (parts) must contribute to the integrationist *telos* ("to develop an integrated, more viable and durable multilateral trading system") of the whole (the world trade community). As long as RTAs generate negative externalities, they remain stumbling blocks to global trade equivalent to public *bads* of the world trade community.[171] Against this backdrop, the federalistic trade constitution pursues the institutional stability of the world trade community by defragmenting compartmentalized sub-trading systems represented by RTAs.

The characteristically discriminatory, and therefore fragmenting, elements lurk behind legal texts of RTAs. In particular, the notoriously labyrinthine rules of origin are regarded as being as protectionist as tariffs.[172] Any radical attempt to undo this original distortion at the

[167] Richard Baldwin and Dany Jaimovich, "Contagious FTAs: New Evidence on the Domino Theory of Regionalism," *Vox* (September 2, 2010), available at www.voxeu.org/article/contagious-ftas-new-evidence-domino-theory-regionalism.

[168] Mark Beeson, "ASEAN plus Three and the Rise of Reactionary Regionalism," 25 (2003) *Contemporary Southeast Asia*, 251; see "Asia-Pacific Leaders Announce Major Regional Trade Talks," 16 *Bridges Weekly Trade News Digest* (November 21, 2012).

[169] Jayant Menon, "Regional Consolidation, Cross-Regional Tie-Ups, or Multilateralisation of East Asian FTAs?: Relative Impacts When Preference Utilisation is Incomplete," *Vox* (April 10, 2013), available at www.voxeu.org/article/asian-noodle-bowl-when-preferences-are-underused.

[170] Moshe Hirsch, "The Sociology of International Economic Law: Sociological Analysis of the Regulation of Regional Agreements in the World Trading System," 19 (2008) *European Journal of International Law*, 277, 290–1.

[171] See Sungjoon Cho, "Global Integration and the Complete Public Goods," 8 (2008) *Chicago Journal of International Law*, 553.

[172] A. Estevadeordal *et al.*, *Bridging Regional Trade Agreements in the Americas* (2009).

formation stage appears out of the question. The legal vacuum around GATT Article XXIV is simply too vast. First of all, it would be unrealistic to contemplate invalidating the existence of any preexisting RTA for its failure to meet internal (paragraph 8) or external (paragraph 5) requirements under Article XXIV. Furthermore, whether any given RTA would satisfy these requirements remains an "economic test," which the WTO tribunal is not well qualified to answer.[173] To the relief of the Appellate Body, disputing parties in *Turkey – Textiles* did not raise the potentially combustible issue of the WTO compatibility of the EU–Turkey Association Agreement in question.

Given the situation, the federalistic trade constitution concerns the *operation*, not the formation, stage of RTAs: preexisting RTAs are *fait accompli*. The federalistic trade constitution systemizes the WTO and RTAs into an orderly configuration, both jurisdictionally and substantively. First, the federalistic trade constitution tends to render an unwaivable jurisdiction *vis-à-vis* RTAs on overlapping trade issues. In other words, the federalistic trade constitution permits no abstention doctrine under which the WTO tribunal may decline to exercise its own jurisdiction by deferring the entire ruling to RTAs.

The Appellate Body underscored this point in *Mexico – Soft Drinks* by highlighting an explicit jurisdictional mandate stipulated under various provisions of the WTO Dispute Settlement Understanding (DSU).[174] Some scholars attempt to overcome the rigor of this mandate under the DSU and render an exclusive jurisdiction to an RTA tribunal under certain conditions. They invoke various domestic and international law doctrines to justify their position.[175] However, the existence of this abstention may undermine the federalistic trade constitution and subsequently the autonomy of the world trade community.

173 Panel Report, *Turkey – Restrictions on Imports of Textile and Clothing Products*, ¶IX.120, WT/DS34/R (November 19, 1999).

174 Appellate Body Report, *Mexico – Tax Measures on Soft Drinks and Other Beverages*, ¶ 47, WT/DS308/AB/R (circulated on March 6, 2006).

175 See e.g., Joost Pauwelyn and Luiz Eduardo Salles, "Forum Shopping Before International Tribunals: (Real) Concerns, (Im)Possible Solutions," 42 (2009) *Cornell International Law Journal*, 77, 102–13 (advocating the rendering of a jurisdiction to RTA tribunals based on principles of *res judicata* or *forum non conveniens*); Caroline Henckels, "Overcoming Jurisdictional Isolationism at the WTO–FTA Nexus: A Potential Approach for the WTO," 19 (2008) *European Journal of International Law*, 571 (arguing that the WTO tribunal should, based on the principle of comity, concede its jurisdiction to an RTA tribunal under certain circumstances).

Substantively, the federalistic trade constitution may constrain an RTA's normative operation.[176] *Turkey – Textiles* is a case in point. In this dispute, India sued Turkey for the latter's sudden imposition of quotas against the former's textile exports. Turkey attempted to justify its quotas based on paragraph 8 of Article XXIV of GATT, which requires members of a customs union to follow the same external trade policies as other customs union members. Here, Turkey allegedly followed the EU's preexisting quotas against India.

However, the Appellate Body rejected this ostensibly plausible defense from Turkey by creating the Article XXIV version of the less trade-restrictive alternative test. The Appellate Body highlighted that an RTA is permitted only if it does not negatively affect a non-member, which was India in this case, under paragraphs 4 and 5 of Article XXIV. Thus, Turkey should have adopted a policy, such as certificates of origin, which would have been less trade-restrictive to India than quotas. Nonetheless, tensions remain between globalism and regionalism after the ruling in *Turkey – Textiles*. In particular, the new less trade-restrictive alternative test tends to impose a border control requirement on RTA members, which, from their own perspective, contradicts the very purpose of RTAs.[177]

C. *Defragmentation as interdiscourse between the WTO and RTAs*

If the federalistic trade constitution is a newly defined social structure of the world trade community, it is symbolic interaction among individuals and groups, such as judges and tribunals, that actually shape the WTO's social structure.[178] Discourse, to be more precise interdiscourse, between the WTO and RTAs may multilateralize RTAs and therefore defragment

[176] Thomas Cottier and Marina Foltea, "Constitutional Functions of the WTO and Regional Trade Agreements," in Lorand Bartels and Federico Ortino (eds.), *Regional Trade Agreements and the WTO Legal System* (2006), pp. 43, 44 (contending that the WTO rules should override those of RTAs to prevent any unnecessary trade distortions); but see Joost Pauwelyn, "Legal Avenues to 'Multilateralizing Regionalism': Beyond Article XXIV," in Richard Baldwin and Patrick Low (eds.), *Multilateralizing Regionalism: Challenges for the Global Trading System* (2009) (denying such a federalistic relationship between the WTO and RTAs).

[177] Joel P. Trachtman, "Decisions of the Appellate Body of the World Trade Organization (Turkey – Restrictions on Imports of Textile and Clothing Products)," 11 (2000) *European Journal of International Law*, 217, 217.

[178] Hirsch, *supra* note 170, 291–2.

the world trade community.[179] Modalities of such interdiscourse may vary, as seen in Chapter 4, ranging from negotiation to adjudication to peer review. Negotiation has produced little progress in this area due mainly to the highly political nature of RTAs. Negotiating parties have largely avoided any binding actions in the area, although "clarifying and improving" disciplines over RTAs was one of the Doha Round agendas.

On the other hand, adjudicative discourse has gained much traction under the new WTO system. Paragraph 12 of the WTO Understanding on the Interpretation of Article XXIV of the General Agreement on Tariffs and Trade 1994 explicitly declared that *any* issue concerning GATT Article XXIV could be subject to the WTO dispute settlement procedure. This institutional innovation, subjecting trade regionalism to legal disciplines, can be understood, for the purpose of this book, as an expansion of an avenue for adjudicative discourse. More interlocution, in the form of claims, arguments, and defenses, in the course of adjudicating trade regionalism could not only address the chronic legal vacuum in this area but also widen discursive space between the WTO and RTAs.

Yet the more practical issue would be to what extent the WTO tribunal should accommodate RTA norms in the WTO dispute resolution process. The gist of the federalistic trade constitution is that while the WTO interacts with RTAs, it still maintains its autonomy and operational closure.[180] If the WTO were to allow RTAs to control its own operation, the effect would be tantamount to the WTO being dissolved or assimilated into the environment, that is, into the terrain of RTAs.[181]

The Appellate Body reaffirmed this point in *Argentina – Poultry* and *Brazil – Retreaded Tyres*. Both disputes involved previous decisions under the Common Market of the Southern Cone (MERCOSUR). In *Argentina – Poultry*, Argentina claimed that the WTO panel should

[179] See generally Richard Baldwin and Philip Thornton, *Multilateralizing Regionalism: Ideas for a WTO Action Plan on Regionalism* (2008).

[180] *Cf.* Kyung Kwak and Gabrielle Marceau, "Overlaps and Conflicts of Jurisdiction Between the WTO and RTAs," Paper Presented at World Trade Organization Conference on Regional Trade Agreements (April 26, 2002), available at www.wto.int/english/tratop_e/region_e/sem_april02_e/marceau.pdf (arguing that the doctrine of *forum non conveniens*, which operates in the context of domestic jurisdictions, does not apply to public international law tribunal proceedings).

[181] But *cf.* Joost Pauwelyn, "Going Global, Regional, or Both? Dispute Settlement in the Southern African Development Community (SADC) and Overlaps with the WTO and Other Jurisdictions," 13 (2004) *Minnesota Journal of Global Trade*, 231, 254–5 (arguing that RTA laws may be accepted as a *defense* in the related WTO proceeding under some condition).

reject Brazil's complaint either jurisdictionally or substantively because Argentina prevailed in an earlier MERCOSUR dispute on the same Brazilian measure. In *Brazil – Retreaded Tyres*, Brazil argued that its apparent discrimination against non-MERCOSUR countries, such as the EU, should be justified since it had simply followed its obligation under MERCOSUR. Yet the Appellate Body rejected all these attempts to impose RTA decisions on the WTO.[182] Likewise, the Appellate Body in *Mexico – Soft Drinks* refused to apply non-WTO norms, such as NAFTA, in adjudicating a WTO dispute.[183]

Of course, this operational closure does not translate into the WTO's clinical disconnection from RTAs. The WTO tribunal can take into account any relevant decisions by RTA tribunals that guide its own reasoning process.[184] The WTO tribunal may reference relevant RTA rules not as a matter of law but as a matter of *fact*, which is analogous to judicial notice in domestic courts. Vertical trade constitution is a similar type of discursive engagement witnessed in domestic courts.[185] The WTO court's discursive space for accommodating RTA decisions tends to be largest when an RTA-consistent measure may also be justified within the context of general exceptions (GATT Article XX), such as a legitimate public health or environmental measure.

The next question is whether and how RTA tribunals receive WTO norms in their own disputes. Here, the NAFTA *Tariffication* case offers a paradigmatic example.[186] In this dispute, the United States accused Canada of the latter's sudden tariff increase on certain agricultural products, which on its face would have violated the latter's NAFTA commitments. However, Canada justified this technical violation as an inevitable outcome of its compliance with the WTO commitment of tariffication, namely, converting agricultural quotas to tariffs. The WTO Agreement on Agriculture provides such a tariffication scheme because

182 Panel Report, *Argentina – Definitive Anti-Dumping Duties on Poultry from Brazil*, ¶ 7.41, WT/DS241/R (May 18, 2003).

183 Appellate Body Report, *Mexico – Tax Measures on Soft Drinks and Other Beverage*, 56, WT/DS308/AB/R (March 24, 2006).

184 *Cf.* Davey and Sapir, *supra* note 55, 18 (arguing that the WTO tribunal might reference RTA norms "to the extent it is necessary to determine rights and obligations under the WTO agreements").

185 Appellate Body Report, *Brazil – Measures Affecting Imports of Retreaded Tyres*, 246–47, WT/DS332/AB/R, (December 17, 2007).

186 Final Report of the Panel, *NAFTA – Tariffs Applied by Canada to Certain U.S.-Origin Agricultural Products*, No. CDA-95-2008-01 (December 2, 1996).

tariffs are regarded as a lesser evil than quotas due to the former's transparency.

Given the situation, a literal, inward-looking interpretation of NAFTA by the panel would have found Canada's tariff increase inconsistent with its NAFTA commitment.[187] Yet the NAFTA panel, citing the WTO Agreement on Agriculture and its tariffication scheme, eventually upheld Canada's tariffication scheme. This is the same kind of discursive engagement that one might identify in the *Charming Betsy* doctrine in the United States. Essentially, the NAFTA panel interpreted relevant NAFTA provisions in a way that avoided any conflict with the WTO norms.[188]

Considering that both the WTO and RTA tribunals largely share epistemic grounds, such as basic trade norms, this discursive engagement appears plausible. In fact, an increasing number of RTA tribunals cite or adopt WTO jurisprudence regarding both its procedural and substantive law.[189] To facilitate discursive engagement between the WTO Appellate Body and RTA tribunals, the latter should be allowed to inquire, or refer to, the WTO Appellate Body on issues that concern possible conflicts with WTO norms. Upon such referral from an RTA tribunal, the WTO Appellate Body may issue an advisory opinion on the WTO compatibility of the measure in question before the RTA tribunal. RTAs' discretion to refer appears to have recently gained much traction as some RTAs contemplate requiring their tribunals to adopt WTO jurisprudence on issues of overlapping obligations.[190]

If adjudication provides a formal avenue for discourse between the WTO and RTAs, peer review is a forum for rather informal, yet possibly more practical, discourse. For example, the WTO's Trade Policy Review Mechanism (TPRM) can provide a useful avenue to engage those WTO members who also belong to certain regional trading blocs. The primary tool of TPRM, which is peer pressure, offers a good surveillance mechanism

[187] See Dale E. McNiel, "The NAFTA Panel Decision on Canadian Tariff-Rate Quotas: Imagining a Tariffying Bargain," 22 (1997) *Yale Journal of International Law*, 345, 348 (criticizing the NAFTA panel's interpretation in the *Tariffication* case).

[188] For a similar observation, see Locknie Hsu, "Applicability of WTO Law in Regional Trade Agreements: Identifying the Links," in Lorand Bartels and Federico Ortino (eds.), *Regional Trade Agreements and the WTO Legal System* (2006), pp. 543–9.

[189] See Gabrielle Marceau *et al.*, "The WTO's Influence on Other Dispute Settlement Mechanisms: A Lighthouse in the Storm of Fragmentation," 47 (2013) *Journal of World Trade*, 481.

[190] See, e.g., Article 20.5 (Rules of Interpretation) of the Australia-Korea Free Trade Agreement (Draft), available at dfat.gov.au/fta/kafta/downloads/KAFTA-chapter-20.pdf (last visited March 6, 2014).

over suspicious intra-bloc measures.[191] This kind of surveillance under peer pressure, which has recently been put into practice under the banner of "Transparency Mechanism,"[192] tends to secure a great horizontality of the WTO *vis-à-vis* regional trading blocs, as it practically prevents controversial intra-bloc policies from escalating into formal disputes.[193]

In fact, RTAs may establish a similar discursive forum. As seen in the recent "Best Practice for RTAs/FTAs in APEC,"[194] members of RTAs may first make the texts of RTAs, including annexes and schedules, readily available to the WTO so that WTO members can study those texts and locate any part of RTAs that might potentially conflict with WTO norms. While the current TPRM is a country-specific review, RTAs, if called upon by some WTO members, may voluntarily undergo a TPRM-like peer review to discuss the WTO compatibility of their operation. Such RTA-initiated peer review tends to create an opportunity for RTAs to communicate with WTO members. The WTO Secretariat may also attend meetings of RTAs as an observer to monitor their activities.

In those areas that remain uncovered by the WTO, other WTO members can learn from the experience of RTAs. Under these circumstances, RTAs may function as test laboratories.[195] For example, in order to fight climate change and achieve green development, APEC members decided in 2011 to reduce their applied tariffs on environmental goods to 5 percent or less by the end of 2015.[196] In 2012, they reaffirmed their commitment by

191 Sutherland Report, *supra* note 57, pp. 26–7.

192 WTO, "Transparency Mechanism for RTAs," www.wto.org/english/tratop_e/region_e/trans_mecha_e.htm (last visited October 28, 2013).

193 *Ibid.*; see also Youri Devuyst and Asja Serdarevic, "The World Trade Organization and Regional Trade Agreements: Bridging the Constitutional Credibility Gap," 18 (2007) *Duke Journal of Comparative and International Law*, 1, 8 (opposing the WTO's direct determination on the validity of RTAs but instead proposing indirect supervision over RTAs through transparency and peer review); see also Petros C. Mavroidis, "Always Look at the Bright Side of Non-Delivery: WTO and Preferential Trade Agreements, Yesterday and Today," 10 (2011) *World Trade Review*, 375 (arguing that the new Transparency Mechanism should be used to generate vibrant RTA discussions within the WTO).

194 Asia-Pacific Economic Cooperation, "Best Practice for RTAs/FTAs in APEC," Forum Doc. No 2004/CSOM/028rev1 (November 17–18, 2004), available at www.apec.org/Home/Groups/Other-Groups/~/media/D3CEA02503D04FB49D9859EA10D29520.ashx.

195 See John H. Jackson, "Regional Trade Blocs and the GATT," 16 (1993) *World Economy*, 121, 130.

196 APEC, "Environmental Goods and Services (EGS)," available at egs.apec.org/ (last visited October 23, 2013).

announcing the detailed list of products ("Annex C – APEC List of Environmental Goods") covered by such an ambitious plan.[197]

Note that this project holds the same potential as the WTO Information Technology Agreement (ITA). As seen in the ITA experience, the original pluralist nature of these pioneering projects tends to turn into a multilateral nature as more members join the projects. Indeed, this shared spirit has reverberated to the WTO in an expanded fashion. Once this WTO pact on liberalizing trade in environmental goods takes effect, the benefits will be shared among *all* WTO members, including those who did not participate in the negotiation, based on the most-favored-nation principle.[198] This is a typical example of social learning: as more WTO members learn and familiarize themselves with new areas, they become more willing to embrace these novel fields.

In a similar manner, both the WTO and RTAs may share the same regulatory language because both subscribe to the same regulatory references, such as widely accepted international norms and standards. While RTAs may retain some local variations, sharing the same regulatory baselines with the WTO leaves regulatory dialogue between RTAs and the WTO open. In fact, this initial form of regulatory convergence between RTAs and the WTO has already happened in the area of trade facilitation over relevant norms and standards, such as the World Customs Organization ("WCO") Kyoto Convention and the WCO Arusha Declaration.[199]

In sum, various means of interdiscourse between the WTO and RTAs are capable of broadening their shared grounds. Each mode of discourse tends to retain its own pros and cons. While a formal mode of discourse, such as adjudication, may deliver a concrete result, it tends to lack flexibility and practicality, two characteristics that an informal mode of discourse might provide. The eventual effectiveness of the federalistic trade constitution depends on the frequency, intensity, and depth of symbolic interactions engineered by these means of interdiscourse between the WTO and RTAs.

[197] APEC, Annex C – APEC List of Environmental Goods, available at www.apec.org/Meeting-Papers/Leaders-Declarations/2012/2012_aelm/2012_aelm_annexC.aspx (last visited October 23, 2013).

[198] Daniel Pruzin, "Key WTO Ministers Cite Need for 'Realism, Pragmatism' in Setting Post-Bali Work Plan," *Bloomberg* (January 25, 2014).

[199] Evdokia Moïsé, "Trade Facilitation," in *Regionalism and the Multilateral Trading System* (2003), p. 92.

6

Evaluation: the legitimacy of the world trade community

Man cannot become attached to higher aims and submit to a rule if he sees nothing above him to which he belongs.

– Émile Durkheim[1]

After reconstructing the world trading system as a community of law from a social perspective in Chapters 3, 4, and 5, this chapter aims to evaluate the legitimacy of the new framework. Although concepts of legitimacy may vary, for the purpose of this book, the legitimacy of the world trade community can be defined as a generalized perception that its operation is appropriate and desirable among members of the community as well as non-members. Naturally, the legitimacy of the world trade community is inextricably linked to social aspects of its existence and operation, such as its intra- and extra-community dynamics.

Internal legitimacy concerns whether or how much the intra-community dynamics of the WTO community, shaped by its norms and discourse, are acceptable to the internal actors of the community, such as WTO member states and individual economic players within them. This aspect of legitimacy concerns meaning-maintenance within the WTO's symbolic universe and thus keeps its symbolic order integrated by precluding internal disorder. In contrast, external legitimacy represents whether and how much the extra-community dynamics, which concern the WTO's social relationship with surrounding non-trade systems, are sustainable in the long-run.

I. The social concept of legitimacy

In general, the concept of legitimacy as an evaluative criterion for a polity or an institution can be defined both narrowly and

[1] Émile Durkheim, *On Suicide: A Study in Sociology* (1897).

broadly.[2] A narrow definition mainly concerns formal legal procedures,[3] while a broad one regards societal acceptability of the polity or institution.[4] Notably, these narrow and broad concepts of legitimacy are often associated with a paradigmatic position on the WTO. Under the contractarian framework, one tends to lean toward a narrow view of legitimacy, as this view highlights the inter-*state* nature of the WTO. According to this view, the WTO is a legitimate tool as long as its members duly negotiated, signed, and ratified the WTO Agreement. Conversely, in the narrow view, the legitimacy of an autonomous organization, such as the WTO, on its own terms might be inconceivable in the absence of direct sovereign control.

Yet, such formal legality derived from state consent would not exhaust foundations for the WTO's legitimacy.[5] Even though the WTO is a member-driven organization, WTO members often blame the WTO system itself, not merely other members, for various alleged failures and poor performance of WTO procedures for negotiation and dispute settlement.[6] Likewise, the dramatic expansion of the WTO operation in general ever since its creation, ranging from the size of its membership to the caseload of its dispute settlement mechanism, is often credited to the WTO itself *qua* organization, not necessarily its members.

This book mainly addresses the second (broad) notion of legitimacy. The legitimacy of the world trade community, at least from a social perspective, is conceptually distinguishable from the kind of legitimacy attributed to aggregated consents of member states. Instead, the legitimacy of the world trade community can be defined as a generalized perception among its members that its operation is desirable or appropriate "within some socially constructed system of norms, values, beliefs,

[2] Part of the discussion in this chapter draws on Sungjoon Cho, "A Quest for WTO's Legitimacy," 4 (2005) *World Trade Review*, 391.

[3] See Joseph H. H. Weiler, "The Transformation of Europe," 100 (1991) *Yale Law Journal*, 2403, 2468–9. For example, Thomas Franck scrutinized the legitimacy of international rules by focusing on a "rule's and a rule-making process' legitimacy," and regarded legitimacy in terms of the "compliance pull" of such rules. Thomas M. Franck, *The Power of Legitimacy among Nations* (1990), p. 49.

[4] Weiler, *supra* note 3, 2468–9.

[5] *Cf.* Jürgen Habermas, "Between Facts and Norms: An Author's Reflections," 76 (1999) *Denver University Law Review*, 937, 938.

[6] See e.g., Doug Palmer, "WTO Becoming a 'Kangaroo Court' – U.S. Senator," *Reuters* (September 26, 2002) (reporting Max Baucus' condemnation of the WTO tribunal as a "kangaroo court").

and definitions."[7] It may be a newly constructed interest, such as a long-term, diffuse, and communal interest, that WTO members have learned to value, and therefore legitimize, within the WTO community.[8]

Defined broadly as social acceptability, the WTO's legitimacy is closely related to social aspects of its existence and operation, such as its intra- and extra-community dynamics. Internal legitimacy concerns the intra-community dynamics, while external legitimacy deals with the extra-community dynamics. Each dimension of legitimacy denotes certain properties that define this evaluative concept.

First, "trust" characterizes internal legitimacy. Internal legitimacy concerns whether and how much the intra-community dynamics of the world trade community, shaped by its norms and discourse, are acceptable to the internal actors of the community, such as WTO member states and the individual economic players within them. Second, "sustainability" demonstrates external legitimacy. External legitimacy represents whether and how much the extra-community dynamics, which concern the WTO's social relationship with surrounding non-trade systems, supports the existence and operation of the world trade community in the long-run.

II. Internal legitimacy

A. *Legitimacy as trust*

Repeated discourses tend to self-remedy any irregularities in the operation of the WTO system[9] because as WTO members share more social knowledge they expand their shared cultural-normative grounds. Therefore, to the extent that norms and discourse structure WTO members' actions, their mutual expectations stabilize around certain default behavioral patterns. These regularized patterns generate certain "trust" in other WTO members and their actions. Note that the notion of trust is not necessarily a moral one: it is a *social* concept based on stabilized expectations. It is a belief that "things could not be any other

7 Mark C. Suchman, "Managing Legitimacy: Strategic and Institutional Approaches," 20 (1995) *Academy of Management Review*, 571; W. Richard Scott, *Institutions and Organizations* (2nd edn, 2000).

8 Laurence R. Helfer and Anne-Marie Slaughter, "Why States Create International Tribunals: A Response to Professors Posner & Yoo," 93 (2005) *California Law Review*, 899, 911.

9 *Cf.* T. K. Das and Bing-Sheng Teng, "Between Trust and Control: Developing Confidence in Partner Cooperation in Alliances," 23 (1998) *Academy of Management Review*, 491, 504.

way."[10] This notion of trust is an essential factor that explains the legitimacy of the world trade community. Given that trust is presumed within the world trade community, so is its legitimacy.

To fully understand the presumption of trust, and subsequently trust-driven legitimacy, it is imperative to recognize the self-referential nature of trade discourse. The intrinsic nature of legitimacy of the world trade community originates from the linguistic trait of WTO norms. As is often seen in a language, WTO members' unquestioned reliance on the grammar and syntax of WTO norms tends to render their observance with the WTO language a default pattern. This mutual trust embedded in the WTO language is a strong indicator for legitimacy.[11] In other words, the very fact that we are communicating among ourselves via the WTO language (norms) itself attests to its legitimacy. Each WTO member follows the WTO norms because any deviation would render communication impossible.[12] A linguistic designation of certain WTO concepts, such as "risk assessment," carries with it a default legitimation: any domestic conduct done in the name of risk assessment, within the meaning of the SPS Agreement, is instantaneously legitimated until further challenged.[13]

From this perspective, compliance is not necessarily a binary, behavioral concept, but may be reconstructed as a social, identity-forming commitment. A purely behavioral understanding of compliance as a revealed form of preferences often leads to a tautological definition of state interest: any deviance from a certain norm would translate into its invalidation.[14] Therefore, a prior commitment to norms, internalized within norm abiders, is a necessary component for compliance. Such norm acceptability constitutes an essential ground for legitimacy of any community of law, including the WTO.

In order to articulate this self-legitimizing nature of WTO discourse, it is worth revisiting the internal dynamics of the WTO trade community discussed in Chapter 4. The WTO jurisprudence, as the

[10] Julia Black, "Constructing and Contesting Legitimacy and Accountability in Polycentric Regulatory Regimes," 2 (2008) *Regulation and Governance*, 137, 147.

[11] *Cf.* Habermas, *supra* note 5, 938.

[12] *Cf.* Lynne G. Zucker, "The Role of Institutionalization in Cultural Persistence," 42 (1977) *American Sociological Review*, 726, 726; Alfred Schutz, *Collected Papers: The Problem of Social Reality* (Maurice Natanson ed., 1962); Peter L. Berger and Thomas Luckmann, *The Social Construction of Reality* (1967).

[13] *Cf.* Berger and Luckmann, *supra* note 12, p. 94.

[14] Audie Klotz, *Norms in International Relations: The Struggle against Apartheid* (1995), p. 30.

world trade community's *acquis*, enables participants of the community, both member states and individual economic players (e.g., producers and consumers), to communicate with each other under the common grammar and syntax of international trade law. This communication may be direct (e.g., participating in a WTO litigation as parties) or indirect (e.g., engaging in international business transactions). The bottom line is that through this trade language the community participants reflect upon other parties' behaviors and choose their own courses of action.[15] This socialization process tends to gradually cultivate a culture of amenability, which is often backed by "communitarian peer pressure."[16] Thus, the WTO norms are ubiquitous in our everyday lives, not residing exclusively in their Geneva headquarters.[17]

As norm-sponsors, trade lawyers, government officials, and scholars maintain and develop trade discourse by making it used, heard, and therefore relevant in managing trade relations among WTO members. This epistemic foundation of their involvement tends to legitimize trade discourse and consequent trade norms. At minimum, their role can be bureaucratic in a Weberian sense;[18] at maximum, their role can be constitutive, identity-building and therefore legitimacy-building.

Two salient consequences from rhetorical practices within the WTO further substantiate the aforementioned default pattern of legitimacy. First, routine and repeated intersubjective interactions among members are powerful enough to reconstruct the nature of global governance within the WTO's context. Both density and frequency of interaction (discourse) within the WTO tend to produce an authority narrative distinct from that derived from a positivistic understanding of treaty compliance.

Second, because the rhetorical process is also didactic, various norm entrepreneurs cultivated by the process tend to transmit and preserve its normative value.[19] The WTO discourse produces learning within its community: not only simple learning that regulates certain behaviors but also

[15] In this sense, Robert Keohane coined constructivism as "reflectivism." Robert O. Keohane, "International Institutions: Two Approaches," 32 (1988) *International Studies Quarterly* 379.

[16] Louis Henkin, *How Nations Behave: Law and Foreign Policy* (1979), p. 47.

[17] See Robert Wolfe, "See You in Geneva? Legal (Mis)Representations of the Trading System," 11 (2005) *European Journal of International Relations*, 339, 342.

[18] See Nicolas Greenwood Onuf, "Global Law-Making and Legal Thought," in Nicolas Greenwood Onuf (ed.), *Law-Making in the Global Community* (1982), pp. 36–7.

[19] Jutta Brunnée and Stephen J. Toope, "International Law and Constructivism: Elements of an Interactional Theory of International Law," 39 (2000) *Columbia Journal of*

complex learning that constructs the very identity of the organization.[20] This complex learning as *social* learning is critical in that it habituates WTO members' culture of compliance or norm-sponsoring. For this purpose, discursive agents, such as the WTO Appellate Body or the WTO Secretariat, often signal the appropriateness of certain WTO norms or policies in various avenues, including press releases, public forums and workshops.

In sum, engaging in discourse means creating and broadening a deliberative space for participants of the WTO community, which in and of itself is a process of legitimation.[21] Even though this international public sphere lacks a formal positivistic institutionalization, it can still provide a sufficient level of cultural solidification and functional satisfaction, which in turn might serve as a form of legitimation.[22]

Importantly, the traditional rationalist model would not share the aforementioned social concept of the WTO's legitimacy. Under the rationalist framework, the legitimacy of the WTO is determined by the logic of consequences, that is to say, whether the WTO achieves its functional goals, such as enhancing market access through trade liberalization and lowering transaction costs by resolving disputes. Likewise, under the rationalist framework, the compliance pull, which is the conventional barometer for legitimacy, originates from these utilitarian considerations. Under rationalism, WTO members would respond rationally to pre-given preferences, i.e., the payoff matrices composed of varying sets of utilities (increased exports) and disutilities (increased imports). Therefore, these theories seldom heed norm-internalization as trust-building that requires no explicit intervening process, such as reward or retaliation.[23]

According to rationalists, it *pays* to comply, and therefore compliance is in sync with the titular national interest. More often than not, the political economy works in a way that defines such an interest narrowly as a direct, short-term gain, such as a temporary commercial boon to certain well-connected domestic industries, rather than a long-term gain to the general welfare of the whole economy. Nonetheless, one could,

Transnational Law, 19, 28; Alexander Wendt, "Collective Identity Formation and the International State," 88 (1994) *The American Political Science Review*, 384, 391; Martha Finnemore and Kathryn Sikkink, "International Norm Dynamics and Political Change," 52 (1998) *International Organization*, 887, 895; *cf.* Peter Goodrich, *Legal Discourse: Studies in Linguistics, Rhetoric and Legal Analysis* (1987), p. 63 (highlighting a "heuristic" value of language in the legal discourse).

20 Alexander Wendt, *Social Theory of International Politics* (1999), pp. 326–7.

21 *Cf.* Habermas, *supra* note 5, 940.

22 Jürgen Habermas, *The Divided West* (2006), pp. 142–3.

23 Zucker, *supra* note 12, 726.

and in a sense *should*, reconfigure the national interest rather broadly as the long-term, diffused, and systemic interest. The very existence of a well-operating world trading system is an essential public good, particularly in this highly interdependent world. This structural interest can be institutionalized, educated, habituated, and normativized among WTO members. After all, the initial utilitarian logic may turn into the logic of appropriateness.

Just as different sets of logic explain different notions of legitimacy, so too do different sets of logic explain different concepts of trust. Given the ignominious history of interwar economic balkanization, the GATT began with a contract built upon mutual distrust. Despite Article II of GATT, which legally binds every outcome of tariff negotiation, GATT contracting parties were constantly suspicious of others' opportunistic behavior or cheating. This lack of trust necessitated a monitoring mechanism, and thus the parties invented the dispute resolution procedure.[24] This original architecture of GATT might have translated into a rational project in the sense that it aimed to lower contracting parties' transaction costs by reducing uncertainty. In general, formal rules and procedures tend to enhance trust in the system itself.[25] As Kenneth Arrow aptly observed, even a commercial transaction holds within itself a certain degree of trust in the system, such as trust in the law of contracts or protection of private property.[26]

However, in the absence of trust in *others*, the trust in the system alone might not be able to prevent those opportunistic behaviors. The original GATT might have institutionalized trust in the system so that it managed to maintain reciprocal bargains among contracting parties. Yet it did not create a culture of fellowship among its members. It was only after the institutional evolution, as discussed in Chapter 3, that trust in others gradually emerged through socialization and norm-building. As discussed in Chapter 3, the community paradigm envisions anticipation about a trustee's appropriate (norm-abiding) behavior, which often connotes an assumption of risk of betrayal.[27] In sum, trust represents "social

[24] R. Leifer and P. K. Mills, "An Information Processing Approach for Deciding upon Control Strategies and Reducing Control Loss in Emerging Organizations," 22 (1996) *Journal of Management*, 113, 117.

[25] *Cf.* Sim B. Sitkin, "On the Positive Effect of Legalization on Trust," in *Research on Negotiations in Organizations* (5th edn, 1995), pp. 185, 189.

[26] Kenneth J. Arrow, "Gifts and Exchanges," 1 (1972) *Philosophy and Public Affairs*, 343, 357.

[27] See generally James S. Coleman, *Foundations of Social Theory* (1990).

capital" in the sense that it facilitates cooperation among members of the community.[28]

Perhaps two differing notions of reciprocity may further elucidate the aforementioned nexus between trust and legitimacy. First, a narrow, strategic version of reciprocity represents a conventional *quid pro quo* situation that is common in our economic and political life. The rationalist framework is based on this notion of reciprocity. Here, trust in the system does not automatically translate into trust in fellow members. Therefore, the WTO system may still fail to manage opportunistic behaviors of some members since those members may regard others not as partners but as mere objects of manipulation.[29] In contrast, a broad, diffuse notion of reciprocity embraces a social, relational reciprocity. Here, reciprocity is a trust-driven anticipation of certain behavioral patterns. Mutually practised and habituated, this notion of reciprocity is self-fulfilling and thereby generates different qualities of cooperation, or conflict, than a narrow concept of reciprocity.

Which version of logic (consequence or appropriateness) or reciprocity (narrow or broad) would prevail in a given situation remains an empirical question. For example, the recent Doha deadlock might be best explained as the prevalence of the logic of consequence over the logic of appropriateness. The mercantilist calculation trumped the ideational goal of development.[30] WTO members still regard a trade negotiation merely as a joint, not a collective, project. In the Doha Round, they largely failed to take seriously the potential damage to the trust level among WTO members that the Doha debacle could precipitate, perhaps except for a trade facilitation deal in Bali at the end of 2013.

In contrast, the WTO dispute settlement mechanism, discussed as adjudicative discourse in Chapter 4, can be best explained in terms of the logic of appropriateness. Its long, solid history of successful operation is a strong empirical confirmation of WTO members' habituated practice. Granted, rationalists might interpret this distinctive success of the WTO dispute settlement mechanism as its eventual adherence to WTO members' interests. However, the moment rationalists construct the

28 Moshe Hirsch, "The Sociology of International Investment Law," in Z. Douglas, J. Pauwelyn and J. E. Viñuales (eds.), *The Foundations of International Investment Law: Bringing Theory into Practice* (2014).

29 *Cf.* Anoop Madhok, "Revisiting Multinational Firms' Tolerance for Joint Ventures: A Trust-Based Approach," 26 (1995) *Journal of International Business Studies*, 117.

30 See generally Sungjoon Cho, "The Demise of Development in the Doha Round Negotiations," 45 (2010) *Texas International Law Journal*, 573.

national *interest* as systematic, discursive, and long-term, rather than episodic, transactional, and short-term, they tend to depart from their conventional theoretical premise.

B. *The internal legitimacy crisis*

If trust-driven legitimacy is taken for granted in the daily operation of the WTO community, as discussed above, the crisis of legitimacy indicates that such presumption no longer stands. This is a crisis of trust. Severe erosion or lack of trust among WTO members tends to precipitate conflicts and undermines what Anthony Giddens described as "ontological security."[31] Then, the next question is how to meet those unfulfilled conditions for trust-building that are taken for granted in the social paradigm of the world trade community. Those unfulfilled conditions, among others, concern basic competences of WTO members, which enable WTO members to effectively participate in various forms of WTO discourse. If some WTO members are not equipped with the necessary proficiency in the WTO language, they might not fully engage with the rest of the members of the WTO community. Even if they speak the WTO language, if they still could not afford to present themselves in one of those discursive forums, they might not truly belong to the world trade community. Naturally, neither trust nor compliance pull would flow from those members.

Jürgen Habermas' communicative action theory sheds critical light on these situations where the default pattern of trust-legitimacy might be destabilized. Any WTO norm cannot claim its validity in the absence of "ethics of discourse," that is to say, unless all participants of the WTO's community approve the norm through a practical discourse.[32] This discourse ethics in turn presupposes that all WTO members, as participants of the WTO discourse, must be communicatively competent, that is to say, capable of speaking to, questioning and deliberating with one another ("ideal speech situation").[33] Likewise, a "jurisgenerative

[31] Anthony Giddens, *Modernity and Self-Identity* (1991).

[32] *Cf.* Jürgen Habermas, *Moral Consciousness and Communicative Action* (1990), p. 66.

[33] Jürgen Habermas, *On the Pragmatics of Social Interaction: Preliminary Studies in the Theory of Communicative Action* (Barbara Fultner trans., 2001), p. 97. Rather than describing the reality, this is "construct against which the quality of actual deliberations can be measured." See Ian Johnstone, *The Power of Deliberation: International Law, Politics and Organizations* (2011), p. 15.

communicative power" can only originate from "undamaged intersubjectivity found in nondistorted communication."[34]

Note that the discourse ethics or ideal speech situation does not necessarily hinge on an absolute unanimity or a universal consensus. Rather, its presumption is based on a reasonable set of discourse with sufficient numbers of interlocutors from all corners of the world trade community.[35] Any myth of normalcy that would eradicate legitimate differences to impose agreements within the community[36] could not bring modernity to the WTO. After all, the WTO discourse is an "imaginative engagement" which serves to recognize WTO members in the end, not a tool of manufacturing consensus about values.[37]

Within the WTO context, however, such an ideal speech situation is often disabled by certain factors, in particular the capacity gap in developing countries.[38] It is vital to acknowledge that power and resources are not distributed evenly among members of the WTO community: some are "burdened societies"[39] and others "hegemons."[40] Most developing countries lack the financial, technical, and human resources necessary to allow them to meaningfully take part in WTO discourse, such as negotiation, adjudication, committee deliberations, or other peer review mechanisms.[41] Thus, they are often unable to make their positions and preferences heard, considered, and materialized into WTO norms.[42]

34 Habermas, *supra* note 5, 148.

35 James Bohman and William Rehg, "Jürgen Habermas," *The Stanford Encyclopedia of Philosophy* (May 17, 2007), available at plato.stanford.edu/entries/habermas/.

36 Daniel K. Tarullo, "Logic, Myth and the International Economic Order," 26 (1985) *Harvard International Law Journal*, 533, 550.

37 Kwame Anthony Appiah, *Cosmopolitanism: Ethics in a World of Strangers (Issues of Our Time)* (2006), pp. 85, 99.

38 Emanuela Ceva and Andrea Fracasso, "Seeking Mutual Understanding: A Discourse-Theoretical Analysis of the WTO Dispute Settlement System," 9 (2010) *World Trade Review*, 457, 480 (observing that "some Members may *de facto* end up being excluded from active participation in the [Dispute Settlement System], either because of its costs or as a result of unequal power relations").

39 John Rawls, *The Law of Peoples* (2002), p. 106.

40 José E. Alvarez, "Hegemonic International Law Revisited," 97 (2003) *American Journal of International Law* 873, 888.

41 Developing countries have consistently raised this issue in the WTO. See, e.g., Communication from Egypt, Special and Differential Treatment for Developing Countries in the Multilateral Trading System, WT/GC/W/109, WT/COMTD/W/49 (November 5, 1998).

42 See, e.g., Joseph A. Conti, "Learning to Dispute: Repeat Participation, Expertise, and Reputation at the World Trade Organization," 35 (2010) *Law and Social Inquiry* 625,

Moreover, the WTO discourse might be operated in a strategic manner to exploit the uneven distribution of resources. For example, as experienced parties choose whether to settle, they can structure WTO disputes in a way that maximizes their strategic interests.[43] From this perspective, because developing countries are innately in a disadvantageous position in trade negotiations with developed countries, developing countries might suffer from certain protectionist policies adopted by developed countries, such as farm subsidies and other protectionist devices.

Considering that approximately three quarters of WTO members are developing countries, the poor discursive conditions that developing countries suffer pose a threat to the legitimacy of the world trade community. Because legal discourse sustains the WTO community, developing countries' limited access to such discourse, whether it results from lack of power or incapacity, appears to be unfair. Worse still, legal discourse under such uneven discursive conditions may actually reinforce the original status of inequality.[44] Thus, those who are excluded from the agora of the WTO discourse due to the lack of capacity tend to build resistance and resentment toward the WTO community.[45]

This serious "participation gap"[46] may even fuel the neo-colonialist notion that trade is still the "controlling preoccupation of colonial governance."[47] At the same time, in a phenomenon known as "actor mismatch,"[48] such discursive exclusion may complicate the

626–7 (observing that only a limited number of WTO members have participated in the WTO dispute settlement procedures); *ibid.*, 651 (quoting a trade official who reportedly said that "we're big and we're rich and we can hire lots of people to do the dirty work."); Marc L. Busch and Eric Reinhardt, "Developing Countries and GATT/WTO Dispute Settlement," 37 (2003) *Journal of World Trade*, 719 (spotlighting the significance of legal capacity necessary to participate in the WTO process).

43 Conti, *supra* note 42.

44 Alison Young and Austin Sarat, "Introduction to 'Beyond Criticism: Law, Power, and Ethics'," 3 (1994) *Social and Legal Studies*, 323.

45 José E. Alvarez, "The New Dispute Settlers: (Half) Truths and Consequences," 38 (2003) *Texas International Law Journal*, 405, 417.

46 David Held, "From Executive to Cosmopolitan Multilateralism," in David Held and Mathias Koenig-Archibugi (eds.), *Taming Globalization: Frontiers of Governance* (2003), p. 163.

47 Anthony Anghie, *Imperialism, Sovereignty, and the Making of International Law* (2004), p. 269; see also B. S. Chimni, "International Institutions Today: An Imperial Global State in the Making," 15 (2004) *European Journal of International Law*, 1 (arguing that a "transnational capitalist class" (TCC) has recently shaped international economic norms and institutions to its advantage and that these imperial developments deepened the North–South divide).

48 Terence C. Halliday, "Recursivity of Global Normmaking: A Sociological Agenda," 5 (2009) *Annual Review of Law and Social Sciences* 16.1, 16.15–16.

internalization process of WTO norms in those developing countries. If developing countries as main stakeholders of the WTO system are excluded from the norm-generating and norm-sustaining discourse, they will have very few incentives to implement such norms into their domestic legal systems.

The legitimacy crisis, if left unchecked, may potentially destabilize the world trade community by creating an unhealthy gap between formal ("mechanical") and actual ("organic") solidarity among its members.[49] The world trade community must address these uneven discursive conditions in order to avoid those pathological consequences. For example, the traditional development aid must be customized to deliver effective tools to enhance developing countries' discursive competence. In this regard, some organizations, such as the "Advisory Centre on WTO Law," hold great potential to aid developing countries in gaining access to high quality legal service in the WTO litigation at subsidized rates.[50]

In particular, the Advisory Center may aid developing countries' third-party participation, which provides developing countries with unique opportunities to cultivate their discursive capacity via the process of learning by doing. They can closely watch those disputants with high proficiency in trade language and absorb the necessary skills and knowledge. Importantly, third-party participation helps those developing countries familiarize themselves with discursive conditions of the WTO adjudicative discourse by "de-dramatiz[ing]" the litigation setting.[51] It is worthwhile to underscore that developing countries' discursive access as a necessary condition for the legitimacy of the world trade community is a potential, not actualized, criterion. In other words, the WTO would not become legitimate merely because poor countries participate in the same *number* of disputes as rich ones. Rather, when a poor country elects to litigate in the WTO, it must not be discouraged from doing so for unfair reasons.[52]

49 Émile Durkheim called this gap "anomie." Émile Durkheim, *The Division of Labor in Society* (1893), pp. 368–70.

50 Chad P. Bown, "The WTO Dispute Settlement System Would Survive without Doha," *Vox* (June 19, 2010), available at www.voxeu.org/article/wto-dispute-settlement-system-would-survive-without-doha.

51 Jan Bohanes and Fernanda Garza, "Going beyond Stereotypes: Participation of Developing Countries in WTO Dispute Settlement," 4 (2012) *Trade Law and Development*, 45, 117.

52 *Ibid.*

III. External legitimacy

A. *Legitimacy as nexus*

One of the most routine attacks on the WTO's alleged lack of legitimacy has steadily been undertaken by what might be dubbed "weak publics," including many non-governmental actors, such as individual economic players, non-governmental organizations (NGOs), and civil society.[53] This "global associational revolution"[54] renders the conventional state-centered governance less sustainable than before. At the same time, the success of GATT and the launch of the WTO have generated both high expectations among observers and attention from a broad audience.[55] The increasing prominence of the WTO has recently spotlighted an external legitimacy, which connotes this extended society's perception of the WTO.

The focal point of their criticism is that the WTO's alleged insulated operative structure is disconnected from its external environment. In the absence of *inter*discourse between the WTO and non-WTO systems, it would be difficult to envision that the WTO's own social value would ever be recognized in a global public sphere. This extended public sphere is an important platform in which ordinary people may discuss and debate trade and trade-related (social) issues. In this regard, transparency is key to the WTO's external legitimacy in that it enhances the visibility and communicativeness of the WTO's operation to the outside world.[56]

In fact, the WTO has already been cognizant of the vitality of external legitimacy, and it has recently moved in this direction by augmenting its engagement with its environment through such means as broader

[53] Asher Alkoby, "Global Networks and International Environmental Lawmaking: A Discourse Approach," 8 (2008) *Chicago Journal of International Law*, 377, 385.

[54] Report by the Consultative Board to the Director-General, Supachai Panitchpakdi, "The Future of the WTO: Addressing Institutional Challenges in the New Millennium," (2004), at ¶ 176 [hereinafter "Sutherland Report"].

[55] See Steve Charnovitz, "Triangulating the World Trade Organization," 96 (2002) *American Journal of International Law*, 28, 29; Sylvia Ostry, "The WTO and International Governance," in Klaus Günter Deutsch and Bernhard Speyer (eds.), *The World Trade Organization Millennium Round: Freer Trade in the Twenty-First Century* (2001), pp. 285, 290, 293.

[56] See Paul B. Stephan, "Accountability and International Lawmaking: Rules, Rents and Legitimacy," 17 (1996–97) *Northwestern Journal of International Law and Business* 681, 726–7 (arguing that "the greater the quantity and quality of information generated during the formation of the rule, the more willing would be the decision-maker to respect the international norm.").

de-restriction of official documents, expanded web posting, and improved public access to various WTO activities.[57] These relatively recent WTO external policies tend to promote the WTO's positive image and enhance its visibility in general.[58] Such active engagement can also help check the WTO from being disconnected from its surroundings or reverting to the fatal pro-trade bias under the old GATT. It facilitates cross-fertilization between the WTO and non-WTO systems, such as international environmental law or international health law, and thus contributes to better reconciliation between trade and non-trade values.

In this global public sphere, the WTO and non-WTO systems share a certain level of common cultural grounds and thus promote integration between them.[59] Even without constitutional foundations in a domestic sense, the global public sphere may still deserve a form of legitimization on its own terms. In this post-Westphalian world, a state is not the exhaustive form of legitimating or organizing mechanisms.[60] Different modalities of public spheres can exist, varying in their density, maturity and institutional configuration.

For example, one might envision a public sphere comprised of loose transnational networks among NGOs, members of civil society, and even policymakers that is capable of providing a limited yet still effective base for legitimating the WTO operation by informing the WTO's decision-making process.[61] One should not immediately reject any discursive quality of such an open-ended deliberation process.[62]

However, the global public sphere should also legitimate itself before it is ready to exert such influence, albeit indirect. Here, the legitimacy of such an imaginative deliberative sphere is not without reservations. In the same vein, the Sutherland Report raised some caution. First of all, the

[57] Sutherland Report, *supra* note 54, pp. 183–5. [58] Cho, *supra* note 2, 391.

[59] Habermas, *supra* note 22, pp. 142–3.

[60] Neil Walker, "The Idea of Constitutional Pluralism," 65 (2002) *Modern Law Review*, 317, 320–1.

[61] Habermas, *supra* note 22, p. 142 ("the auxiliary role of a supportive global public sphere though it can exercise only indirect influence: the spontaneous activity of a weak public sphere that does not have formal legal access to binding decisions at least makes possible a form of legitimacy via a loose linkage of discussion and decision.").

[62] Stephen K. White, "Reason, Modernity, and Democracy," in Stephen K. White (ed.), *The Cambridge Companion to Habermas* (1995); see also Robert Howse, "Moving the WTO Forward – One Case at a Time," 42 (2009) *Cornell International Law Journal*, 223, 227 (observing that the unwritten practice of the WTO tribunal's accepting *amicus* briefs from NGOs tends to empower them to make their views heard in the WTO through various means, including lobbying and advocacy).

Report warned that the global public sphere might overburden developing countries by "adding parallel tracks" in trade negotiations.[63] Moreover, if the global public sphere should get over-involved in the deal-making process, the WTO's fundamental member-driven structure would be jeopardized. Although the conventional state-centered structure of the WTO might unduly eclipse increasingly important actors, such as private business, the limited social base for legitimacy in the global public sphere should not easily sidestep the formal, state-centered notion of legitimacy without any additional grounds for legitimation.[64] In fact, not all NGOs, the Report observed, are transparent or accountable themselves.[65]

B. *The external legitimacy crisis*

In this book, the world trade community is defined as a community of *law*. After all, the WTO norms, for the purpose of the book, are the WTO language that restores, mediates, and reproduces the daily operation of the WTO. Yet the WTO still might not make itself understood to the outside world with its own language, that is to say, its own norms. As long as outsiders find the WTO norms unintelligible and even undesirable, its existence and operation tend to be in conflict with non-WTO systems, and it thus becomes increasingly unsustainable.

For example, certain legal interpretations that would depart from widely shared views outside of the WTO and thus remain purely those of insiders could undermine the WTO's external legitimacy. As Professor Joseph Weiler trenchantly observes, juridification within the WTO tends to inevitably empower lawyers and subject the WTO to the "rule of lawyers," not necessarily to the "rule of law."[66]

63 Sutherland Report, *supra* note 54, p. 198.

64 *Cf.* Joel P. Trachtman, "The WTO, Legitimacy and Development," 4 (2012) *Trade Law and Development*, 12, 14 (observing that "nor is it a foregone conclusion that greater participation at an international level is better, where there is already good participation at a domestic level.").

65 Sutherland Report, *supra* note 54, pp. 197, 209.

66 Joseph H. H. Weiler, "The Rule of Lawyers and the Ethos of Diplomats: Reflections on the Internal and External Legitimacy of WTO Dispute Settlement," 35 (2001) *Journal of World Trade*, 191. Karen Alter also observed that governments would be tempted to abuse adjudication for political reasons, not for the sake of genuine deliberation, such as "to embarrass other countries" or "to create a bargaining chip." Karen J. Alter, "Resolving or Exacerbating Disputes?: The WTO's New Dispute Resolution System," 79 (2003) *International Affairs*, 783, 794.

At this juncture, it is imperative to firmly recognize the limit of the WTO language as a communicative device. As the late Robert Hudec observed, certain disputes ("wrong cases") might be better de-litigated to avoid any further political escalation.[67] Any misguided instrumentalization of the WTO language for narrow commercial or political purposes would risk rendering the WTO language even more inaudible to outside ears. In this regard, excessively lengthy and esoteric WTO panel reports, such as those in *EC – Biotech*[68] and *Airbus – Boeing*,[69] would distance, not invite, a broad audience outside of the WTO. The limit of the WTO language in fact shares a common paradox of contemporary legal culture, which is a highly elitist (epistemic) nature of legal language (knowledge).[70]

One possible solution to this potential threat to external legitimacy is to convert the esoteric nature of the WTO language into an exoteric one that could somehow relate to the outside world. This transition could be a useful tool to enhance the WTO's external legitimacy. This "social marketing" of the WTO may broaden the user base of the WTO language and help augment its external legitimacy. Enhanced external legitimacy could empower the WTO enough to disabuse the public of those mercantilist myths preached by special interests and politicians who cater to those interests. Also, a better informed public would engage in better deliberation that would in turn shape better trade policy. It is for this purpose that this book proposes a "Basic Law of International Trade" in Chapter 4. Trade scholars and the WTO Secretariat should work together to create such an accessible heuristic on the WTO and its operation. Such a heuristic will accord the world trade community a badly needed upgraded version of the WTO language.

[67] See Alter, *supra* note 66, 788; José E. Alvarez, "How Not To Link: Institutional Conundrums of an Expanded Trade Regime," 7 (2001) *Widener Law Symposium Journal*, 1, 15.

[68] Panel Report, *European Communities – Measures Affecting the Approval and Marketing of Biotech Products*, WT/DS291, WT/DS292, WT/DS293 (September 29, 2006).

[69] Panel Report, *European Communities and Certain Member States – Measures Affecting Trade in Large Civil Aircraft*, WT/DS316/R/ (June 30, 2010).

[70] Peter Goodrich, *Legal Discourse: Studies in Linguistics, Rhetoric and Legal Analysis* (1987), p. 7.

7

Conclusion: building the world trade community

The empires of the future are the empires of the mind.

– Winston Churchill[1]

I. The community-building agenda

The recent stalemate in the Doha Round put the world trading system at a crossroads. The conventional trading system framework, based on a rationalist model, has left a number of descriptive and prescriptive dilemmas, as discussed in Chapter 3. Some of these dilemmas, such as political obsession with mercantilism, are responsible for the current problems facing the world trading system. The world trading system urgently needs a new way of thinking: the field of the world trading system must embrace an alternative paradigm to the traditional rationalist framework.

Against this background, this book offers a novel thesis that questions the tacit rationalist assumptions embedded in the conventional contractarian model. This project is unique in that it employs a *social* framework, embracing the notion of "community." This concept produces a critical theoretical lens through which the concept of community not only describes the WTO's operation but also offers prescriptive policies to improve the WTO's operation. The new community model can help WTO members rethink the nature of the WTO and generate new policies to tackle some of the most daunting challenges faced by the WTO today, such as development failure.

Then, the next question is what should be done to fully realize the WTO's community potential. Admittedly, this community-building agenda exceeds the original mandate of this book, as it deserves an independent endeavor of its own. At the same time, however, it would

[1] Winston Churchill, Speech at Harvard University (September 6, 1943).

be a serious disservice if the book that has committed to reconstruct the WTO system as a community failed to at least suggest some pathways through which such an endeavor may materialize in the future. In particular, the community-building agenda is inextricably linked to the legitimacy of the world trade community, as discussed in Chapter 6.

In this regard, this final chapter proposes three pathways to build, and also to enhance, the world trade community: communicative competence, public education, and enlightened leadership. Improving the WTO discourse begins with communicatively empowering those left marginalized in the world trading system by enhancing their communicative competence. The ethics of the WTO discourse mandate that every participant of the world trade community exercise its rights to communicate to acquire its own effective space for deliberation.[2] Finally, it argues that more powerful and capable members of the WTO, such as the United States and the EU, must exercise their leadership roles to enhance the world trade community.

Before turning to these three community-building pathways, it is worth noting an unexpected sign, or momentum, of community-building that emerged in the recent WTO Ministerial Conference in Bali, Indonesia.

II. A new hope in Bali?

The small yet momentous package delivered at the Ninth WTO Ministerial Conference in Bali in December 2013 vindicates an urgent call for new thinking about the world trading system. The key component of the Bali Package is the Trade Facilitation Agreement, which aims to streamline customs administration.[3] Of course, one might find the actual package disappointing: one commentator called it a "ribbon," not even a package.[4] Nonetheless, it is not the size of the package but the fact that it was indeed delivered that matters. In retrospect, most, if not all, commentators were pessimistic about any delivery at all. That pessimism would make sense from the typical realist perspective. For example,

[2] *Cf.* Jürgen Habermas, "Between Facts and Norms: The Author's Reflections," 76 (1999) *Denver University Law Review*, 937, 940.

[3] The Protocol of Amendment for the Trade Facilitation Agreement remains unadopted as of September 20, 2014. See "WTO Trade Facilitation Deal in Limbo as Deadline Passes without Resolution," 18(25) *Bridges* (July 31, 2014).

[4] Richard Baldwin, "WTO Agreement: The Bali Ribbon," *Vox* (December 12, 2013), available at www.voxeu.org/article/wto-agreement-bali-ribbon.

India had a big election in the following year and did not want to be boxed in over such sensitive issues as food security. The United States had already thrown its weight behind mega-regional deals, such as the Trans-Pacific Partnership (TPP) and the Transatlantic Trade and Investment Partnership (TTIP).

Nonetheless, most WTO members, including India and the United States, did not want to lose the Trade Facilitation Agreement. A general consensus seems to have emerged among WTO members that they have now been interconnected with one another through global value chains. For a moment, WTO members suspended a tacit commitment to the taken-for-granted mercantilist attitude.[5] Ironically, WTO delegates in Bali could deliver the deal only by stopping bargaining. For that moment, at least, WTO delegates appeared to realize that the old bargaining model based on an instant *quid pro quo* mentality might not always work. They subscribed to the critical proposition that trade is not a game of winning or losing and that a trading nation might not always need to outsmart its trading partner to get a better deal.

It is vital to appreciate that streamlining customs administration is a communal project from which *every* economic player involved, not only exporters and importers but also retailers, wholesalers, shippers, forwarders, warehouse owners, insurers, bankers, and consumers, can benefit on its own terms. With contemporary cutting-edge information technology, even small and medium-sized enterprises can participate in trade.[6] In particular, cutting red tape at the border will greatly reduce transaction costs incurred to trade activities and thus enable once-marginalized economic players in developing countries to tap into the global market. Indubitably, the mainstreaming of trade offers an effective path to development.[7]

[5] The WTO Director-General Roberto Azevêdo also attributed the Bali deal to a "collective awareness" among WTO members that: "(1) the agreement being pursued was desirable for everyone and, above all, doable for everyone; (2) a positive outcome would not produce winners and losers, nor a north south divide (both developed and developing countries would need to work for the agreement); (3) the multilateral trading system needs to be reinvigorated to benefit everyone, particularly the smallest countries and those with least capacity to manage the intricacies of large scale trade negotiations." WTO, "'Bali Is Just the Start' – Azevêdo," *WTO News* (January 6, 2014), available at www.wto.org/english/news_e/spra_e/spra4_e.htm.

[6] See Harold McGraw III, "Seize This Chance to Ease Cross-Border Trade," *Financial Times* (December 3, 2013), 12.

[7] See Sungjoon Cho, "A New Trade Pact for the 21st Century," *National Law Journal* (August 13, 2012).

The moment we recognize the (potential) value of trade facilitation, we tend to admit, albeit implicitly, that the world trade system could be a "community," rather than a mere contractarian arrangement made up of haggling. World trade need not be a sport competition of winners or losers. Everybody can win if the winners' circle is adequately widened.

This new perspective has even more merit considering the very nature of the WTO's future homework, such as services, food security, and non-tariff barriers. The remaining hardest nuts to crack ahead seem to hinge not on episodic, big time bargains but more on workman-like, diurnal regulatory dialogue that could widen shared grounds among members; not overnight by negotiations, but only incrementally by mutual understanding. Perhaps the sober recognition of this vital operational flexibility, which leaves room for talk and therefore learning among WTO members, could be another accomplishment of the Bali deal.[8] The Bali package certainly departs from the bargaining rigidity symbolized by the single-undertaking principle. This room for talk is essential under the social framework proposed in this book. Learning, and subsequently better understanding, not bargaining, is key to overcoming new barriers borne not of protectionism but of different ways of thinking and living. For that purpose, the WTO *qua* organization must reinforce its research and education functions so that it proactively assists its members in reaching a better understanding of those difficult issues.

III. Communicative competence

As discussed in Chapter 6, certain distortions in the discourse undermine the communitarian base of the WTO. These distortions may hinder the construction of the WTO norms and culture. Perhaps the most serious distortion stems from the lack of communicative competence of developing countries. Because of their weak political status as well as deficient capacity, most developing countries have much less communicative competence than developed countries. Given that three quarters of the WTO membership are developing countries, this is a serious problem. The WTO community should make education and training more available to those members lacking capacity so that they can equip themselves with adequate discursive proficiencies necessary to participate in the trade discourse.

[8] See Uri Dadush, "How Can the World Trade Organization Stay Relevant?," *World Economic Forum* (January 14, 2014), available at forumblog.org/2014/01/how-can-the-world-trade-organization-stay-relevant/.

Moreover, those financially distressed members should also be able to take advantage of various formal and informal avenues for WTO talks, such as negotiation, adjudication and committee meetings.[9]

Then, how could the world trade community help developing countries augment their communicative competence? First of all, legal provisions for development assistance are legion. A wide variety of provisions as to financial and technical assistance are scattered in every nook and corner of the WTO agreements. Yet they are mostly hortatory and lacking any binding effect. So often, empathetic pledges for development aid have ended up with mere lip service. The point is that aid, no matter how appealing it may be as a quick fix for communicative incompetence, cannot but largely remain a mirage given the fact that any development aid requires domestic political decisions unpopular to most domestic constituencies.[10]

Given that donations from member states are politically infeasible, the WTO *qua* organization should seriously contemplate collecting fees from member states for its various services, such as those involving the dispute settlement procedures patterned after the World Intellectual Property Organization (WIPO). With additional resources, the WTO Secretariat would be able to augment the current training programs in some developing member countries. In addition, development agencies, such as the World Bank, might also collaborate with the WTO to educate and train government officials from developing member countries in order to enhance their communicative competence for the WTO discourse. In particular, the current "Aid for Trade" program should channel more financial resources to education and training in WTO norms and practices.

One rare successful community-building project currently in action is the "Standards and Trade Development Facility (STDF)."[11] The STDF is

[9] See, e.g., Gregory Shaffer, "A Structural Theory of WTO Dispute Settlement: Why Institutional Choice Lies at the Center of the GMO Case," 41 (2008) *New York University Journal of International Law and Policy*, 1, 54 (highlighting asymmetric distribution of power, experiences and resources available to developed countries for the WTO negotiation); Christina L. Davis and Sarah Blodgett Bermeo, "Who Files? Developing Country Participation in GATT/WTO Adjudication," 71 (2009) *Journal of Politics* 1033, 1035 (observing that with capacity-building developing countries can actively participate in activities of the international institutions).

[10] See, generally, Sonia E. Rolland, *Development at the World Trade Organization* (2012).

[11] Standards and Trade Development Facility, available at www.standardsfacility.org/en/index.htm (last visited February 28, 2014).

a global partnership comprised of five international organizations: the WTO, the World Bank, the World Health Organization (WHO), the World Organization for Animal Health (OIE), and the UN Food and Agriculture Organization (FAO). It is a recognized "knowledge platform" in which WTO members can exchange information, share experiences, and locate and distribute good practice on SPS-related technical cooperation.[12] Its main goal is to help developing countries build their regulatory capacity so that they can implement the SPS Agreement and thus enhance their products' access to developed countries' markets. In other words, the STDF helps developing countries participate in trade discourse in an effective way by augmenting their proficiency in trade language, such as the SPS Agreement. An independent review agency has recently concluded that projects under the STDF have been "highly relevant to the needs of the beneficiaries."[13] Here, the STDF sets a vital model for future community-building projects within the world trade community.

IV. Information sharing

Even if participants in the WTO discourse are discursively competent, that is to say, capable of communicating with one another in terms of WTO norms, the lack of available information might still impede their effective discourse. Misinformation might be worse than a sheer lack of information because it tends to distort knowledge formation within the world trade community. As seen in a number of scandals involving human health, inaccurate information saddled with public fear could wreak havoc on world trade. Gaining access to adequate and accurate information remains a key to "risk communication."[14]

On the other hand, an asymmetrical distribution of information could precipitate a discursively unethical situation in which powerful members monopolize and exploit valuable information regarding trade and trade-related regulatory policies. Not only collecting but also processing information requires substantial resources. Unfortunately, many developing

12 Standards and Trade Development Facility, Facilitating SPS-related Technical Cooperation (Year), available at www.standardsfacility.org/Files/KeyDocs/STDFFactSheet_EN.pdf.

13 WTO, "WTO and Partners Praised for Assistance on Food Safety, Animal and Plant Health," available at www.wto.org/english/news_e/news13_e/sps_29nov13_e.htm (last visited February 28, 2014).

14 See, generally, WHO, "Food Safety: Risk Communication," available at www.who.int/foodsafety/micro/riskcommunication/en/ (last visited October 22, 2013).

countries have insufficient access to information related to their trading partners' trade policies and statistics.

This information deficit is problematic to some developing countries for two main reasons. First, it would be very costly, if not impossible, for exporters from those developing countries to acquire necessary information about their potential export markets, such as importing countries' trade and trade-related policies. Second, it would complicate foreign private businesses' plans to collaborate with local businesses within the context of global value chains. Additional costs incurred to foreign investors in familiarizing those local businesses in developing countries with trade and trade-related policies and other related information would be a serious disincentive to potential foreign investment.

Indeed, the WTO has already responded to these challenges to some extent. To its credit, the WTO official website provides both WTO members and the public with a variety of information on trade and trade-related policies and other related facts. In particular, its "Documents Online" service offers both comprehensive and detailed records of WTO discourse in such avenues as meetings, councils, committees, and working groups.[15] More recently, the WTO has commissioned an extended version of the "Integrated Trade Intelligence Portal" (I-TIP) that contains all WTO members' trade policy information, including information on trade in services.[16]

The future challenge of the WTO in this regard is how to make all these information channels more user-friendly, that is, more readily accessible to potential users. Certain improvements, such as easier search functions and prioritization of certain frequently invoked items, could contribute to a substantial increase in those information channels' utility.

V. Public education

While the WTO remains an inter-governmental organization, such a formal institutional arrangement may not be equated with its deeper

[15] WTO, "Documents and Resources," available at www.wto.org/english/res_e/res_e.htm (last visited October 22, 2013).

[16] WTO, "WTO Extends Scope of the Integrated Trade Intelligence Portal," available at www.wto.org/english/news_e/news13_e/serv_23jul13_e.htm (last visited October 22, 2013).

identity, that is to say, the world trade community. The world trade community goes beyond a mere inter-governmental contract under which a breach may be bought at a certain price as the efficient breach doctrine suggests.[17] The true value of a well-functioning multilateral trading system pierces the veil of sovereignty, reaching out to ordinary *people*. As Professor John Jackson suggests, the global trading system exists to secure predictability and stability on the basis of which countless individual economic decisions can be made.[18] Likewise, the *Section 301* panel (1999) underscored that the world trade system is comprised of not only states but also individual economic players that are negatively affected by the lack of stability of the system.[19]

In this regard, the aforementioned agenda for a heightened level of communicative rationality and an extended deliberative space is not limited to developing countries. The agenda equally pertains to individual economic players, such as manufacturers, importers, distributors, wholesalers, retailers, shippers, forwarders, warehouse owners, bankers, customs brokers, customs lawyers, and consumers, who are actually running the WTO system behind the veil of member states. To the extent that these individual economic players operate within the normative gravitational force of the WTO's constitution, they also engage in everyday trade discourse. This is why the exigency for social marketing as to the WTO language is as pressing from a broad public standpoint as it is from a development perspective. Once the general public is educated and capable of *speaking* the WTO language, it can inoculate itself against protectionist banners and make informed political decisions on mercantilist trade policies. Then, and only then, can the WTO language, and the WTO norms it symbolizes, become truly constructive, as the language unifies divergent interests and projects scattered throughout the community.[20] This should be the WTO's reconstituted future.

In order to educate the public about WTO jurisprudence, two conditions should be met. First of all, to enable a direct legal discourse

[17] The WTO's prototype, i.e., the GATT 1947, did manifest this *contract*-like nature in its earlier stage of institutional development. See Sungjoon Cho, "The Nature of Remedies in International Trade Law," 65 (2004) *University of Pittsburgh Law Review*, 763, 766–7.

[18] John H. Jackson, "Fragmentation or Unification among International Institutions: the World Trade Organization," 31 (1999) *New York University Journal of International Law and Policy*, 823, 825.

[19] Panel Report, *United States – Sections 301–310 of the Trade Act of 1974*, ¶ 7.76, WT/DS152/R (January 27, 2000).

[20] Ronald Dworkin, *Law's Empire* (1986), p. 413.

between the global trading system and domestic constituencies, an accessible yet comprehensive heuristic of international trade law should be created. Unfortunately, it appears quite daunting, if not impossible, for ordinary people to gain meaningful access to the WTO language.

For example, WTO panel reports are written in a way which even scholars trained in the field have trouble reading and digesting.[21] To ordinary people, these lengthy reports are full of esoteric WTO semantics and codes, which few individuals would actually venture to read, let alone comprehend. To the extent that panel reports remain arcane, international trade law cannot be effectively reached, understood or used by people. Here, trade law scholars bear the primary responsibility of decoding an esoteric WTO language into an exoteric common language.[22] They should convert an unintelligible array of algorithms to a plain set of heuristics for common people. This task would be greatly facilitated by codification and dissemination of the "Basic Law of International Trade," discussed in Chapter 4.

Second, a reachable platform, be it a website or a newsletter, where people can gain access to this heuristic, should also be provided. A public, non-commercial service in its true sense can help people better access this educational and consultative avenue. Importantly, such a platform should be designed with due appreciation for the necessity of social marketing. In other words, such a platform should enable intuitive and compelling communication to ordinary people.[23] In this regard, the WTO Secretariat may explore various

21 Karen J. Alter, "Resolving or Exacerbating Disputes?: The WTO's New Dispute Resolution System," 79 (2003) *International Affairs* 783, 794 (observing that "the larger public has no real knowledge or appreciation of the workings of international legal bodies"). Alter also argues for "page limits on submissions" and rulings that are "concise, well written and crafted in plain language" so that the public and media can better understand normative messages of the WTO. *Ibid.*, 798.

22 See, e.g., Joseph A. Conti, *Between Law and Diplomacy: The Social Contexts of Disputing at the World Trade Organization* (2011), p. 188 (proposing to "establish a WTO bar to professionalize the training of WTO delegates, more deeply institutionalize service commitments, and share responsibility with states for increasing the scale and quality of the international legal profession."); *cf.* Gerald Postema, "Implicit Law," in Willem J. Witteveen and Wibren van der Burg (eds.), *Rediscovering Fuller: Essays on Implicit Law and Institutional Design* (1999), pp. 265, 264 (observing that norm interpretation must take into account "how citizens are likely to understand, and expect their fellow citizens to understand the language they use and the decisions they make.").

23 See e.g., Social Marketing Institute, "Social Marketing," available at www.social-marketing.org/sm.html (last visited October 22, 2013).

educational projects through partnerships with like-minded organizations – private and public.[24]

For example, a WTO member may establish a "WTO Center" in its territory to serve this discursive purpose of research, education, and consultation. WTO members must realize their own stakes in enhancing the legitimacy of the WTO. They have to invest more resources and personnel in these kinds of projects and empower the Secretariat to effectively implement them. Certainly, NGOs can also lend a hand in disseminating WTO rules to the public and educating them. Besides challenging the WTO's legitimacy, NGOs can actually contribute to it.

VI. Enlightened leadership

As discussed above, some developing country members hold a unique position within the world trade community in that their communicative competence must be augmented before they can fully engage in the WTO discourse. Some powerful developed members of the WTO, such as the United States and the EU, might be said to retain the obverse side of such a position. The enormous magnitude of benefits and influences that members like the United States and the EU hold in the world trade community tends to assign them a special leadership role of overseeing the general welfare of the community.

This type of leadership is not unprecedented. In fact, the very genesis of the old GATT system after the Second World War was attributable in no small part to the essential leadership role played by the United States and its vision of a well-operating multilateral trading system as an international public good.[25] Unfortunately, however, such a leadership

[24] Regarding some pilot projects along this line, see, e.g., WTO, "WTO Chairs Programme," available at www.wto.org/english/tratop_e/devel_e/train_e/chairs_prog_e.htm (last visited October 22, 2013) ("support trade-related teaching by providing WTO support for the development and delivery of courses on trade policy and WTO-related matters in academic institutions;" "encourage and extend outreach/communication – universities awarded the WTO Chairs are expected to organize public activities aimed at disseminating research and promoting discussion regarding international trade and trade cooperation"); WTO, "Agriculture: Committee Going Public on Farm Trade Concerns," available at www.wto.org/english/news_e/news10_e/ag_com_10mar10_e.htm (last visited October 22, 2013) ("mak[ing] members' exchanges on their policies more readily available to the public").

[25] See Jagdish Bhagwati and Douglas A. Irwin, "The Return of the Reciprocitarians: US Trade Policy Today," 10 (1987) *World Economy*, 109.

role could not be found in the recent Doha Round negotiations.[26] The political power that those influential developed countries exercised in the Doha Round talks was not converted into genuine leadership, which would have transcended myopic national interests.

To transform selfish hegemons into responsible community leaders would require a social perspective, that is, a sincere recognition that the WTO is not merely comprised of zero-sum commercial bargains but is indeed a community in which everyone is dependent on everyone else and thus collective, positive-sum welfare is possible. Indeed, the world trade community witnessed a flash of enlightenment when major developed countries played a critical role in launching the Doha Round in 2001 only two months after the September 11 terrorist attacks. WTO members then shared the urgent need to herald to the panicking international community a propitious message of common prosperity. The same kind of enlightened leadership is called for to revive the comatose Doha Round.

After all, the Doha *Development* Round might not be reduced entirely to a set of mercantilist deals. Its main goal itself is nothing but community-building, for which development and poverty reduction play a key role. Leaders of developed countries must realize that genuine peace and security derive from global citizens who have a decent amount of food to eat and decent kinds of work to do. Trade can help us attain this. The total financial burden of those titular concessions borne by major developed countries necessary to help deliver the Doha's success would be trivial compared to their astronomical security spending to keep their countries safe. Investing in the world trade community is truly a cost-efficient peacemaking solution.

Epilogue

My analysis in this book is not meant to be exhaustive. It is my sincere hope that my endeavor will stimulate further theoretical debates and empirical pursuits in this area. At the same time, I hope that some of the

[26] See, e.g., Robert E. Baldwin, "The World Trading System without American Leadership," *Vox* (May 17, 2010), available at www.voxeu.org/article/world-trading-system-without-us-leadership (observing the lack of the US leadership in the Doha Round talks); Tim Castle, "Doha Trade Round Lost If No Deal by July," *Reuters.com* (May 25, 2011 4:31 PM), available at in.reuters.com/article/2011/05/25/idINIndia-57267920110525 (quoting Jagdish Bhagwati who ascribed the Doha crisis to a "deficit of political leadership").

insights developed in the book will be of useful guidance in studying other international organizations besides the WTO.

Finally, to the extent that this book concerns the world trade community of law, readers of the book have already engaged in the trade discourse and have become participants of the community. As an interlocutor yourself within the world trade community, your further involvement in the trade discourse can make a difference to the future of the WTO.

INDEX

Lightning Source UK Ltd.
Milton Keynes UK
UKOW07n1936211214

243513UK00002B/17/P